William J. Crawford (Ed.)
Multiple Perspectives on Learner Interaction

Studies on Language Acquisition

―

Series Editors
Luke Plonsky
Martha Young-Scholten

Volume 60

Multiple Perspectives on Learner Interaction

The Corpus of Collaborative Oral Tasks

Edited by
William J. Crawford

ISBN 978-1-5015-2144-7
e-ISBN (PDF) 978-1-5015-1137-0
e-ISBN (EPUB) 978-1-5015-1128-8
ISSN 1861-4248

Library of Congress Control Number: 2021938555

Bibliographic information published by the Deutsche Nationalbibliothek
The Deutsche Nationalbibliothek lists this publication in the Deutsche Nationalbibliografie; detailed bibliographic data are available on the Internet at http://dnb.dnb.de.

© 2023 Walter de Gruyter GmbH, Berlin/Boston
This volume is text- and page-identical with the hardback published in 2021.
Typesetting: Integra Software Services Pvt. Ltd.
Printing and binding: CPI books GmbH, Leck

www.degruyter.com

Acknowledgements

Funding for the construction of the CCOT was provided by research grants awarded to the Kim McDonough by the Canada Research Chairs Program (950-221304). I am grateful for the cooperation of the Program in Intensive English at Northern Arizona University for making the audio files available for analysis and to the students who granted us access to their interactions as well as the research assistants who transcribed the audio files: Zach Alderton, Jessica Bate, Megan Callahan, Yuan Chen, Maxim Lavallee, Pham Quynh Mai Nguyen, and June Ruivivar.

Many of the students taking the Ph.D. seminar, Discourse and Register Variation, in the fall of 2016 worked on earlier versions of the CCOT and made significant contributions to its format.

I would also like to thank the anonymous reviewers who provided valuable feedback on these chapters as well as Doug Biber, Jesse Egbert, and Tove Larsson for useful discussions and feedback. Finally, Seda Acikara and Amanda Black at Northern Arizona University deserve thanks for their help in manuscript preparation.

Contents

Acknowledgements —— V

William J. Crawford
Introduction —— 1

William J. Crawford and Kim McDonough
Introduction to the Corpus of Collaborative Oral Tasks —— 7

Mohammed Alquraishi and William J. Crawford
A Multi-Dimensional Analysis of the Corpus of Collaborative Oral Tasks —— 17

Tatiana Nekrasova-Beker
Use of Phrase-Frames in L2 Students' Oral Production Across Proficiency Sub-Levels —— 41

Kim McDonough and Pakize Uludag
Individual and Shared Assessment of ESL students' Paired Oral Test Performance: Examining Rater Judgments and Lexico-grammatical Features —— 69

Tony Becker
Exploring Multiple Profiles of Highly Collaborative Paired Oral Tasks in an L2 Speaking Test of English —— 91

Shelley Staples
Exploring the Impact of Situational Characteristics on the Linguistic Features of Spoken Oral Assessment Tasks —— 123

SungEun Choi, Mark McAndrews and Okim Kang
Effects of Task and Gender on Interactive Spoken Fluency and the Mediating Role of Alignment —— 145

Romy Ghanem
ESL Students' Use of Suprasegmental Features in Informative and Opinion-Based Tasks —— 173

Appendix
A Detailed Description of Tasks in the Corpus of Collaborative Oral Tasks (CCOT) —— 199

About the Contributors —— 273

Index —— 275

William J. Crawford
Introduction

Multiple Perspectives on Learner Interaction: The Corpus of Collaborative Oral Tasks

Corpus linguistic methods have become increasingly prominent in the field of Second Language Acquisition and Teaching (SLAT). Various handbooks focusing on the application of corpora to second language studies (Granger, Gilquin and Meunier 2015, Tracy-Ventura and Paquot 2020, Jablonkai and Csomay to appear) as well as a journal dedicated solely to learner corpus research (*The International Journal of Learner Corpus Research*) illustrate the sustained influence of corpus linguistics on the SLAT field. Furthermore, as seen in the special issue of *The International Journal of Learner Corpus Research*, which uses the Trinity Lancaster Corpus (Brezina, Gablasova and McEnery 2019), as well as the recent availability of The University of Pittsburgh English Language Institute Corpus (Juffs, Han and Naismith 2020), the use of shared corpora is an important trend that can promote the application of corpus linguistic methods to describing, interpreting, and theorizing about second language performance.

The impact of these handbooks and interest in shared corpora should be seen as tangible evidence for the future potential of learner corpus research (LCR) as noted, for example, by Granger (2009). Despite the prevalence of (learner) corpus research and its application to SLAT, the two fields have been seen as disparate, a position which has led some to describe a disconnect between SLAT and LCR. McEnery, Brezina, Gablasova and Banerjee (2019), for example, point to a descriptive – theoretical divide in LCR and SLAT, noting that while some corpus research seeks to inform theoretical perspectives such as Usage-Based theories (Römer and Garner 2019), the vast majority of corpus studies in SLAT adopt a descriptive approach.

The future of SLAT and LCR, however, is bright. The use of advanced statistical techniques that are increasingly possible using corpora (Gries 2015; Larsson, Plonsky and Hancock 2020) allows future theoretically based quantitative researchers to explore various ways of combining corpus data and SLA theory as seen, for example, in the recent volume *Learner Corpus Research Meets Second Language Acquisition* (Le Bruyn and Paquot 2021). Alternatively, those SLAT researchers taking a more descriptive or qualitative approach may benefit from corpus data to help generalize or triangulate their analyses (Baker and Egbert 2019).

Furthermore, corpus-based approaches to language description such as Register Analysis can also be seen as theoretical.

Since Biber's (1988) work on the grammatical differences in spoken and written language, an entire discipline of linguistic studies has been developed to demonstrate how co-occurring linguistic features are markers of different registers. This research has been used to demonstrate how a good deal of linguistic variation can be attributed to specific functions found in various situations of use. A register approach to language description has not only been very useful in describing registers but it has also been increasingly influential in the field of SLAT as seen, for example, the identification of the noun phrase as the locus of grammatical complexity in both L1 and L2 writing (Biber, Gray, Poonpon 2011, Parkinson and Musgrave 2014). Further examples of the use of register to account for language use are found in the present volume. Staples (chapter 6) uses situational characteristic to predict variation which is supported by the analysis of functionally interpretable lexico-grammatical and phonological features. Choi, McAndrews and Kang (chapter 5) also examine variation in tasks to promote communicative purpose as an important task variable. Although these studies are not designed to test a theory, both studies provide notable examples of how Register Analysis can be used by SLAT researchers to predict and interpret linguistic variation.

The present volume includes corpus-based research that focuses specifically on peer interaction in the Corpus of Collaborative Oral Tasks (CCOT). Interactionist research in SLAT (see Loewen and Sato 2018 for an overview of peer interaction research) has explored peer interaction by reference to numerous variables, including: interactional behavior (negotiation of meaning/form, the role of input/output); task characteristics (task complexity, task conditions, task structure, task repetition); linguistic features (targeted features, incidental features); interactional contexts (modality, instructional setting); and, participant information (proficiency, L1 use, individual differences). As noted by Sato and Ballinger (2016), peer interaction studies in second language contexts have been theoretically motivated by interaction theory (Long 1983), sociocultural theory (Aljafreh and Lantolf 1994) or by a combination of the two (Socio-cognitive theory, Sato and Ballinger 2016: 13). However, perhaps due to the interest of many SLAT researchers in testing theoretical models which generally include a relatively small number of participants than would be appropriate to use for descriptive purposes, there has been very little descriptive research involving peer interaction. The present volume addresses the benefits of describing peer interaction by reference to a single corpus, the Corpus of Collaborative oral Tasks (CCOT). The volume contains a detailed description of the CCOT (Chapter 1) as well as seven studies focusing on various aspects of peer interaction, including papers that describe task performances, consider language development, and investigate the assessment of collaboration.

Chapters 2–5 in this volume look specifically at lexico-grammatical features in peer interactions. In chapter 2, Alquraishi and Crawford use Multi-Dimensional analysis in an exploratory study that identifies five dimensions of variation in the entire CCOT and illustrates the extent to which the language used in some of these dimensions are formulaic. In chapter 3, Nekrasova-Beker addresses the issue of proficiency and formulaic language through an analysis of p-frames in the CCOT and relates her findings to previous research supporting the developmental aspect of p-frame use. Chapters 4 and 5 are focused on assessment and collaboration. In chapter 4, McDonough and Uludag consider the differences between shared and individual ratings of task performances and the specific lexico-grammatical features associated with collaboration. Using a different rubric than what was used in the original CCOT ratings, they found no difference in the shared or individual ratings and identified a smaller range of lexico-grammatical features associated with collaboration than found in previous research. In chapter 5, Becker, looks specifically at the lexico-grammatical features of tasks that were rated as being highly collaborative. Through the use of Cluster Analysis, Becker identifies different types (profiles) of highly collaborative language. This study extends work on identifying linguistic features of collaboration by illustrating that collaboration can be achieved in multiple ways.

Chapters 6–8 contribute to an understanding of the role that the communicative purposes of tasks play in peer interaction. These three studies are especially notable in that they include phonological analysis of task performances. In chapter 6, Choi, McAndrews and Kang use Mediation Analysis to investigate how both fluency and syntactic alignment are influenced by task type and gender pairings of the task participants. The study finds that tasks requiring participants to choose from multiple alternatives resulted in a higher speaking rate than tasks that involved persuasion or decision-making. They further report that that gender pairing did not have a significant effect on fluency but that same gender pairs tended to be more syntactically aligned during task performances and that higher degrees of syntactic alignment were related to higher degrees of utterance fluency. In Chapter 7, Staples uses a "register linguistic" approach to describe lexico-grammatical, interactional, and fluency features across tasks that vary in their communicative purpose and expected levels of interactiveness. Through the use of Bootstrapping, Staples identifies a range of linguistic features that vary across task types with respect to both lexico-grammatical and fluency features with no real difference in the use of interactional features, a finding which will aid future research in deciding what specific linguistic features may be relevant in various types of tasks. The final chapter of this volume by Ghanem investigates suprasegmental variation in opinion-based and information-based tasks through Multiple Regression with results showing a complex relationship between the use of pronunciation features across both tasks. Ghanem's study not only identifies specific pronunciation features related to specific types of tasks but also raises the need to address a range of pronunciation features in second language classrooms.

The studies in this volume include a variety of ways that the CCOT can inform our understanding of peer interaction and task variation through the use of learner corpora. Furthermore, many of these chapters use advanced quantitative procedures (e.g., Factor Analysis, Cluster Analysis, Bootstrapping, Mediation Analysis, and Multiple Regression) that exemplify various ways to use corpus data to explore learner performance. The use of a single corpus is one productive way that the field of SLAT in general can use corpus data to pursue questions of interest both inside and outside of the corpus linguistic tradition and, to borrow a concept from Le Bruyn and Paquot (2021), to find spaces where LCR and SLAT can "meet."

References

Aljafreh, Ali & James Lantolf. 1994. Negative feedback as regulation and second language learning in the Zone of Proximal Development. *The Modern Language Journal* 78(4). 465–483.

Baker, Paul. & Jesse Egbert. (Eds.). 2019. Triangulating corpus linguistics with other linguistic research methods. New York, NY: Routledge.

Biber, Douglas. 1988. *Variation across speech and writing*. Cambridge: Cambridge University Press.

Biber, Douglas, Bethany Gray & Kornwipa Poonpon. 2011. Should we use characteristics of conversation to measure grammatical complexity in L2 writing development?. *TESOL Quarterly* 45(1). 5–35.

Brezina, Vaclav, Dana Gablasova & Tony McEnery. 2019. Corpus-based approaches to spoken L2 production: Evidence from the Trinity Lancaster Corpus. *International Journal of Learner Corpus Research* 5(2). 119–284.

Granger, Sylviane. 2009. The contribution of learner corpora to second language acquisition and foreign language teaching: A critical evaluation. In K. Aijmer (Ed.), Corpora and language teaching, 13–32. Amsterdam, The Netherlands: John Benjamins.

Granger, Sylviane, Gaëtanelle Gilquin & Fanny Meunier (Eds.) 2015. *The Cambridge Handbook of learner corpus research* (Cambridge Handbooks in Language and Linguistics). Cambridge: Cambridge University Press.

Gries, S. T. 2015. Statistics for learner corpus research. In S. Granger, G. Gilquin, & F. Meunier (Eds.), *The Cambridge handbook of learner corpus research*, 160–181. Cambridge, UK: Cambridge University Press.

Jablonkai, Reka & Eniko Csomay (Eds.) To appear. *The Routledge Handbook of Corpora in English Language. Teaching and Learning*. New York: Routledge.

Juffs, Alan., Han, Na-Rei Han & Ben Naismith. 2020. *The University of Pittsburgh English Language Corpus (PELIC)* [Data set]. https://github.com/ELI-Data-Mining-Group/PELIC-dataset

Larsson, Tove, Luke Plonsky & Gregory R. Hancock. 2020. On the benefits of structural equation modeling for corpus linguists. *Corpora Linguistics and linguistic theory* AOP. Le Bruyn, Bert & Magali Paquot (Eds.). 2021. *Learner Corpus Research Meets Second Language Acquisition*. Cambridge: Cambridge University Press.

Long, Michael. 1983. Linguistic and conversational adjustments in non-native speakers. *Studies in Second Language Acquisition* 5(2). 177–193.

McEnerey, Tony, Vaclav Brezina, Dana Gablasova & Jayanti Banerjee. 2019. Corpus linguistics, learner Corpora, and SLA: Employing technology to analyze language use. *Annual Review of Applied Linguistics* 39. 74–92.

Parkinson, Jean & Jill Musgrave. 2014. Development of noun phrase complexity in the writing of English for Academic Purposes students, *Journal of English for Academic Purposes* 14. 48–59.

Römer, Ute & Eric Garner. 2019. The development of verb constructions in spoken learner English: Tracing effects of usage and proficiency. *International Journal of Learner Corpus Research* 5(2). 207–230.

Sato, Masatoshi & Susan Balinger (Eds.). 2016. *Peer interaction and second language learning: Pedagogical potential and research agenda*. New York: Routledge.

Tracy-Ventura, Nicole & Magali Paquot (Eds.). 2020. *Routledge handbook of second language acquisition and corpora*. New York: Routledge.

William J. Crawford and Kim McDonough
Introduction to the Corpus of Collaborative Oral Tasks

1 Introduction

Learner corpora and corpus approaches to understanding second language (L2) learning have become increasingly influential in the fields of L2 teaching and acquisition as evidenced by recent handbooks dedicated expressly to these topics (Granger, Gilquin and Meunier 2015; Paquot and Tracy-Ventura 2021). As corpora are used to address a range of research issues in the field of L2 acquisition, language data needs to be broad enough to permit different types of research questions yet narrow enough to control for specific learner and contextual variables. One challenge for learner corpus research is the scarcity of spoken corpora as compared to written corpora. For example, the Université Catholique de Louvain's Center for English Corpus Linguistics (CECL) list of learner corpora around the world (https://uclouvain.be/en/research-institutes/ilc/cecl/learner-corpora-around-the-world.html) contains descriptions of 181 corpora of which only 61 (34%) contain spoken performances. Furthermore, the spoken data in these corpora are either monologic tasks or contain interviews between native-speakers (or highly proficient non-native speakers) and learners; none of the corpora included on this website are focused on learner-learner interactions. Given the interest of interaction in SLA (e.g., Mackey and Goo 2007; Loewen and Sato 2018) peer interaction data is certainly an area where learner corpus research can be used to explore questions of interest to SLA researchers. This need is, in part, addressed by the Corpus of Collaborative Oral Tasks (CCOT). This chapter describes the design of the CCOT by reference to (a) the instructional context where the data was collected, (b) the tasks learners carried out, (c) learner background information, and (d) data formatting. At the end of this volume, the appendix provides the task directions and prompts for all 24 tasks in the CCOT, including any differences in tasks that were used multiple times (see section 2.2 for more information on tasks).

2 CCOT Description

2.1 Context

The CCOT consists of timed paired oral assessments administered between August 2009 and August 2012. The corpus contains 775 conversations (576 participants) totaling 268,324 words. These conversations were produced by students in the Program in Intensive English (PIE) at Northern Arizona University, a program which focused on English for Academic Purposes at the time. Most students in the program had not met the university's minimum English language proficiency requirement, but they could be admitted to degree programs upon passing the highest level in the program. The entire curriculum was comprised of classes on Reading and Writing (6 hours/week), Listening and Speaking (6 hours/week), Content-Based Instruction (6 hours/week), Extensive Reading class (2 hours/week) and elective courses focusing on topics such as social media, marketing, or making a short informative video (2 hours/week).

The interactions included in the corpus were given to students as part of the achievement tests administered in Listening and Speaking classes each semester. The achievement tests were used as a formative assessment and comprised 40% of the final grade in each class. Some semesters these achievement tests were given three times during a 16-week semester (e.g., week 5, week 10, and week 15); in other semesters the achievement tests were given two times during a 16-week semester (e.g., week 7 and week 15). During the shorter summer semesters (either 5- or 10-week formats), the exams were given at the end of the semester. Each Listening and Speaking achievement test contained discrete point test items such as fill-in-the-blank or multiple choice focusing on listening comprehension (40% of the grade) and vocabulary (20%), and one or two speaking tasks (40%). Some exams used both an individual and collaborative task and other exams used only the collaborative task. When there were two tasks, the paired speaking task accounted for 20%. When the paired speaking task was the only spoken task, it accounted for 40% of the final grade.

The paired oral tests complemented the topics in the Speaking and Listening classes to ensure that the students were familiar with the content of the test and related vocabulary. Although the students were not told in advance the specific topic they would discuss, they were informed that the content was related to the course themes and they were familiar with the test format and its function as an achievement test. During the test administration, partners were self-selected and received the same instructions on the use of individual digital audio-recorders. The directions are provided in (1).

(1) Recording directions
- Look on the side of the recorder for a grey button labeled "hold".
- Slide the hold button in the opposite direction of the arrow. The screen should activate.
- When you're ready to start talking, press "Rec" to begin recording. The "Rec" button has a red circle on it. If a red light on the back of the recorder is glowing, and the numbers on the screen are changing, then the machine is recording.
- Say your name and whether you are "Student A" or "Student B" to begin the test. For example,
  - My name is John Smith. I am Student A.
  - My name is Mary Johnson. I am Student B.
- If you have any problems, raise your hand and ask the teacher for help.

Each paired test was rated by two PIE instructors using an analytic rubric with three subcomponents most often scored on a five-point scale: collaboration (how well the participants worked together and responded to the ideas of their partner); task completion (the extent to which all components of the task were completed using relevant content); and, style (the ability to state and support an opinion, persuade their partner, and use language relevant to the task prompts). The raters' scores on each component were averaged and the total average for each component was summed which resulted in an overall maximum score of 12. Over the five-year data collection period, the rubric was modified slightly in some semesters to better align with curricular goals. Such changes included changes to the format, descriptors, or point ranges (e.g. from a 0–4 range to a 2.5–4 range) of the rubrics.

2.2 Tasks

The CCOT consists contains 775 paired interactions of 24 tasks with a total of 268,324 words. Although the tasks varied in terms of content, they shared the same key task characteristics identified by Ellis (2003, 2012): a) tasks were primarily focused on meaning (as opposed to form); b) the tasks contained a functional need to use language (contain some type of 'gap'; c) the tasks allowed learners to use their own linguistic resources to complete the task; and d) the tasks had a clearly defined outcome. Using the task categorization in Pica, Kanagy and Falodun (1993) all of the tasks were two-way, open-ended convergent tasks.

Table 1 shows a general breakdown of the corpus including the general communicative purpose of each task, the level of instruction in which each task was administered (see section 2.3 for more information on proficiency levels), as well as the number of administrations, number of words, and mean words per text.

Table 1: Tasks and word counts in the CCOT.

Task name	Communicative purpose of task	Level of students	Number of tests	Number of words*	Mean words per text
Advertisement	Persuasion	1	73	19,641	269.05
Cancer advice	Persuasion	3	14	5614	401
Chen problem	Decision making	1	56	13,855	247.41
Choosing a patient	Selecting from alternatives	2	104	35,675	343.03
Crime statistics	Selecting from alternatives	3	17	5256	309.18
Election	Selecting from alternatives	2	37	13,779	372.41
Avoid an extreme sport	Persuasion	1	16	5750	359.38
Hiring	Selecting from alternatives	2	16	5024	314
Choosing an extreme sport	Selecting from alternatives	1	17	4532	266.59
Investing in a famous entrepreneur	Selecting from alternatives	2	21	7510	357.62
Investing in science funding	Selecting from alternatives	2	37	14,799	399.97
Matt test score	Decision making	1	18	4187	232.61
Music and vocabulary	Decision making	3	13	4880	375.38
Non verbal communication	Decision making	3	18	8542	474.56
Presentation on healthy food	Decision making	2	27	9016	333.93
Presentation on immigration	Decision making	2	16	5532	345.75
Opening a barbershop	Selecting from alternatives	2	47	19,902	423.45
Awarding a scholarship	Selecting from alternatives	1	16	6556	409.75

Table 1 (continued)

Task name	Communicative purpose of task	Level of students	Number of tests	Number of words*	Mean words per text
Sleep clinic	Selecting from alternatives	2	21	8493	404.43
Spanking	Decision making	1	39	13,557	347.62
Selecting a store to open	Selecting from alternatives	2	46	18,975	412.5
Voluntary simplicity	Decision making	1	78	25,103	321.83
Workplace monitoring	Persuasion	3	15	6687	445.8
Crime and economy	Selecting from alternatives	3	13	5459	419.92
Total			775	268,324	346.22

* Note: these word counts reflect the removal of speaker role (A, B) that are counted as words (e.g., **A**: Hi my name is X).

The students were given 3–5 minutes to complete a given task with completion time ranging from 45 seconds to 7:35 (the average completion time is 2:40). Furthermore, because some of these tasks were given more than once, certain tasks were modified for curricular or administrative reasons. Most of the differences within and across tasks are related to 1) when the task was done in relation to the other parts of the exam; 2) the amount of planning time provided (1–5 minutes); 3) whether the planning was to be done individually, collaboratively, or both; 4) the amount of time to complete a task (2–4 minutes); and, 5) whether grading requirements were shared with the students prior to doing the task; In certain tasks, language models were provided (especially at the lowest proficiency level) to provide students with frames/examples to use during the task assessment. Table 2 lists the tasks along with the number of times each task was used. For tasks that were administered in multiple semesters, this table also indicates whether there were any modifications to the tasks or rubrics. The appendix at the end of this volume describes each task in detail, including any variation in task directions and rubrics.

2.3 Learner Variables

The 775 paired oral tests in the CCOT were produced by 576 PIE students. The number of interactions produced by each student ranged from 1–7 with an average of 1.34 interactions per student. Their language backgrounds and gender are pro-

Table 2: Tasks, types, administration, and differences in the CCOT.

Task name	Number of tests	Number of semesters used	Modifications to task prompt	Modifications to task rubric
Advertisement	73	4	Yes	Yes
Cancer advice	14	1	No	No
Chen problem	56	4	Yes	Yes
Choosing a patient	104	5	Yes	Yes
Crime statistics	17	2	No	No
Election	37	2	Yes	Yes
Avoid an extreme sport	16	2	No	No
Hiring	16	2	No	No
Choosing an extreme sport	17	1	No	No
Investing in a famous entrepreneur	21	1	No	No
Investing in science funding	37	2	No	Yes
Matt test score	18	1	No	No
Music and vocabulary	13	1	No	No
Non verbal communication	18	1	No	No
Presentation on healthy food	27	2	No	No
Presentation on immigration	16	2	No	No
Opening a barbershop	47	2	No	Yes
Awarding a scholarship	16	2	No	No
Sleep clinic	21	3	No	Yes
Spanking	39	3	No	
Selecting a store to open	16	3	Yes	Yes
Voluntary simplicity	78	6	No	Yes
Workplace monitoring	15	2	No	Yes
Crime and economy	13	1	No	No

vided in Table 3. Reflecting the student population at the PIE between 2009–2012, the CCOT students were predominantly Arabic speaking and male (63%). Chinese (Mandarin) speakers were also frequent (26%) with males comprising 57% of the Mandarin speakers and 78% of all speakers in the CCOT.

Table 3: Language backgrounds and gender of CCOT.

First language background	Female	Male	Total
Arabic	48	361	409
Chinese	63	84	147
Japanese	8	2	10
Korean	4	4	8
Pashto	1	–	1
Portuguese	1	–	1
Total	125	451	576

The students belonged to three general proficiency bands as determined by an in-house proficiency test. Level 1 students had scores equivalent to 32 to 44 on the TOEFL iBT, while the Level 2 students had higher scores ranging from 45 to 56. The most proficient students in the corpus (Level 3) had scores equivalent to 57 to 69 on the TOEFL iBT. Although the students were not asked to provide their age, the student population at the time of data collection ranged in age from 18 to 26 years. No information was collected about their prior amount and type of exposure to English or other known L2s.

2.4 Data Preparation and Formatting

Audio-recordings of the paired oral tests were transcribed by a research assistant after which a second research assistant checked the transcript against the audio-recording to correct any errors or omissions. Each participant was assigned a unique personal identification number and all identifying information was removed from the transcripts and audio files. Each task was assigned a unique number and all files were re-named by reference to the task number followed by speaker A and then speaker B. Thus, for the advertising task (02) produced by speakers 048 and 212, the file was designated as "02048 & 02212" with both the text file and the de-identified audio file sharing the same name. The transcripts were converted to text files, which allows researchers to search the files using a range of concordance and other computer programs. The entire CCOT is provided in a single folder with all tasks as well as separate folders for each task. Each task folder contains subfolders of performances at specific times. For example, the task *Hiring* contains two subfolders that correspond to the time the task was administered (Fall 2009, week 10 and Spring 2010, week 10).

Each file contains 5 lines of header information: the time, administration, and participants of the task; the transcriber for each task; the date of transcription; total length of the recording; and the roles and task/speaker numbers for the two participants. The excerpt in (2) shows an example an interaction of the *Advertisement task* (coded as task 02) including the header information.

(2) File header and transcript
    <SP11wk5_Advertisement_02048 & 02212>
    <Transcribed by: June Ruivivar>
    <Date: 10 July 2013>
    <Total length of recording: 1:26>
    <A is 02048; B is 02212>
    B: Look look A, this uh this is view it's it's fantastic. I want take some pictures.
    A: Oh this is the Grand Canyon, you should try this camera.
    B: Oh uh I should try your camera, can you give it to me?
    A: Yeah of course, take it (mimes clicking sound)
    B: Oh what a nice pictures. What kind of your camera, it's very good.
    A: This is the the Sony camera, uh it's very good and very cheap uh you can uh take a picture and you can record from it, uh it's uh videotape or whatever, uh it's ten uh megapixel and it's very good, uh you should try it.
    B: Oh, very nice, it's very clear uh pictures, it's very high quality and I will I will I hope to buy this Sony camera, it's very good.
    A: I hope so.
    B: Oh good.

3 Conclusion

The CCOT provides a relatively large sample of oral learner interaction during collaborative assessment tasks and includes both text files and sound files of each performance as well as assessments of each tasks. The construction of the corpus allows for analyses of the entire dataset as well as sub-components of the corpus to address a variety of research questions as seen in the various chapters of this volume. The description of the CCOT provided in this chapter, along with the task information found in the appendix to this volume provides researchers with a good starting point to pursue various questions of interest to both learner corpus and SLA researchers.

The CCOT also has some limitations. For example, because the CCOT was built from an existing assessment data and "repurposed" to construct a corpus, the tasks do not encompass a wide range of task variables to include important task variables such as task complexity or task sequencing. Even in cases where a similar task was used in different semesters, there are often differences in the tasks or in the rubrics used to assess them. These differences are noted and it is possible to determine if these differences play a role in task performance but these difference may also be problematic for some questions of interest to researchers. Furthermore, there are some participants who did a task more than once (with a different partner) so researchers who want to control for this variable will need to search the corpus by speaker and select files to include and remove in their analyses. Additionally, the corpus includes a high number of speakers from two language background (Arabic and Chinese) which make up 96.5% of the CCOT. Of these two language backgrounds, Arabic speakers comprise 71% of all participants with 62.6% of all participants being Arabic-speaking males. The large number of speakers from a single language background and gender do not comprise a representative sample of students in intensive language programs focusing on English. Furthermore, 78% of the participants in the CCOT are male which reflects the population of students at the time of collection but is not equally balanced with respect to gender. Future corpora that focus on learner-learner interaction could include a wider range of task types and native language backgrounds in order to gain a more representative sample. Nevertheless, the CCOT is a valuable and freely available corpus that can be used for a variety of research purposes as illustrated in the present volume. It is our hope that researchers can use the CCOT to explore a range of research issues and that those interested in building learner corpora focusing on spoken interaction can address some of the limitations of the CCOT in the future.

References

Ellis, Rod. 2003. *Task-based language learning and teaching*. Oxford: Oxford University Press.

Ellis, Rod. 2012. *Language teaching research and language pedagogy*. Hoboken, NJ: Wiley & Sons.

Paquot, Magali & Nicole Tracy-Ventura (Eds.). 2021. *The Routledge handbook of second language acquisition and corpora*. New York: Routledge.

Granger, Sylviane, Gaëtanelle Gilquin & Fanny Meunier (Eds.). 2015. *The Cambridge handbook of learner corpus research*. Cambridge: Cambridge University Press.

Loewen, Sean & Masatoshi Sato. 2018. Interaction and instructed second language acquisition. *Language Teaching* 51(3). 285–329.

Mackey, Alison & Jaemyung Goo. 2007. Interaction research in SLA: A meta-analysis and research synthesis. In A. Mackey (Ed.), *Conversational interaction in second language acquisition: a series of empirical studies*, 407–453. Oxford: Oxford University Press.

Pica, Teresa, Ruth Kanagy, & Joseph Falodun. 1993. Choosing and using communication tasks for second language instruction. In G. Crookes & S. Gass (Eds.), *Tasks and Language Learning: Integrating Theory and Practice* Vol. 1, 9–34. Clevedon, Avon: Multilingual Matters.

Mohammed Alquraishi and William J. Crawford
A Multi-Dimensional Analysis of the Corpus of Collaborative Oral Tasks

1 Introduction

Describing linguistic performance in tasks has been a main concern of researchers in the field of Task-Based Language Teaching (TBLT). Studies analyzing the effects of task characteristics on spoken linguistic performance have established that task design variables influence the linguistic performance of tasks (e.g., Ellis 2009; Tavakoli 2009) where variables such as information familiarity, monologic vs. dialogic tasks, amount of information, and planning time have been shown to influence the language produced in tasks (Skehan and Foster 2008). This literature has provided valuable contributions to the field of SLA research by proposing theoretical frameworks contributing to our knowledge of teaching languages and performing empirical investigations of task performances (e.g., Pica, Kanagy and Falodun 1993; Ellis 2009; Robinson 2015; Skehan 2015).

The majority of TBLT studies of this type use various pre-determined measures of complexity, accuracy, lexical variety, and fluency (CALF) as means of investigating language variation across task conditions with the broad concept of grammatical complexity (often operationalized using unit-based measures such as T-units or AS-units) being the construct that has been used to show grammatical variation in task performances. Although this approach to understanding complexity can be very useful in understanding development or inform the construct of proficiency (i.e., more complex is indicative of development or a higher proficiency level), such complexity measures have been criticized as being functionally uninterpretable (e.g., the work on complexity in written language as seen in Biber, Gray and Staples 2014; Biber, Gray and Poonpon 2011). Consequently, pre-determined grammatical complexity measures might fail to describe the language that is used during task performances.

One way of addressing the methodological limitations of pre-determined complexity measures is to investigate and interpret linguistic variation through the use of corpus methods that include a wide range of lexico-grammatical features. Corpus analyses of this type provide more fine-grained indicators of language variation as opposed to broad and pre-determined measures. In addition, register analysis, as one approach to examining linguistic variation, links contextual elements of language production to language variation through functional interpretations (Biber 1988; Biber and Conrad 2009). Such functional interpretations are meaningful for the TBLT field as they allow for the investigation of nuanced relationships among task variables and task performance. Nonetheless, the type of investigations found in register analysis studies has not been commonly used in conjunction with task variables in the TBLT literature.

In addition to the need to identify empirically determined features that are functionally interpretable, the concept of co-occurrent features is also of strong value. The relevance of identifying linguistic features that appear together to fulfil specific discourse functions has been mentioned in previous SLA work (Friginal et al. 2014; Jarvis et. al. 2003); however, with the exception of a few studies (See Lambert and Kormos 2014 for writing and Yuan and Ellis 2003 for speaking), this type of analysis has not been a popular way of understanding linguistic variation in task performances.

As task-based researchers have used the construct of complexity to investigate linguistic differences across tasks, we see the need to ask a more general question: *What does L2 collaborative oral task language look like*? In this exploratory study, we address this question through the use of Multi-Dimensional Analysis (MDA) to describe task language and identify co-occurring linguistic features that are then interpreted functionally. Taking such a broad perspective on variation in task performance is possible using the CCOT which controls for variables such as context and provides a large enough dataset to permit an MDA. In proposing an MDA approach to task language, we acknowledge that our research goal may not be of relevance to those TBLT researchers who are interested in language development, particularly with respect to role that complexity plays in the development of interlanguage; nevertheless, we believe that this study provides TBLT researchers with an empirically-based description of L2 interactive peer tasks that are used for assessment purposes and can serve as the basis for future studies that are interested in variation in task performance by reference to functionally-interpretable co-occurring linguistic features.

It is important to note that MD analyses of L2 spoken assessment performances are not uncommon, but the focus of this study is different from previous ones. Previous studies have, for example, used Biber's (1988) dimensions to interpret L2 spoken performance (e.g., Connor-Linton and Shohamy 2001; Pérez-Parades and Sánchez 2015) or have identified dimensions in high stakes summative assessments (Biber, Gray and Staples 2014). Our goal in this paper is to identify shorter task performances that are used for formative assessment purposes and describe linguistic variation in the CCOT.

2 Multi-Dimensional Analysis

Although not traditionally used to explore learner language, Multi-Dimensional Analysis (MDA) has proven to be an influential method of identifying and interpreting patterns of linguistic variation (e.g., Staples, Laflair and Egbert 2017; Biber 1988, 2004, 2006; Csomay 2004). Several MDA studies have contrasted general domains of language use that contain situational variance such as written vs. spoken registers or the registers of the internet (e.g., Biber and Egbert 2018; Biber 1988). Other studies have used MDA to investigate variation in more analogous domains of language use such as focusing on only written or spoken registers (e.g., Staples, Laflair and Egbert 2017; Biber 2004; Csomay 2004; Conrad 1996;) or on a single register such as (Biber 2008).

Whether applied to multiple registers or a single register, MDA identifies and interprets co-occurring linguistic features that vary across groups of texts. In order to identify patterns of functionally interpretable linguistic variation, MDA rely on factor analysis to reduce a large number of linguistic variables to a smaller set of dimensions. The resulting dimensions display groupings of co-occurring variables that reflect underlying trends of variation.

This study uses the methods of conducting an MDA as described in Biber (1988) and includes 43 linguistic features (see Appendix A) that were selected to reflect both spoken interactional and informational registers in previous MDA research (Staples, Laflair and Egbert 2017; Friginal 2009; Csomay 2005; Biber 1988, 2004). We outline each step in our analysis below.

The 43 lexico-grammatical features were first tagged using the Biber Tagger (Biber 1988). The process of checking the corpus for tagging accuracy started with a review of a set of randomly selected texts representing 5% of the total text files to determine areas of concern related to the grammatical features of interest. This review produced a list of linguistic features that showed tagging errors related to nouns, nominalization, attributive adjectives, verbs, *like*, and *wh*-questions. We then examined all tagged files line by line and fixed any tagging errors. In cases where the learner made some production errors, tag determinations were made based on syntactic positions. For example, *he face a problem* vs. *he hit his face*, where *face* in the first example was tagged a verb and in the second was tagged a noun. The line-by-line review provided an opportunity to address tagging errors from the linguistic features identified from the review as well as features that were not identified in our initial accuracy check.

The tagged texts were then processed using the Biber TagCount to extract normalized frequencies (per 1,000 words) for each linguistic feature. After selecting the variables, several steps were taken to determine the best factor solution. The first step was to review the scree plot. Next, several models were constructed to test different factor solutions in terms of constructs presented in the factors and in terms of variance explained. After this process, it was determined that a five-factor solution was the best choice to represent the constructs without under-factoring or over-factoring, as suggested in Biber (1988).

The next step was to extract and rotate the factors using principal factoring and Promax rotation of the factors (e.g., Staples, Laflair and Egbert 2017; Biber 1988). Promax rotation does not assume complete independence among the dimensions, which suits the interconnected nature of linguistic data (Biber 1988). The programming language *R* (R Core Team 2016) and the statistical package *Psych* (Revelle 2016) were used to perform the statistical analyses described here using the *fa* function. After extracting and rotating the factors, the linguistic features on each dimension were reviewed to determine their loading strength. Any feature that had an absolute value lower than 0.3 was removed from the dimension. Additionally, features that loaded on multiple dimensions were removed from the dimensions on which they loaded less strongly. For example, second person pronouns loaded more strongly on Dimension 4 (−0.46), and less strongly on Dimension 3 (0.32), as can be seen in the complete factorial structure in Appendix A.

Based on the assumption that co-occurring features represent underlying functions (Biber 1988), we then interpreted the dimensions. To accomplish this task, dimension scores were calculated for each text to identify texts that represent the dimensions and their functions. Dimension scores were calculated using the *scores* argument in the *fa* function from the statistical package *Psych* (Revelle 2016). The interpretive process involved making sense of the co-occurring linguistic variables by referencing texts with high or low dimension scores. The following five dimensions were identified:

a. Dimension 1: Expression of personal thoughts and judgements
b. Dimension 2: Interactive vs. individual presentation
c. Dimension 3: Reaching agreement vs. informational discourse
d. Dimension 4: Narration of human experiences vs. evaluations of concepts and objects
e. Dimension 5: Expression of preferences

In the following section, we describe and illustrate each of these dimensions by reference to the identified linguistic features and the functions they fulfill in the CCOT.

3 Results and Discussion

The Multi-Dimensional analysis resulted in five linguistic dimensions of language variation that explain 32% of the total variance in the factorial structure.

We acknowledge that this leaves over two thirds of the variation unexplained and raise some possible reasons for the relatively low amount of variance in our discussion of limitations and future directions.

3.1 Dimension 1: Expression of Personal Thoughts and Judgments

As seen in Table 1, five linguistic features comprise the first dimension, all of which load positively: *that* complement clauses; namely, *that* complement clauses controlling verbs of stance and likelihood, *that*-deletion, private verbs, and mental verbs. This dimension explains 9% of the variance in the statistical model.

Table 1: Dimension 1: Expression of personal thoughts and judgements.

Linguistic Feature	Loading
That-deletion	0.95
Stance verbs with *that* complement clauses	0.95
Likelihood verbs with *that* complement Clauses	0.9
Private Verbs	0.79
Mental Verbs	0.62

This combination of features has elements of involved discourse with frequent use of *that*-deletion, and mental and private verbs used to promote ideas and arguments as they relate to task goals. These structures are frequently used by participants, sometimes more than once, within a turn as seen in the example below where structures such as *I see, I mean, I think,* and *I believe* followed by *that*-deletion are heavily utilized.

(1) A: Well I **see** he didn't pass the-this level uh uh w-for nothing. I **mean** he have confident he have uh I **mean** he is good and he will meet a lot of people like him.

  B: I **think** I don't say about the person but I **think** it's about his accent. He should improve his accent. He should b-should improve his skills because he should be he showed everybody uh I **believe** if he have more practice and have more more informations and more and more more pah-and more about his sk-his skills I **think** he he cou-uh he do it very well and everybody understand he-I **think** he now is have some little bit shy about his his accent because uh another person he can't un-understand him very well. (04238&04201, Dimension Score (DS): 3.98)

Texts with low Dimension 1 scores show a pattern of assertive statements that lack the personal positioning of stance. As such, ideas and opinions in texts with low Dimension 1 scores are expressed as truth rather than personal statements that are open for interpretation. This can be illustrated in the following two examples:

(2) A: Uh the smoking is not really good for your health because is going to kill you slowly and I will suggest to the people to quit it. And on other hand, it is spent your money.
    B: The smoking is not not really good for your health because is g – going to kill yourself and I will. (02119&02135, DS: –2.46)

(3) A: Marlboro Gold is the best cigarette in the world. Are you nervous from the work? Just take Marlboro Gold to be relax.
    B: Uh the cigarette make you sick or fight ill and then you will be die. (02100&02575, DS: –2.41)

Examples (2) and (3) show an absence of *that* complement clauses controlled by verbs of stance. In these two examples, statements such as *smoking is not really good for your health* or *Marlboro Gold is the best* are more assertive than the same statements with *I think* added (i.e., *I think smoking is not really good for your health* or *I think Marlboro Gold is the best*).

Texts with high Dimension 1 scores shows a few notable patterns related to the lexical choices associated with this grammatical structure. First, the most frequent verb used with *that* complement clauses is the verb *think*. This verb is found in both private and mental verb lists, which explains the loading pattern of both linguistic features on this dimension. In general, this verb occurs more frequently in the CCOT when compared to other mental and private verbs (e.g., *believe, guess, know, see, feel,* and *mean*). Whereas the verb *think* occurs more than 15 times per thousand words (PTWs), the verb *know* occurs less than five times PTWs, and other verbs (i.e., *believe, guess, & mean*) occur less than once PTWs. Another notable pattern is the frequent occurrence of the verb *think* controlling a *that* complement clause with the first-person pronoun *I*. In fact, the phrase *I think* occurs more than 11 times PTWs in the CCOT while phrases such as *I mean, I believe, I feel,* and *I know* all occur in the CCOT less than once PTWs. Also, participants almost exclusively use *I think* in the present tense, with *I thought* controlling *that* complement clause occurring only three times in raw counts in the CCOT which is the equivalent to 0.01 times PTWs.

The co-occurring features of mental verbs and *that* clauses highlights the formulaic nature associated with this dimension as this structure is used mostly with first person pronoun *I* and the verb *think* to express personal stance that is used to achieve evaluative and epistemic functions. This use of *I think [that]*, Thompson and Mulac (1991) argue, is likely functioning as a formulaic stance marker. They argue that patterns such as: 1) the frequency of using pronouns *I* and *you*, 2) a restricted set of verbs such as *think, believe,* and *guess*, and 3) *that*-deletion all indicate a highly formulaic and adverb-like use of the phrase. This argument is further advanced in Thompson (2002) where she supports the discourse marker interpretation of the structure based on the epistemic and evaluative functions of the phrases, their frequent and formulaic use, and the grammaticalization of such phrases supported by the consistent *that*-deletion. The patterns reported in Thompson and Mulac (1991) and Thompson (2002) are similar to those shown in this dimension, whether in terms of the occurrence of the pronoun *I*, or the frequent occurrence of the verb *think*. It should also be noted here that this formulaic use is not indicative of complexity and studies that choose to use unit measures such as AS-units may be counting as complex something that is formulaic (and quite possibly unanalyzed).

Additionally, the pattern of using the first-person pronoun *I* with the *think* and, to some extent, other verbs (e.g., *believe, mean* and *know*) with *that*-deletion highlights the personal element of expressing thoughts and judgments. This pattern is illustrated in examples (4–6) below. In these examples, participants use Dimension 1 features to situate and frame their thoughts and judgments. The view proposed by Thompson and Mulac (1991) and Thompson (2002) about the use of the *I think [that]* phrase maintains that even though this phrase is formulaic, it also serves epistemic and evaluative functions as a framing device. Moreover, the choice of *think* over verbs such as *believe* and *know* allows task participants to express their stance while maintaining a level of uncertainty. Biber (2006) reports that student-centered registers have more verbs such as *think* and *guess*, which signal likelihood, controlling *that* complement clauses than verbs of certainty (e.g., *know* and *recognize*). The findings in this study seem to follow this pattern reported in Biber (2006) in relation to student-centered spoken university registers in that the stance expressed is related to likelihood more than certainty. Also, since this structure is used in the present tense, this suggests that participants are expressing stance about ideas and experiences as they relate to the contemporary time of performing the task. Lastly, the frequent use of the verb *think* to control *that* complement clauses is similar to the reported distribution for verbs controlling *that* complement clauses in conversation in Biber et al. (1999).

(4) "I **think** he is uh fa – uh famous guy for uh for the running and uh I **think** he he has uh a lot" (02077 & 02592)

(5) "I **think** we should – the physician should lie uh for the patient because otherwise he will he will be worry and anxious all the time don't you think so? (03192 & 03022)

(6) I **think** Chen is did better then I **think** he good student he need uh friends take care take uh take care of friends this is probably very good about it. (04050 & 04476)

3.2 Dimension 2: Interactive vs. Individual Presentation

Table 2 shows the seven linguistic and interactional features that comprise the second dimension. Turn count, *yes,* word count, discourse particles, and *wh-*questions load on the positive end of Dimension 2 and turn length and word length load on the negative end. The variance explained by this dimension is 7% of the total variance found in the factorial structure.

Table 2: Dimension 2: Interactive vs. individual presentation.

Linguistic Feature	Loading
Turn Count	0.96
Yes	0.56
Word Count	0.49
Discourse Particles	0.42
Wh- Questions	0.33
Word Length	−0.37
Turn Length	−0.6

The positive features on this dimension are reflective of an interactive presentation style. Turn count, which is the highest loading feature on this dimension reflects interactions that have very frequent exchange of turns. These turns are facilitated by the use of discourse particles and *wh-*questions which manage the interactive discourse and elicit contributions from participants. The negative features on this dimension – turn length and word length – are indicative of an individual presentation style. Longer turns along with longer words show a focus on transferring information given in a task to the other participant. Moreover, the complementary distribution of the positive and negative poles of Dimension 2 indicates that texts with longer turns and longer words also have very few turns, discourse particles, and *wh*-questions.

Texts with high Dimension 2 scores show highly interactive exchanges among task participants, as can be seen in Example (7). This specific performance had 53 turns, seven of them are shown here:

(7) B: Oh
    A: Yeah you can uh if you have a problem w – uh with it you can take it back for just you have one year
    B: Oh
    A: Yeah
    B: That's a long time
    A: Yeah
    B: Came – wh – uh how much is it? (02161&02592, DS: 3.87)

Example (7) contains frequent short turns, often only containing one word per turn. These short turns occur frequently in texts with high Dimension 2 scores to the extent that they result in more overall word counts, compared to texts with low Dimension 2 scores. This back-and-forth exchange of turns is facilitated by the use of discourse particles and *wh*-questions. Texts with low Dimension 2 scores, on the other hand, show an individual presentation of the information given to participants in the prompt, as can be seen in Example (8) below. This task performance has only 3 turns and an average of 67 words per turn:

(8) A: I think he should uh proud by his reason but he should he should fit in the American accent because he can improve his accent uh as a good student. And I think he can do this because he have uh... a good grade in the PIE and he should don't worry about the accent because he will improve his accent in the future if he enter in the university.
    B: Hi, my name is B. I'm student B. Uh uh I I agree with uh with you. Uh Chen Chen Chen good student and uh have uh good grade but uh you must uh be change uh accent because uh if you have ne – if you have uh need or something you can' talk with people and people understand uh his uh and uh ... if you if you go if you travel any place you can you can talk with people and you can uh you can talk with people and be and uh uh uh visit uh ... I'm done. (04122&04153, DS: –2.31).

Previous analyses of spoken registers have some of these features loading on the traditional involved vs. informational dimensions. For example, both Biber's (1988) analysis of spoken and written English and Biber's (2004) analysis of conversations show word length loading on the informational discourse function, and features such as discourse particles and *wh*-questions loading on the involved discourse function. Moreover, turn length and word length were shown in Friginal (2009) to function as tools for procedural and one-directional talk.

The features comprising this dimension suggest that functions of positive and negative sides serve two styles of presentation: interactive and individual. The leading features on this dimension, both in negative and positive ends, are associated with turn taking: turn count and turn length. Naturally, these two features are on the opposite ends of the interactive continuum. On the positive side, texts have very high turn counts and short turn lengths. This exchange of turns is facilitated by discourse particles and *wh*-questions. As such, task performances with high Dimension 2 scores are constructed interactively. Task performances with low Dimension 2 scores show a pattern of presenting information in an individual or parallel manner. In these exchanges, participants talk more within turns and hold the floor for a longer time.

3.3 Dimension 3: Reaching Agreement vs. Informational Discourse

As seen in Table 3, Dimension 3 is comprised of eight linguistic features, split equally between the positive and negative poles. The positive pole of the dimension has features associated only with verbs: attitude verbs, public verbs, present tense, and communication verbs and shows a formulaic pattern associated with these features. Inspection of these verbs show that the verb *agree* is the most frequent verb. Texts with high Dimension 3 scores also showed a common pattern of using *agree* in the present tense to reach agreement between participants.

On the negative pole, the linguistic features are associated with nouns and lexical density: place nouns, pre-modifying nouns, nominalization, and type/token ratio. These negative loading features are all indicative of informational focus. Inspection of how these features are used in the corpus shows an informational discourse function. The strongest loading feature on the negative pole of this dimension is place nouns, which refer to both specific (e.g., *China*) and generic places (e.g., *barber shop*). In addition to place nouns, pre-modifying nouns and nominalizations are also utilized to pack and condense information. Finally, type/token ratio is also indicative of dense and more specific information in the discourse.

Table 3: Dimension 3: Reaching agreement vs. informational discourse.

Linguistic Feature	Loading
Attitude verbs	0.58
Public Verbs	0.47
Present Verbs	0.39
Communication Verbs	0.31
T/T Ratio	−0.41
Nominalizations	−0.48
Pre-modifying Nouns	−0.49
Place Nouns	−0.62

Texts with high Dimension 3 scores show how verb-related linguistic features function as tools for reaching agreements among participants as seen in Example (9).

(9) A: Uh, hello B.
    B: Hi hello. How are you?
    A: Uh I **think** from uh Chen's he should he shouldn't **worry** about his accent because if he **pronounce** uh the word correctly, everyone will understand him, what do you **think** about?
    B: Yeah I **think** he he should uh, he should don't be shy and he I **think** he he need to improve his accent like to watch uh more movies and uh listen to English music and hang out with uh American people uh yeah and yeah.
    A: Yeah did you **agree** about uh I think if he **pronounce** the word correctly everyone to understand him. Did you **agree** or not?
    B: Yeah I **agree** with you. Uh because uh uh uh if he if he **pronounce** the word he will do very well in his class and uh in the in the university. Yeah and uh yeah and uh if he uh watch more movies, uh he will he will uh understand and uh **talk** fast maybe.
    A: Yeah. Right. I **agree** with you.
    B: Yeah. Thank you. (04204&04293, DS: 2.58)

As seen in this example, instances of the verb *agree* occur four times in this excerpt. Moreover, verbs such as *think, worry, talk,* and *pronounce* are evident in this excerpt. In addition, the frequent use of present tense also makes this discourse relevant to the ongoing context. In Example (10), the text shows a more nominal discourse as the result of using the negative features of Dimension 3 with frequent use of place nouns, pre-modifying nouns, and nominalizations contributed to serve the informational focus.

(10) A: My name is A, Level 2B student. Um I think **Cutting Edge Barber Shop** and **Hair Design** is a good idea. Is what we can investigate. For for the reas – the reason is have have many strength and opportunities. The stre – the first strength is... we have very good sty – stylistics and barbers with good reputation. Second is... uh it's pro – provides discounts which attracted many students. And the third strength is we have a large **advertising budget**. It can make everybody knows that. Our op – we have two opportunities. The first opportunity is... it is have a good very an – uh advantage location. The second stre – opportunities is... we don't have so much com – competi – com...petition. What do you think about it?

B: My name is B. I'm Level 2B student. I don't think so, the **locations barber shop** and **salon** is located in the **office part**. And uh it's away from where pe – where people shop. And the second uh weakness is the **salon** charges more money than cus – customer used to pay. And uh maybe people don't want to pay for s – pay for more money. And uh th – the threats /---/ on two sides, the **office park** is often under the **c**onstruction and uh people af – are /---/ to find the **location** of the **barber shop**. And the second one is the sta – state raise the taxes on **business**. If you get a s – if you – if people pay for so much ma – money, either or or it's means you se – or we are need to pay for more taxes on **business**. (18525&18377, DS: –2.40)

Texts with high Dimension 3 scores show exchanges utilizing phrases such as *Do you agree with me?* and *I agree with you* to reach consensus between task participants. This use of such phrases is highly formulaic where first and second person pronouns *I* and *you* precede *agree*. To illustrate the extent of this formulaic use, the percentage of instances of *I agree* and *you agree* were compared against all instances of *agree*. This comparison shows that 73.7% of *agree* instances in the corpus were preceded by *I* or *you*, and 60% of them were preceded by *I* or *you* and followed by *with*. Looking at the frequency of the phrases associated with the verb: *I agree* and *you agree*, the two phrases combined occur 2.60 times PTWs, which represents 72% of all *agree* occurrences in the CCOT.

The findings from the positive side of the dimension show some departure from previous MD analyses of spoken registers which highlight the use of present tense in the involved/oral discourse (e.g., Biber 1988; 2004) and attribute the use of public verbs to narrative function (e.g., Biber 1988). The pattern observed in this dimension represents a rather restricted lexical selection from the pool of available attitudinal and public verbs. In both attitudinal and public verbs, *agree* is overwhelmingly more frequent than any other verb and is used in a limited set of phrases.

The features loading on the negative side of this dimension highlight a specific type of informational focus that is unique to the CCOT. Place nouns, which is the strongest negative loading feature in this dimension, shows that the informational density achieved using features in the negative pole of the dimension is associated with reference to places. The other noun-related features: nominalizations, pre-modifying nouns, and type/token ratio are indicative of the informational focus. Inspection of texts with low Dimension 3 scores shows a frequent mention of countries such as *China, New Zealand, United States,* and *Korea*. This mention of such places is accompanied by many nominalizations (e.g., *presentations, attraction, location, business, competition, & construction*) and pre-modifying nouns (e.g., *Barber Shop, Hair Design, office park, & crime rate*).

Moreover, the grouping of features in the negative pole of this dimension is different from the grouping of features representing informational focus in previous MDAs. In Biber (1988), the informational focus was achieved through the use of nouns, longer words, propositions, type/token ratio, and attributive adjectives. Biber's (2004) analysis of conversations shows this function through similar features in addition to nominalizations, relative clauses, abstract nouns, and passive verb phrases. The findings from this study show that some of these features (i.e., place nouns, nominalization, pre-modifying nouns, and type/token ratio) were used to serve the informational focus in a more restricted context than is called for by task topics.

3.4 Dimension 4: Narration of Human Experiences vs. Evaluations of Concepts and Objects

This dimension is comprised of eleven linguistic features, with five of them loading on the positive end of the dimension and six features loading on the negative end. On the positive side, third person pronouns load the strongest, followed by human nouns, quantity nouns, past tense verbs, and perfect aspect. The negative side has the following linguistic features: evaluative adjectives, attributive adjectives, second person pronouns, pronoun *it*, attitude adjectives, and abstract nouns. The list of linguistic features and their loadings is provided in Table 4. This dimension explains 6% of the variance in the factorial structure.

Table 4: Dimension 4: Narration of human experiences vs. evaluations of concepts and objects.

Linguistic Feature	Loading
Third person pronouns	0.75
Human nouns	0.43
Quantity nouns	0.32
Past tense verbs	0.32
Perfect aspect	0.3
Abstract nouns	−0.34
Attitudinal adjectives	−0.41
Pronoun *it*	−0.45
Second person pronouns	−0.46
Attributive adjectives	−0.53
Evaluative adjectives	−0.6

Inspection of texts with high Dimension 4 scores shows that the positive features are used to describe people's situations and past experiences as they relate to tasks. The function is highlighted by the use of third person pronouns (e.g., *he, she, his, her* and *they*) where reference to people, together or individually, is very frequent. This reference is often accompanied by human nouns (e.g., *patient* and *student*), and quantity nouns (e.g., *pounds* and *hours*), both of which provide more information about the people being discussed and their experiences. Lastly, past tense and perfect aspect let the participants discuss the events and conditions that have relevance to the stories of the people at the center of the task.

Texts with low Dimension 4 scores utilize attributive and evaluative adjectives to serve the function of evaluating concepts and objects that are presented in the tasks. Second person pronouns and the pronoun *it* both help serve this function as well. The pronoun *you* in particular is commonly used in these texts to reference a generalized *you* while making an evaluative argument (e.g., simple life makes *you* feel good). Also, the pronoun *it* is often used to refer to these concepts and objects (e.g., *simple life* and *camera*) and avoid repetition. Beside adjectives and pronouns, this function is served to some extent by utilizing abstract nouns (e.g., *simple*, *modern*, and *lifestyle*).

Example (11) is taken from a text with high Dimension 4 scores; third person pronouns (*she, her, he,* and *his*) occur frequently in reference to the person being described and their experience. This description is also achieved by using human and quantity nouns and, as these experiences are the accumulation of past events, a description of others' experiences utilizes past tense and perfect aspect.

(11) A: Yeah I'm gonna to talk about Melia. **She** is a student in uh university I uh think **she** is a good student **she** has a lot of things to do. So uh **she** don't have **she** don't have time to eat uh healthy food uh sh-**she gained** fifteen **pound** uh so **her** clothes don't **her** clothes don't fit **her** uh **she** start class-classes from eight until seven p.m. then **she** study at the li-the library uh **she she** buy snacks from the library uh **she** don't have any time to make uh healthy food because of that the **she** she gain fifteen **pounds**.

B: Oh and Joe has uh t-another problem too uh **he**'s a great uh student but uh **he-he** has a problem with **his** weight. Uh since **he** wa-he-uh **he was** a b-**he was** a boy **he has** uh always **been** at least twenty five uh **pounds** overweight. Uh ob-obesity uh obesity runs uh in **his** family. **He** can't uh **he he** has uh many junk. Uh **he**'s uh /---/ **he**'s uh on a diet **he**'s on uh **he**'s on a diet but just uh doesn't lose uh weight. Uh **he**'s al-**he**'s uh worried about uh diabetes-diabetes. Uh **he he** sits at his uh desk for long **hours** every day **he** can't move uh like a-a-another-another guys or w-with **his** friend. (05141&05434, DS: 2.23).

Texts with low Dimension 4 scores illustrate the evaluative function of the constellation of attributive and evaluative adjectives, second person pronouns and *it* pronoun, and abstract nouns. Example (12) clearly shows the ways in which adjectives are used to evaluate and advocate for the concept of lifestyle. Also, the excerpt shows the dual use of *you*, one where it refers to the interactant and another where it refers to a generalized *you*.

(12) A: My name is A uh level3C.

B: Uh my name is B uh I'm in level3C speaking task one. I'm student B. Uh so I think living in a **big** city uh is gives **you** uh an opportunity to see the **modern life style** and helps **you** to get a **good** job. Living in a **modern life** is amazing because uh **big** cities uh offered lot of shops and uh malls and stores that **you** can buy stuff so **you** should uh live in a **big** city where **you** can uh live...**nice life**. What do **you** think?

A: In fact I disagree with B because in my **opinion** the **simple life** it is **good** because **you** have uh **better** world and this help **your** health and uh the **simple life** is very **good** because **you** can uh self-sufficient that's all. (23080&23118, DS: –2.5)

The narrative function has been identified in most MDAs. In Biber (1988), this function was achieved using past tense, third-person pronouns, perfect aspect, and public verbs. Biber's (2004) analysis of conversations includes the use of past tense, third person pronouns, perfect aspect, communication verbs controlling complement clauses, and *that*-deletion. Human and quantity nouns in this dimension are a unique addition to the narrative function that further specifies the characteristics of narrative function in the CCOT. As such, narration of experiences in the CCOT is highlighted by the use human and quantity nouns.

Additionally, features loading negatively on Dimension 4 represent the function of evaluating concepts and objects. The features leading this side of the dimension are evaluative adjectives and attributive adjectives. These features are used to evaluate concepts and objects in an effort to persuade interlocutors. In the following examples, we can see these features and the themes common in this side of the dimension: *Simple life, modern life, big city, good job,* and *professional camera*. These examples illustrate the evaluative function being applied to concepts such as *life* and *job* or objects such as *camera*.

The other features carry this function forward through the use of second person pronouns and the pronoun *it*. Second person pronouns seem to function in two ways: 1) referring to the interlocutor, and 2) referring to a generic and generalized *you*. In the latter, the speaker mentions the benefits for both the interlocutor and others who might benefit when adopting a concept or buying a product. This generic use of *you* is a colloquial and informal alternative to using *one* for generic reference (Quirk et al. 1985), which fits the interactive and informal context of the CCOT. The pronoun *it* is also frequently occurring as speakers refer to the concepts or objects they are evaluating. The use of pronouns *you* and *it* around attributive and evaluative adjectives can be seen in examples (13–15) below.

(13) "When **you** call h – and buy **it you** get a gift it's a bag so **it**'s a **good good good** things" (02268&02295)

(14) "I think living in a **big** city uh is gives **you** uh an opportunity to see the **modern life style** and helps *you* to get a **good** job. Living in a **modern life** is **amazing** because uh **big** cities uh offered lot of shops and uh malls and stores that **you** can buy stuff so **you** should uh live in a **big** city where **you** can uh live…**nice** life." (23080&23118)

(15) "This is the the Sony camera, uh **it**'s very **good** and very **cheap** uh **you** can uh take a picture and **you** can record from **it**, uh **it**'s uh videotape or whatever, uh **it**'s ten uh megapixel and **it**'s very **good**, uh **you** should try **it**." (02048&02212)

As for the complementary distribution of the narrative and the evaluative functions of this dimension, a possible reason for such distribution is whether tasks relate to human experiences or to evaluation of concepts and objects. From this perspective, tasks that have human experiences as a prominent part of their design require using the narrative function to achieve task goals. On the other hand, tasks that have concepts or objects as the prominent elements require the use of the evaluative function to achieve task goals.

3.5 Dimension 5: Expression of Preferences

This dimension is comprised of three features, one loading positively and two loading negatively. The positive side has common nouns loading weakly, just above the cut-off point (0.38). The negative side has infinitives and *to*-complement clauses controlled by stance verbs. The list of linguistic features and their loadings is provided in Table 5. This dimension explains 4% of the variance in the statistical model. Here, we only interpret the negative side of the dimension as one feature with weak loading on the positive side does not provide enough information for interpretation.

Table 5: Dimension 5: Expression of preferences.

Linguistic Feature	Loading
Common nouns	0.38
Stance verbs controlled by *to* clause	−0.72
Infinitives	−0.77

Inspection of texts with low Dimension 5 scores shows that these two features serve the communicative function of expressing preferences. The expression of preferences uses highly formulaic and restricted lexical features. Infinitive structures in these texts use the verb *want* almost exclusively, both in its original form *want* and its contracted form *wanna*. As seen in Examples (16–17), this expression of preferences can be related to the interactants performing the task (*What do you want to do; I want to do …*) or to people that are referenced in the task (*Tom wants to visit; Sarah wants to learn*).

(16) A: Hi B. What do you **want to do** sport in the summer?
B: Hi A. I **want to do** uh… deep-sea diving sport.
A: Why you **wanna** *do* this sport?
B: Because uh the sport of deep sea diving… (10168&10267, DS: −3.04)

In this excerpt, the interactants are asking about and expressing their own preferences. In the following excerpt the expression of preferences is in relation to people other than the interactants themselves:

(17) A: Tom **wants to visit** popular tourist attraction, Japane – Japan Kyoto... and **wants to buy** many souvenir is Korean Gyeongju.
B: And Sarah **wants to learn** about new culture... it is Africa and one more Sarah **wants to visit** a well-preserved area, it's Kyoto. (19424&19410, DS: –6.42)

The expression of preferences and desires in this dimension is achieved by using two features: infinitives and *to* complement clauses controlled by stance verbs. Inspection of texts with high Dimension 5 scores showed a pattern of using these features to express preference.

This dimension highlights the formulaic use of *want* to express preferences, whether personal as in *I want*, or reported as in *Tom wants* or *she wants*. To confirm this pattern, the frequency of several stance verbs controlling *to* complement clauses were compared to see if other verbs were adding to the loading of these features. The most frequent verb controlling *to* complement clauses was *want*, occurring 2.2 times PTWs while verbs such as *hope, need, like, mean, decide, agree, love, prefer* all occurred with a rate of less than one time PTWs. This frequency distribution supports the interpretation that this dimension functions primarily as a way to express preference.

Similar to Dimensions 1 and 3, Dimension 5 represents another instance of a highly formulaic use of a specific structure. The frequency distribution highlights the formulaic nature of using the *want to* structure to express preferences. This dimension, similar to the first dimension, is centered around one grammatical structure: *to* complement clauses controlled by stance verbs. The choice of verbs used in this grammatical structure is limited to a few verbs with *want* being the most frequent one. The verb *like*, which expresses desire similar to *want*, is not used as frequently by CCOT participants to express desires and preferences. All of these elements point to a highly formulaic use of this structure to express preferences.

Moreover, the frequent use of *want to* in this dimension is similar to Biber's (2006) findings that most stance *to* complement clauses in spoken university language are controlled by verbs of desire (e.g., *want* and *like*). However, while the use of this structure in the CCOT is to report on preferences, Biber (2006) shows that these verbs are used rather as directives as in *I want you to open your books*. The function of expressing preference works as a response to task conditions that necessitate conveying personal or other's preferences in order to achieve task goals.

4 Conclusion

This study used an MDA to explore linguistic variation in the CCOT and identified five linguistic dimensions that represent areas of linguistic variation. This exploratory MDA did not find a large amount of variance in the CCOT (32%) which suggests that the task performances were quite similar across task types and proficiency levels with respect to the selected lexico-grammatical features (for more information on tasks and proficiency levels, see chapter 1). The study has identified a highly formulaic use of several grammatical structures: *I think [that]*, *I/you agree with*, and *want to*. The formulaic nature of these phrases was shown in several ways. For instance, the verbs *think*, *agree*, and *want* were commonly the most frequent of their semantic classes (i.e., private verbs, public verbs, and desire verbs). Formulaic structures were also shown by the displaying of extended phrases occurring frequently (e.g., *you agree with*). These formulaic uses of the three phrases speak to the importance of formulaic language use in learners' task performance.

The MDA also highlighted interaction-related features as a separate dimension that was distinct from other features of involvement. Many studies have shown involvement features to be in complementary distribution with informational features. However, this study found a different pattern where one dimension (Dimension 2) consists of turn taking variables, and features such as *wh*-questions, word length, and discourse markers. This marking of interactional style suggests that interaction is an important construct when it comes to collaborative task performance and that these features of interaction suggest that there is a difference between interaction and involvement.

The current study also showed unique additions to several functions that are common in many MDAs. For instance, stance expressions are highlighted here in two separate dimensions, one serving an evaluative framing function, and another serving the function of expressing preferences and desires. Similarly, an informational focus was marked in this study by the presence of place nouns and a specific use of lexical choices for nominalizations and pre-modifying nouns. As such, noun features such as nominalizations and pre-modifying nouns were prevalent in the presence of place nouns. The narrative function was also marked by the use of human and quantity nouns. Moreover, involvement functions and features found in previous MDA studies were spread across different dimensions rather than representing a single involvement function (e.g., second and third person pronouns on contrasting ends of Dimension 4, *that*-deletion and private verbs on Dimension 1, and *wh*-questions on Dimension 2). All of these specific patterns show interactive task performances to have unique linguistic characteristics and functions that warrant their analysis as a unique register.

5 Implications and Future Directions

The current study has shown the viability and benefits of using MDA to explore linguistic performance in L2 collaborative oral tasks. The variables used in this study covered a wide range of linguistic and interactional features and the resulting linguistic analysis showed patterns of co-occurring lexico-grammatical features in paired oral L2 language tasks. As mentioned above, this MDA only identified 32% of the variance in the entire CCOT. There are at least two reasons for this. First, the variation is dependent on the linguistic features included in the study. Many MDAs include a wider range of features than the 43 included in the present study which raises the possibility that a wider set of features may uncover more variation than what was found in the present study. Second, the general purpose of the tasks in the CCOT, tasks used for formative assessment purposes and given 2–3 times during a given 16 week semester, may have resulted in a familiarity with the task that did not lead to much variation. In other words, the general communicative purpose of the task and the frequency with which they were administered lead to a more homogenous linguistic performance than similar tasks that were administered for different purposes.

The exploratory approach to investigating linguistic performance adopted here can serve language researchers in identifying patterns of linguistic variation and specific functions necessitated by task conditions. The current study identified some of these functions, but it is likely that there are many other functions and patterns of linguistic variation that could be identified in subsequent analyses. For this to happen, the linguistic and interactive features included in the analyses should cover a wider range of features and/or expand analyses to include potentially relevant domains of linguistic performance (e.g., linguistic errors or phonology features).

Future studies can explore links between specific tasks and linguistic variation. We fully acknowledge that this study did not explore variation across different tasks as our goal was to identify co-occurring linguistic features in the CCOT. A more detailed exploration of these links can be found in Alquraishi (2020) who showed that some tasks elicited more interactive performances and some elicited fewer interactive performances and explored some reasons for these differences.

The current study is not without limitations. This study included a wide range of linguistic and interactional variables in the initial pool of variables. However, several of these variables were not included in the factor analysis because they were infrequent, or they were not suitable for factoring solutions. The latter group might represent variables that are frequent across the dataset to the extent that they are not showing specific trends of loading on dimensions. Examples of these variables are first-person pronouns and filled pauses. Both of these variables, while frequent, were not included in the analysis because of commonality patterns. Nonetheless, these variables are of relevance to the overall linguistic performance even though they do not show specific patterns associated with certain dimensions. In other words, the functions of these variables are of interest to the linguistic performance despite them not being salient on any of the dimensions. Thus, future studies should pay attention to variables that are frequent yet not suitable for inclusion in the factor analysis as these frequent features are clearly representative of task language and in need of interpretation.

Another limitation of the current study is that some of the included variables contain a certain amount of variation in what they represent (e.g., public and communication verbs). This issue was raised when discussing some of the semantic categories of verbs in Dimension 1; however, this overlap became apparent after doing the linguistic analysis and investigating the manifestations of such semantic categories. There are benefits to be gained from including these variables in future analyses, as different semantic manifestations of verbs or nouns might be present. In other words, while it turned out that two linguistic variables were represented by a limited set of overlapping lexical units, it is not necessarily the case for future studies where other lexical units might be present. However, care should be taken when interpreting co-occurrence patterns to see if the variables are representing the same lexical units.

References

Alquraishi, Mohammed. 2020. Studying Linguistic Variation in Interactive Spoken Assessment Tasks and its Relation to Task Characteristics (Doctoral dissertation). Available from ProQuest Dissertations and Theses Global database. (UMI No. pending).
Biber, Douglas. 1988. *Variation across speech and writing*. Cambridge: New York, NY, USA: Cambridge University Press.
Biber, Douglas. 2004. Conversation text types: A multi-dimensional analysis. In *Le poids des mots: Proc. of the 7th International Conference on the Statistical Analysis of Textual Data* Louvain: Presses Universitaires de Louvain. 15–34.
Biber, Douglas. 2006. *University language: A corpus-based study of spoken and written registers*. John Benjamins Publishing.
Biber, Douglas & Susan Conrad. 2009. *Register, genre, and style*. Cambridge University Press.
Biber, Douglas & Jesse Egbert. 2018. *Register variation online*. Cambridge University Press.
Biber, Douglas, Bethany Gray & Kornwipa Poonpon. 2011. Should we use characteristics of conversation to measure grammatical complexity in L2 writing development? *TESOL Quarterly* 45(1). 5–35.
Biber, Douglas, Bethany Gray & Shelley Staples. 2014. Predicting patterns of grammatical complexity across language exam task types and proficiency levels. *Applied Linguistics* 37(5). 639–668.

Biber, Douglas, Stig Johansson, Geoffrey Leech, Susan Conrad & Edward Finegan. 1999. *Longman grammar of written and spoken English*. Harlow: Longman.

Connor-Linton, Jeff & Elana Shohamy. 2001. Register validation, oral proficiency, sampling and the promise of multi-dimensional analysis. In Susan Conrad & Douglas Biber (Eds.), *Variation in English: Multidimensional Studies*, 124–137. Harlow: Pearson Education.

Conrad, Susan. 1996. Investigating academic texts with corpus-based techniques: An example from biology. *Linguistics and Education* 8(3). 299–326.

Csomay, Eniko. 2004. Linguistic variation within university classroom talk: A corpus- based perspective. *Linguistics and Education* 15(3). 243–274.

Egbert, Jesse & Douglas Biber. 2018. Do all roads lead to Rome? Modeling register variation with factor analysis and discriminant analysis. *Corpus Linguistics and Linguistic Theory* 14(2). 233–273.

Ellis, Rod. 2009. The differential effects of three types of task planning on the fluency, complexity, and accuracy in L2 oral production. *Applied Linguistics* 30(4). 474–509.

Friginal, Eric. 2009. *The language of outsourced call centers: A corpus-based study of cross-cultural interaction* (Vol. 34). John Benjamins Publishing.

Friginal, Eric, Man Li & Sara Weigle. 2014. Revisiting multiple profiles of learner compositions: A comparison of highly rated NS and NNS essays. *Journal of Second Language Writing* 23. 1–16.

Lambert, Craig & Judit Kormos. 2014. Complexity, accuracy, and fluency in task-based L2 research: Toward more developmentally based measures of second language acquisition. *Applied Linguistics* 35(5). 607–614.

Pérez-Paredes, Pascal & Maria Sánchez Tornel. 2015. A multidimensional analysis of learner language during story reconstruction in interviews. In Marcus Callies & Sandra Götz (Eds.), *Learner Corpora in Language Testing and Assessment*, 141–162. Amsterdam: John Benjamins.

Pica, Teresa, Ruth Kanagy & Joseph Falodun. 1993. Choosing and using communication tasks for second language instruction. In Graham Crookes & Susan Gass (Eds.), *Tasks and Language Learning: Integrating Theory and Practice* (Vol 1), 9–34. Clevedon, England: Multilingual Matters.

Quirk, Randolph, Leech Greenbaum, Geoffrey Leech & Jan Svartvik. 1985. *A comprehensive grammar of the English language*. London, GB: Longman.

R Core Team. 2016. R: A language and environment for statistical computing. R Foundation for Statistical Computing, Vienna, Austria. URL http://www.R-project.org/research synthesis.

Revelle, William. 2016. Psych: Procedures for psychological, psychometric, and personality research. Evanston, Illinois.

Robinson, Peter. 2015. The Cognition Hypothesis, second language task demands, and the SSARC model of pedagogic task sequencing. In Martin Bygate (Ed.), *Domains and directions in the development of TBLT: A decade of plenaries from the international conference,* 87–122. Amsterdam: John Benjamins Publishing Company.

Skehan, Peter. 2015. Limited attention capacity and cognition: Two hypotheses regarding second language performance on tasks. In Martin. Bygate (Ed.), *Domains and directions in the development of TBLT: A decade of plenaries from the international conference*, 123–156. Amsterdam: John Benjamins Publishing Company.

Skehan, Peter & Peter Foster. 2008. Complexity, accuracy, fluency and lexis in task- based performance: A meta-analysis of the Ealing research. In Siska Van Daele, Alex. Housen, Folkert Kuiken, Michel Pierrard & Ineke. Vedder (Eds.), *Complexity, accuracy, and fluency in second language use, learning, and teaching*, 207–226. University of Brussels Press.

Staples, Shelley, Geoffrey Laflair & Jesse Egbert. 2017. Comparing language use in oral proficiency interviews to target domains: Conversational, academic, and professional discourse. *The Modern Language Journal* 101(1).194–213.
Tavakoli, Parvaneh. 2009. Assessing L2 task performance: Understanding effects of task design. *System* 37(3). 482–495.
Thompson, Sandra. 2002. "Object complements" and conversation: Towards a realistic account. *Studies in Language* 26(1). 125–163.
Thompson, Sandra & Anthony Mulac. 1991. The discourse conditions for the use of the complementizer *that* in conversational English. *Journal of Pragmatics* 15(3). 237–251.
Yuan, Fangyuan & Rod Ellis. 2003. The effects of pre-task planning and on-line planning on fluency, complexity and accuracy in L2 monologic oral production. *Applied Linguistics* 24(1). 1–27.

Appendix A
Factorial Structure of All Included Features

Variable	Dimension 1	Dimension 2	Dimension 3	Dimension 4	Dimension 5
Turn Count	0.03	0.96	−0.27	−0.04	0.13
Turn Length	−0.05	−0.6	−0.09	0.13	−0.16
Private verb	0.79	0.13	−0.01	0.03	−0.11
That-deletion	0.95	0.03	−0.01	−0.01	0.1
Present verb	0.29	−0.01	0.39	0	−0.09
Second person pronoun	−0.09	0.19	0.32	−0.46	0.1
Emphatic	−0.04	0.13	0.04	0.06	−0.01
Pronoun *it*	−0.12	0.23	−0.06	−0.45	−0.07
sub_conj_caus	−0.04	−0.3	0.3	−0.03	0.05
Disc Particle	−0.05	0.42	0.04	0.02	0.16
Pro nom	0.06	0.03	0.02	−0.17	−0.02
Wh-questions	0.01	0.33	0.04	−0.14	0.09
coord_conj_cls	−0.08	0.03	−0.25	−0.03	−0.16
Prepositions	−0.03	−0.19	0.05	0.11	0.2
Attributive adjectives	0.06	−0.26	−0.2	−0.53	0.1
3 person pronoun	0.04	−0.21	0.4	0.75	−0.08
Infinitive	−0.06	−0.26	−0.15	0.1	−0.77
Common nouns	−0.09	−0.28	−0.17	0	0.38

(continued)

Variable	Dimension 1	Dimension 2	Dimension 3	Dimension 4	Dimension 5
Pre-modifying nouns	0.05	−0.05	−0.49	−0.04	0.08
th_vb_likely	0.9	−0.05	−0.01	−0.04	0.12
th_vb_stance_all	0.95	0.03	−0.02	−0.03	0.05
to_vb_stance_all	−0.08	−0.13	−0.14	0.12	−0.72
Human nouns	−0.02	−0.19	0.04	0.43	0
Place nouns	0.03	0.03	−0.62	−0.2	−0.1
Evaluative adjectives	0.1	−0.17	0.04	−0.6	0.12
Mental verbs	0.62	−0.04	0.21	0.13	−0.28
Word length	0.2	−0.37	−0.2	−0.03	0.05
Yes	0.08	0.56	0.01	−0.03	0.1
1 word repetition	0.05	−0.02	0.1	0.08	0.06
Comm. verbs	−0.06	0	0.31	0.1	−0.02
T/T ratio	0.11	0.32	−0.41	0.31	0.05
Word count	0.11	0.49	−0.48	0.05	0
Abstract nouns	0.07	−0.26	0.01	−0.34	0.26
Quantity nouns	−0.16	0.04	0.04	0.32	0.16
jj_att_other	0.06	0	0.14	−0.41	−0.07
Necessity modals	0.03	−0.13	0.27	0.29	−0.06
Attitudinal verbs_other	0.11	−0.14	0.58	0.14	0.13
Past verbs	−0.03	0.08	0.12	0.32	0.05
Perfect aspect	−0.04	0.03	0.05	0.3	0.09
Public verbs	0.02	−0.08	0.47	0.04	0.16
Nominalization	0.09	−0.06	−0.48	−0.06	−0.12
Adverbs	0.07	0.16	0.06	0.24	0.17
Contractions	−0.13	0.16	0.21	−0.14	−0.11

Tatiana Nekrasova-Beker
Use of Phrase-frames in L2 Students' Oral Production across Proficiency Sub-levels

1 Introduction

Second language (L2) development is a complex construct, with a number of different operationalizations having been proposed over the years by researchers, including (among others) linguists, psychologists, and education specialists. Moving away from a modular view of language theory and language acquisition, more recent perspectives on L2 development highlight the multi-faceted nature of the L2 learning process and recognize the interconnectedness of lexis and grammar in authentic language. This recognition of the meaningful role that lexico-grammatical patterns of various types play in communicating meaning in a natural language (see Sinclair 2008) prompted a plethora of studies focusing on different types of phraseological units and their use by both first (L1) and second language (L2) learners.

With phraseological patterns viewed as essential units of language representation and use that blur the distinction between grammar and lexicon, language learning can be conceptualized as the learning of various types of phrases at different levels of complexity, from completely frozen to more productive, which, in turn, offers a unique perspective to explore language development through examining learners' inventory of phraseological units and how it changes across time (or proficiency levels). While there are a number of language patterns that have been examined in previous research (e.g., Bestgen and Granger 2018; Ellis and Ferreira-Junior 2009; Eskildsen and Cadierno 2007; Granger and Bestgen 2014; Li, Eskildsen and Cadierno 2014; Römer, O'Donnell and Ellis 2014), the present study explores L2 learners' use of a specific phraseological unit – *phrase-frame* (hereafter *p-frame*) – across three proficiency sub-levels (from low-intermediate to high-intermediate) and two L1 groups (Arabic and Chinese) in the Corpus of Collaborative Oral Tasks (CCOT, Crawford and McDonough, this volume).

A p-frame, introduced by Fletcher (2002–2012), is a frequent discontinuous multi-word lexical pattern that consists of a lexical chunk with a variable slot. P-frames, also referred to as *formulaic frames* (Biber 2009) and *lexical frames* (Gray and Biber 2013), can be conceptualized as generalizations of recurrent patterns in which, due to their semi-fixed nature, it becomes possible to explore internal variation. Many previous studies on p-frames have been carried out with discipline-specific texts, in which, as Römer (2010) observed, the analysis of internal variation within structures as well as their functions and distributions across texts were examined to help uncover the 'phraseological profile' of a text type. There is also a growing body of research that targeted the use of p-frames by L1 and L2 learners in mostly written data (e.g., Garner 2016; Römer 2019; Römer and Berger 2019), although a few studies have examined L2 learner oral production (Römer and Banerjee 2017; Römer and Garner 2019). In the current study, a similar approach has been adopted to describe the phraseological profile of L2 learner oral use at three different proficiency sub-levels and between two L1 groups in order to explore the potential effects of proficiency and L1 on learners' inventory of frequent patterns employed to accomplish speaking tasks. In order to contextualize the study, the next section offers a brief overview of current research on the use of recurrent multiword sequences by L2 learners, followed by a more detailed discussion of studies that specifically targeted p-frames in learner language.

2 Literature Review

2.1 Use of Recurrent Multiword Sequences by L2 Learners

A traditional approach to exploring L2 development involves conducting a longitudinal case study during which large quantities of production data are collected from one or several L2 learners in order to discover and examine their usage patterns and how they change over time. A plethora of L2 constructions have been examined using such a design, including (but not limited to) negation patterns (Eskildsen and Cadierno 2007), *can* patterns (Eskildsen 2008), question constructions (Eskildsen 2011; Nekrasova-Beker 2016) and motion constructions (Li, Eskildsen and Cadierno 2014). With rich data samples collected from the participants, this research has generated important findings about how the process of language development unfolds. Specifically, previous studies provided support for exemplar-based learning and offered evidence for the proposed path of L2 development, from frequent, concrete language patterns to more productive constructions that were also used to express a broader set of communicative meanings. While the case study approach employed in these longitudinal studies produced a series of detailed accounts of construction development in L2 learners and highlighted the variability in the use of linguistic patterns both within and between individuals, these studies employed small-scale datasets and, therefore, the implications could only be limited to the specific situational contexts targeted in the studies.

Cross-sectional corpus-based investigations of language use by groups of L2 learners offer an alternative approach to the case study design by allowing one to conduct analyses of language data from larger numbers of participants as well as to make comparisons across proficiency levels, participants' native language, gender, L2 experiences, and other contextual features of interest. Studies that examined the use of language patterns by L2 learners typically focused on a specific type of multi-word sequences, including collocations, various types of formulaic language, and n-grams or lexical bundles. Previous research on the use of collocations and formulaic expressions by L2 learners has generated a wealth of important findings about the development of L2 phraseology, emphasizing the potential effects of the amount of language exposure as well as learners' L1. Specifically, in their overview of the main findings obtained from learner corpus research studies, Paquot and Granger (2012) highlighted the prominence of L1 as a factor that typically impacted learners' phraseological production. Some findings seem to suggest that a large proportion of collocational errors could be accounted for by L1 influence (e.g., Laufer and Waldman 2011). In addition, there is evidence that EFL learners' use of phraseological patterns, in terms of both underuse and overuse, is also linked to learners' mother tongue, including such factors as L1-L2 typological differences (Wang 2016), whether a structure is present or absent in an L1, whether an L1 has a direct equivalent of the target structure (Gilquin and Granger 2011) and the frequency with which the target structure is employed in an L1 (Paquot 2013). The next section provides an overview of research conducted specifically on p-frames in order to further contextualize the present investigation and to introduce the research questions asked in the study.

2.2 Analyses of P-Frames in L1 and L2 Corpora

A great amount of research targeting p-frames has been carried out to investigate the phraseology of specialized texts, and these studies have informed a number of methodological decisions made in the current investigation. Specifically, an argument presented in previous studies regarding the use of an inductive approach to generating p-frames by considering all possible n-grams in a corpus in order to capture the most variable patterns (Cunningham 2017; Gray and Biber 2013), as well as the measures proposed to capture slot variability (Biber 2009; Gray and Biber 2013; Römer 2010) have been particularly instrumental for the purposes of the present study. In general, these studies have also provided ample evidence of the suitability of the p-frame approach for the purposes of capturing and demonstrating variability across different text types as well as differentiating between more and less formulaic discourse (Grabowski 2015; Forsyth and Grabowski 2015;

Fuster-Márquez 2014; Fuster-Márquez and Pennock-Speck 2015; Lu, Yoon and Kisselev 2018). Furthermore, research conducted by Biber (2009) and Gray and Biber (2013) also illustrated that there are important phraseological differences between conversation and academic prose, with p-frames identified in conversation being less variable and often composed of verbs and verb phrase structures.

Studies that have explored the use of p-frames in learner corpora constitute another body of research that motivated the current study. Specifically, Römer (2009) examined the use of p-frames in the collections of apprentice writing samples produced by both native and non-native speakers of English and compared it to the use of p-frames by expert writers. The results indicated that native and non-native apprentice writers utilized many of the same p-frames, but with deviating frequencies, and that the variability in p-frame use was attributed to the amount of expertise with the language rather than an issue of nativeness, although much variation across p-frames was also topic-specific. In another study that also focused on student academic writing, O'Donnell, Römer and Ellis (2013) employed a p-frame approach to explore the development of formulaic language in L1 and L2 learners and, more specifically, if learners' language use became less formulaic and more creative with an increase in proficiency. The authors targeted p-frames as one of the units of analysis in the study, along with n-grams and MI-defined formulas. The results showed that neither expertise nor native language status were significant factors for the use of p-frames by L1 and L2 writers.

In another study, Garner (2016) examined the use of p-frames by L1 German learners of English across five proficiency levels (i.e., CEFR levels A1–C1). The study tested the prediction put forward by the usage-based approach about language users employing more diverse and less predictable structures as their language proficiency increases by analyzing the use of the 100 most frequent four-word p-frames from low to high proficiency levels. The results of the study revealed that, indeed, L2 writers at higher levels of language proficiency tended to exhibit a higher degree of variability of p-frames that were also used to communicate a wider variety of discourse functions. Likewise, Juknevičienė and Grabowski (2018) explored formulaicity of learner writing by focusing on p-frames employed by L1 Lithuanian and Polish learners of English. In addition to comparing the use of p-frames in L2 learners of English from two different language backgrounds in order to examine L1-transfer effects, the study also tested the suitability of p-frames as units of analysis in phraseological research targeting recurrent multi-word constructions. The results of the study highlighted the similarities between the two learner groups in their use of p-frames. Specifically, compared to native speakers, L2 learners from both languages tended to use less frequent p-frames and underused p-frames that were based on function words. The authors concluded that the similarities identified between the two learner groups in their use of p-frames, including a number of shared p-frames, illustrated the developmental issues that learners in both L1 groups were facing.

Finally, more recent research conducted by Römer and colleagues explored the use of p-frames by L2 learners and native speakers in both written and oral data, focusing specifically on language development. For example, Römer and Berger (2019) investigated the development of verb constructions in learner writing extracted from the Education First-Cambridge Open Language Database (EFCAMDAT) and reported an overall increase in the productivity of patterns as participants became more proficient in their L2, and this pattern applied across multiple L1 groups. Furthermore, a series of correlation analyses revealed that in their acquisition of verb-argument constructions learners across L1 backgrounds and proficiency levels were influenced by the verb frequencies in L1 usage. Interestingly, the authors reported that the two learner L1 groups largely overlapped in their repertoire of verbs used in the constructions, and the correlations were higher at lower levels of L2 proficiency while showing a decrease at the higher proficiency levels as learners became more diverse (and less similar) in their inventory of p-frames. In another study examining the EFCAMDAT datasets, Römer (2019) further explored, among other questions, the role of formulaic sequences in the acquisition of verb-argument constructions by L2 learners, noting that a set of initially fixed sequences exhibited more variability and became more diverse functionally at higher levels of language proficiency. As the author herself observed, "[c]oncrete sequences of words develop into more abstract constructions" (Römer 2019: 285), the finding that corroborated earlier analyses of construction development by individual learners. Lastly, Römer and Garner (2019) analyzed the development of verb constructions in spoken data produced by L2 English learners from L1 Romance backgrounds that was extracted from the Trinity Lancaster Corpus Sample. The results of this analysis indicated that higher proficiency learners were closer to the pattern exhibited by L1 users, also showing that their inventory of verbs in each construction was more predictable. In addition, learners from different L1 groups but at the same proficiency level were reported to have used very similar verbs in their constructions, suggesting that there was little L1 influence on participants' use of verb-argument constructions detected in this study. Finally, the study provided additional evidence that intermediate and advanced L2 learners were sensitive to L1-based usage patterns. The authors, however, urged caution when interpreting these results, as the study did not control for potential effects of the speaking tasks that were used to collect data from learners at different proficiency levels.

In reviewing previous research on the use of phraseological patterns by L2 learners, it becomes evident that focusing on p-frames as a unit of analysis can offer a unique perspective on language patterning in L2 phraseology and how these patterns change with proficiency. While previous studies that examined n-grams and p-frames in learner corpora have offered strong evidence that such patterns become more variable and complex with an increase in language exposure (proficiency), this research mostly targeted differences across distinct proficiency levels (e.g., from low to high or from A1 to C2 on the CEFR). Thus, it remains unclear if the p-frame approach can be as suitable to reveal the phraseological profile of L2 use within a given level (i.e., intermediate). In addition, few studies (at least at the time of writing this chapter) have examined the use of p-frames in learner oral production, and even fewer of them utilized corpora designed to control for task characteristics. All of these aspects motivated the present investigation which aims to further contribute to the on-going explorations of learner 'phraseological profiles.'

Considering the overall trajectory of research investigating the use of p-frames in learner language, this study examines the use of p-frames in oral production of L2 learners within a single (i.e., intermediate) proficiency level. The study asks the following research questions:

(1) Are there any differences in the variability of p-frames produced by L2 learners across three sub-levels of intermediate English language proficiency?

(2) Are there any differences in the functional characteristics of p-frames produced by L2 learners across three sub-levels of intermediate English language proficiency?

Based on findings obtained in previous research, it was expected that learners' use of p-frames across the three sub-levels would differ, with lower proficiency learners producing more fixed p-frames that would be functionally less diverse compared to patterns identified in high-intermediate learner data which would include more variable p-frames that would also be more diverse functionally.

In addition, motivated by previous research that examined the role of L1 on learners' phraseological patterns in L2 use, this study also explores if there are any differences in the use of p-frames that could be (potentially) attributed to participants' L1 by carrying out a small-scale analysis on a sample of Arabic and Chinese oral production data. This analysis was guided by research question 3:

(3) Are there any differences in the variability and functional characteristics of p-frames produced by L2 learners of intermediate English language proficiency who are from different L1 backgrounds?

3 Method

3.1 Description of Corpora

The oral production data analyzed in the current study were elicited from the CCOT which included 775 dyadic interactions produced by L2 students as part of their achievement tests taken during a given semester of study over 10 semesters (for more information about the corpus see Crawford and McDonough, this volume; Crawford, McDonough, and Brun-Mercer 2019). The corpus included data from participants at three proficiency sub-levels (low-intermediate or sub-level 1, mid-intermediate or sub-level 2, and high-intermediate or sub-level 3), which was determined by an in-house exam that generated proficiency scores comparable to the TOEFL iBT (see Table 1).

Table 1: Participant information.

Sub-level	N	TOEFL iBT scores	L1 background
1	305	32–44	Arabic (81%), Chinese (15%), Korean (2%), Japanese (1%), Pashto (1%)
2	334 (130 progressed from level 1)	45–56	Arabic (76%), Chinese (21%), Japanese (2%), Korean, Pashto, Portuguese (1%)
3	104 (24 progressed from level 2)	57–69	Chinese (59%), Arabic (33%), Japanese (6%), Korean (2%)

During each achievement test, participants completed a paired oral task during which they were instructed to exchange information on a range of topics related to the content targeted in the listening and speaking courses, such as discussing the possibilities of different scientific projects that could be accomplished with a given budget or discussing different types of non-verbal communication that might be useful to an international student in various situations. Participants in each level carried out a set of unique tasks (see Table 2). Orthographic transcriptions of each dyadic interaction were used to compile the sub-corpora of L2 data analyzed in the present study.

Each individual file was examined to only include the interaction between the participants. Information about task characteristics (e.g., the time when the task was administered, the length of the conversation, participant IDs, the task type), transcriber's comments (e.g., how the participant roles were assigned or any additional notes about recorded interactions), as well as information recorded by the participants prior to the actual interaction (statements of their level, task, and roles) were not included in the sub-corpora. Furthermore, data from several participants who carried out the same task twice with different partners were manually removed from the transcripts, which affected the data files from five participants at level 1, six participants at level 2, and four participants at level 3. Finally, while a large number of participants took the speaking test once (accounting for 37% of the data), the majority of them conducted two or more recordings. In several instances, the data from participants who completed four or more tasks at each level (6% of all data) were also manually removed from the corpora to minimize possible idiosyncratic effects. Ideally, the number of individual contributions per level should be consistent (e.g., each participant completes two tasks in each level). In the present study, however, a modest corpus size at each level as well as the general design of the CCOT prevented the researcher from removing additional data from each level (see Table 2 for the breakdown of the resulting corpora).

Table 2: Corpora of L2 collaborative oral tasks.

Sub-level	Number of task types	Number of participant contributions	Number of tokens
1	8	604	89,829
2	10	705	134,015
3	6	171	35,160

3.2 Identification and Analysis of Target P-Frames

Each of the three corpora were analyzed using a free program *kfNgram* (Fletcher 2002–2012) which automatically extracted 4-word sequences and then generated p-frames with variable slots in all four positions. Considering the lower level of language proficiency for some participants as well as the relatively small sizes of the sub-corpora utilized in the study, it was deemed appropriate to focus on 4-word sequences, as longer stretches would be far less frequent to represent a reliable pattern. Similar to previous research (e.g., Gray and Biber 2013; Fuster-Márquez and Pennock-Speck 2015), the target structures were identified using an inductive approach by considering every possible 4-word sequence generated in the corpus in order to capture highly variable p-frames in the analysis. In order to be able to relate the results of the present study to the findings obtained in previous research on the use of p-frames by L2 learners (e.g., Garner 2016; Römer 2009) as well as the findings reported in Biber (2009) and Gray and Biber (2013) about the occurrence of p-frames in conversation, only p-frames with internal variation in the medial slots (i.e., A*CD and AB*D) were considered. Furthermore, the interactive nature of the CCOT data resulted in a high concentration of various types of hesitation phenomena (e.g., uh, huh, hmm) being captured in the transcripts and, therefore, included in the generated sequences (e.g., *uh * can uh, uh * do you think*). To be consistent during the identification process, p-frames with hesitation phenomena were not considered, although the specific variants that included such phenomena in a variable slot (e.g., *I think uh it's* identified as one of seven variants of the *I think * it's* p-frame) were retained.

Next, following the methodological procedures established in previous research on p-frames, sequences that did not constitute meaningful units or did not have a distinct pragmatic function (e.g., *the uh * the, have the * and*) were also disregarded. Also, following recommendations outlined in Juknevičienė and Grabowski (2018), topic-specific p-frames were removed (e.g., *I think * life, the simple * is*), as well as any sequences that were taken verbatim from the prompts, since there is evidence indicating that such sequences often misrepresent learners' productive ability and, therefore, they could distort the results generated in a learner corpus (Paquot 2013). Finally, to reduce possible idiosyncratic effects, each candidate p-frame had to occur in at least two separate data sets at each level (i.e., produced by participants during two different tasks). The lists of candidate frames were also checked to ensure that each p-frame included at least two distinct variants in which fillers differed by more than just capitalization and spelling. Considering the exploratory nature of the present investigation, the present study adopted Garner's (2016) approach in selecting the 100 most frequent p-frames identified in each of the three corpora to be considered in the subsequent analyses (see Appendix for a complete list of p-frames listed in order of frequency, along with their normed frequencies per 100,000 words).

Each set of the 100 most frequent p-frames identified in learner corpora was further subjected to three types of analyses to explore the differences in variability and functional characteristics of p-frames employed by L2 learners across levels as well as across L1 groups. First, the variability analysis was carried out to examine the degree to which the slot in each p-frame was variable by computing a *type-token ratio* (TTR), where *type* refers to the number of unique fillers that are used to complete a frame and *token* refers to the total number of occurrences of that frame (see Römer (2010) for a description of a similar measure – a *variant/p-frame ratio* or *VPR*). The TTR indices range from 0 to 1, with more variable slots yielding indices closer to 1. On the other hand, a TTR closer to 0 reveals a more fixed pattern, in which only a limited number of fillers are used by the participants. Following Gray and Biber's (2013) thresholds, the p-frames were further categorized based on the TTR measure into three groups: highly variable p-frames with TTRs greater than .70, variable p-frames with TTRs between .30 and .70, and (relatively) fixed p-frames with TTRs less than .30.

The next analysis targeted the discourse functions of the p-frames. Biber et al.'s (2004) broader taxonomy, initially proposed for lexical bundles, was adopted in the present study in order to be able to relate the results of the study to the findings obtained in previous research conducted with L2 learners as well as research that examined spoken registers. Biber and colleagues identified four main functions of recurrent multiword sequences in English: stance expressions, discourse organizers, referential expressions, and special conversational expressions. According to this taxonomy, stance expressions perform interpersonal functions, such as expressing attitudes or evaluations (e.g., *I think * should, they don't * to, I'm gonna * about*), discourse organizers reflect relationships between parts of discourse (e.g., *do you * about, what * you think, so what * you*), referential expressions refer to physical or abstract entities and identify its specific attribute (e.g., *lot of * and, the * in the, the * of the*), and special conversational expressions are typically used to express politeness or to report during conversation (e.g., *thank you * much, and my * is, A how * you*). Overall, the p-frames were classified based on the primary function they served in the texts by examining concordance lines for each p-frame and its variants.

Finally, to answer the last research question about potential differences in the use of p-frames associated with participants' L1 background, two L1 groups with the most participants were considered – Arabic and Chinese (see Table 1 for more information). The number of participant contributions (which is different from the number of participants, as some participants contributed more than once) from the two language groups at each proficiency sub-level was identified, with 55 participant contributions recorded for Arabic level 3 participants being the smallest count. In order to be able to make comparisons across multiple groups, L1-based sub-corpora were created by combining contributions from 55 participants from each L1 at each of the three proficiency sub-levels (see Table 3), while also following the general procedure of corpus construction outlined in the previous sections. Next, following the overall procedure for the identification of p-frames described above, 35 of the most frequent p-frames employed by the participants at each level in both L1 groups were selected and then analyzed for slot variability and discourse functions. Ideally, a larger number of p-frames should be analyzed at each sub-level to offer reliable findings. However, due to the unequal number of participant contributions in the original corpus and, therefore, smaller L1-based sub-corpora generated in the present study, only 35 p-frames that met the overall identification criteria were selected in each sub-corpus. Therefore, all analyses performed on these data are interpreted with caution.

Table 3: L1-based corpora of L2 collaborative oral tasks.

Sub-level (participant contributions)	Number of tokens	
	Arabic	Chinese
1 (n = 110)	15,315	14,829
2 (n = 110)	15,762	14,015
3 (n = 110)	16,310	15,387

In order to determine if the differences in the distributions of p-frames across various categories (i.e., variability and functional features) were significant across proficiency sub-levels and L1 groups, three different statistical tests were performed. Because the variability data did not meet the assumption of normality, a Kruskal-Wallis H test was carried out to determine if the differences in the TTR indices were statistically significant across the three groups. To carry out pair-wise comparisons, a series of Mann-Whitney U tests with a Bonferroni adjustment were performed. For the functional analyses, chi-square tests were performed to explore if the distribution of p-frames across the functional categories differed across participant groups. Alpha was set at .05 for all statistical tests, unless specified otherwise.

4 Results

To provide a general overview of the frequency profiles of the p-frames identified in the three learner corpora, Table 4 includes information about the mean, median, and maximum and minimum frequencies (normalized per 100,000 words) of the 100 most frequent 4-word p-frames produced by the participants in each group. As illustrated in Table 4, participants in the high intermediate group (sub-level 3) seemed to utilize fewer extremely frequent p-frames in their oral production, compared to participants in the mid-intermediate (sub-level 2) and low intermediate (sub-level 1) groups who showed a wider range of frequencies in their datasets.

Table 4: Frequency distribution (per 100,000 words) of 100 most frequent P-frames across sub-levels.

Sub-level	M (SD)	Median	Minimum frequency	Maximum frequency
1	18.38 (20.94)	13.40	7.80	194.80
2	24.86 (26.76)	16.79	11.94	214.16
3	23.41 (17.57)	17.06	11.38	116.61

4.1 Variability Analysis

To answer the first question about the differences in the variability of p-frames produced by L2 learners across three proficiency sub-levels, Table 5 includes information about the distribution of p-frames across the three categories (fixed, variable, and highly variable) in each group. As illustrated in the table, high intermediate participants employed more p-frames that were of a variable and highly variable nature, especially compared to participants in group 2 (mid-intermediate). A comparison of the median TTRs computed for the use of p-frames in each group (see Table 5) provides additional support for the differences illustrated above – specifically, with an increase in language proficiency, a higher proportion of the frequent p-frames produced by the learners are more variable in nature.

While the results presented in Table 5 seem to be logical and, in general, support the findings obtained in previous research on the use of p-frames by L2 learners across proficiency levels (see Garner 2016), due to the differences in corpora sizes used in the present study (as well as in previous research), these results need to be interpreted with caution, as larger corpora typically yield smaller TTRs. Garner (2016: 39, footnote 2) also acknowledged the sensitivity of the TTR measure to the length of a corpus, but he used it nonetheless, noting that there was "no other measure of lexical diversity for p-frames." While the same measure is used in the present study (and, hence, the same issue pertains to the present investigation), an alternative approach to computing the TTRs is employed below.

Specifically, the TTR indices were recalculated using equal-size samples elicited from the larger corpora (for sub-levels 1 and 2) by using the size of the smallest corpus (i.e., for sub-level 3) as the basis and drawing 35,000 words from each of the two larger corpora. The larger corpora were each divided in five equal parts and the first 7,000 words were drawn from each part. Using kfNgram, the equal-size samples from the two larger corpora were re-analyzed to identify the

Table 5: Distribution of P-frames in the three variability categories across sub-levels.

Sub-level	Fixed (<.30)	Variable (.30 – .70)	Highly variable (>.70)	Median TTR (MAD*)
1	31	50	19	.39 (.17)
2	55	38	7	.28 (.15)
3	13	52	35	.57 (.18)

Note: *MAD stands for Median Absolute Deviation, which is a more appropriate measure of dispersion for data that is not normally distributed. MAD is similar to the interquartile range, but it is a more robust statistic.

new type and token counts for the original p-frames. While this approach is not ideal, as not every original p-frame could be identified in the smaller samples, it was, nevertheless, employed in the present study as an alternative methodological procedure that was worthwhile exploring. Table 6 presents the re-calculated numbers of p-frames across the three variability categories, along with adjusted median TTRs and median absolute deviations identified in samples of 35,000 words drawn from each corpus.

Table 6: Distribution of P-frames in the three variability categories across sub-levels (calculated based on samples of 35,000 words).

Sub-level	Fixed (<.30)	Variable (.30 – .70)	Highly variable (>.70)	Median TTR (MAD)
1 (n = 77)	22	46	9	.43 (.16)
2 (n = 83)	29	38	16	.36 (.19)
3 (n = 100)	13	52	35	.57 (.18)

As shown in Table 6, in terms of variability, the overall trend detected for the use of p-frames across the three participant groups persists, although the differences in the median TTRs identified in equal-size samples are less pronounced. Also, a number of highly variable p-frames that were initially identified in the corpus of low intermediate learners were not included in the smaller sample, bringing the number of highly variable p-frames down for group 1. The adjusted distribution of the TTR values across the three groups was tested for significant differences. A Kruskal-Wallis H test showed that there was a statistically significant difference in median TTR values across participant groups, $H(2) = 21.87$, $p = .000$. Post hoc analyses revealed the following significant pairwise differences: between groups 2 and 3 ($Z = -4.15$, $p = .000$, $r = .31$) and between groups 1 and 3 ($Z = -3.72$, $p = .000$, $r = .28$). No significant difference between the median TTRs of p-frames was found for groups 1 and 2 ($p = .418$). The results of these analyses confirmed that the participants in the high intermediate group were using significantly more variable p-frames with more diverse sets of variants occupying the slots compared to participants in groups 1 (low-intermediate) and 2 (mid-intermediate). Although there were no significant difference between the median TTR values for groups 1 and 2, mid-intermediate participants (group 2) appeared to rely more on p-frames that were less variable compared to the other two groups.

4.2 Functional Analysis

The second research question asked about differences in functional characteristics of p-frames produced by L2 learners across the three sub-levels. To address this question, the function of each of the top 100 p-frames identified for each level was determined by considering the original sub-corpora (as opposed to the 35,000-word samples employed in the previous analysis). Based on the analysis of concordance lines, each p-frame was categorized in one of the four groups. Table 7 shows the distribution of p-frames across the four functional categories in each corpus.

Table 7: Distribution of P-frames in the four functional categories across sub-levels.

Sub-level	Stance p-frames	Referential p-frames	Discourse organizing p-frames	Special conversational p-frames
1	68	8	13	11
2	50	30	8	12
3	57	21	18	4

As shown in Table 7, participants in all three groups relied most heavily on p-frames that expressed stance, followed by referential p-frames in group 2 and group 3, while low intermediate learners produced more p-frames performing discourse-organizing functions. A notable difference is that the number of special conversation p-frames was lower for high intermediate participants. The results of a chi-square test indicated that there were significant differences in the functional characteristics of the p-frames employed across the proficiency groups, $\chi^2(6) = 25.11$, $p = .000$, Cramer's $V = .205$. In order to locate significance, standardized residuals were computed. Higher residuals (> 1.96) have located significance with the frequency of stance and referential p-frames produced by group 1 and group 2, as well as the frequency of special conversational p-frames produced by group 3. In other words, higher frequency of stance p-frames and lower frequency of referential p-frames in group 1, higher frequency of stance and referential p-frames produced in group 2, and lower frequency of special conversation p-frames produced by participants in group 3 all contributed to the statistically significant chi-square statistic value.

4.3 L1 Influence

The last research question asked about the potential influence of learners' L1 on their production of p-frames at the three sub-levels of English proficiency. Table 8 provides a general overview of the frequency distribution for the p-frames produced by L1 Arabic and Chinese learners of English at each of the three proficiency sub-levels. As illustrated in Table 8, the mean frequency of p-frames produced by Arabic and Chinese L1 speakers was consistently higher for high-intermediate learners (i.e., sub-level 3) in both groups.

Table 8: Frequency distribution (per 100,000 words) of 35 most frequent P-frames across sub-levels for Arabic and Chinese learners.

L1/ Level	M (SD)	Median	Minimum frequency	Maximum frequency
Arabic (n=55)				
1	36.38 (29.22)	31.06	20.71	186.36
2	48.78 (47.02)	29.24	20.24	200.18
3	49.57 (31.63)	30.66	24.52	128.76
Chinese (n=55)				
1	39.72 (18.54)	37.83	23.64	104.03
2	39.76 (27.54)	29.44	18.73	128.45
3	47.35 (33.42)	32.49	26.00	201.47

In terms of the potential differences in the variability of p-frames produced by the Arabic and Chinese L2 learners, Table 9 includes the distribution of the 35 most frequent p-frames across the three variability categories for each proficiency sub-level, along with the median TTR and MAD values for each sub-level. As illustrated in Table 9, mid-intermediate learners in both L1 groups produced more p-frames of a fixed nature and fewer p-frames of a highly variable nature compared to the other two sub-levels whose use of fixed, variable, and highly variable p-frames was comparable for both L1 Arabic and Chinese learners. This overall pattern is also reflected in the median TTR indices computed for the p-frames produced by participants in each sub-level within both L1 groups. The overall distribution of the TTR values was tested for significant differences for the two L1 groups as a whole as well as for each proficiency sub-level by performing a series of Mann-Whitney U tests.

The first Mann-Whitney U test indicated that there was a statistically significant difference in median TTR values for the two L1 groups, with Arabic participants overall showing less variation in their use of p-frames than Chinese participants, $U = 4471.00$, $p = .018$. To locate the significance, a series of post hoc analyses were conducted to compare the median TTR indices for each pair of proficiency levels, with alpha adjusted to .017 to control for Type 1 error.

Table 9: Distribution of 35 most frequent P-frames in the three variability categories across sub-levels for Arabic and Chinese learners.

L1/ Level	Fixed (<.30)	Variable (.30 – .70)	Highly variable (>.70)	Median TTR (MAD)
Arabic (n=55)				
1	6	20	9	.50 (.17)
2	21	13	1	.23 (.15)
3	7	17	11	.50 (.21)
Chinese (n=55)				
1	6	16	13	.63 (.17)
2	10	19	6	.43 (.19)
3	3	17	15	.60 (.20)

Note: Calculated Based on Samples from 55 Learners per Sub-level

Three Mann-Whitney U tests revealed that there was one significant pairwise difference for participants in the mid-intermediate level (level 2), with Arabic level 2 participants producing significantly less variable p-frames ($Mdn = .23$) compared to Chinese level 2 participants whose use of p-frames was more variable ($Mdn = .43$), $U = 373.50$, $p = .005$. No significant differences between the median TTRs of p-frames produced by participants from different L1 groups was found for low-intermediate ($p = .275$) and high-intermediate ($p = .418$) sub-levels.

Table 10 shows the distribution of p-frames across the four functional categories in each sub-level of the two L1 groups. As illustrated in the table, participants in both L1 groups followed the overall trend detected for the entire participant pool examined in the study, by relying most heavily on p-frames that expressed stance, followed by referential p-frames, p-frames performing discourse-organizing functions, and special conversation p-frames.

Table 10: Distribution of 35 most frequent P-frames in the four functional categories across sub-levels for Arabic and Chinese learners.

L1/ Level	Stance p-frames	Referential p-frames	Discourse organizing p-frames	Special conversational p-frames
Arabic (n=55)				
1	26	4	3	2
2	21	3	6	5
3	18	9	7	1
Chinese (n=55)				
1	29	4	2	0
2	24	7	1	3
3	23	7	5	0

The results of the chi-square tests, which examined the differences in the functional characteristics of the p-frames across the two L1 groups, while also controlling for proficiency sub-levels within each L1 group, indicated that there were no significant differences in the functional characteristics of the p-frames between Arabic and Chinese participants (low-intermediate: $p = .50$; mid-intermediate: $p = .118$; high-intermediate: $p = .53$). In other words, the participants in both L1 groups were consistent in their use of p-frames of the four discourse types, and although Arabic participants in general utilized more p-frames serving discourse organizing and special conversational functions compared to Chinese participants, these differences were not statistically significant.

5 Discussion

The study asked three research questions about the differences in the variability and functional characteristics of p-frames employed by participants in three sub-levels of intermediate English proficiency and in two L1 groups during oral collaborative interaction. In terms of the variability of p-frames, the results of the median TTR values indicated that the patterns employed by high intermediate participants were more variable compared to the patterns produced by learners in the other two groups, and these differences were statistically significant. This result is consistent with findings obtained in previous research on the use of p-frames by L2 learners across proficiency levels in writing as well as oral production (Garner 2016; Römer 2019; Römer and Berger 2019; Römer and Garner 2019).

Specifically, Garner (2016) observed that the number of variable and highly variable p-frames increased with proficiency, although significant pairwise differences were found only between non-adjacent levels (e.g., A1 and B2, A1 and C1). Considering that the present study examined language production from learners within a single proficiency level, it is noteworthy that the differences were statistically significant. Interestingly, the variability pattern exhibited by the participants across the three groups is not linear, with participants in group 2 producing more fixed p-frames, also reflected in a lower median TTR, compared to participants in group 1. These results suggest that there is a lot of variability in the data, and participants at this level (i.e., an intermediate level in general) tend to utilize both familiar formulaic chunks as well as more productive patterns with which they experiment to see what works and does not work in a language. Compared to beginning learners who might rely exclusively on formulaic patterns (see median TTR values for levels A1 and A2 in Garner 2016), the intermediate participants in the present study exhibited patterns that were more variable in general. Interestingly, Gray and Biber (2013) reported that p-frames identified in conversation were much more fixed compared to the p-frames used in academic writing. The fact that the majority of p-frames identified in the present study were rather variable could be related to the specific genre targeted in the study – collaborative interaction – during which participants had to accomplish a specific task of an academic nature, rather than casually converse about general topics. Garner (2016) argued that the increase in complexity of topics employed for writing tasks in his study might have prompted more advanced learners to produce more productive patterns in order to address the complexity of the tasks. The tasks employed to compile learner corpora analyzed in the present study were consistently complex across sub-levels – participants in all three groups were asked to share opinions, give advice, find a solution to a problem, identify strengths and weaknesses of a proposal, to name a few tasks. All of these scenarios constituted complex communicative situations which could have prompted the learners to adapt their language patterns to meet the demands of those situations, thus contributing to higher variability indices across groups.

The functional analysis of the p-frames across participant groups illustrated the overall preference for p-frames expressing stance, which is not surprising given the highly interactive nature of the tasks that learners engaged in. In addition to that, L2 learners were also reported to overuse stance expressions, especially at lower levels of language proficiency. In the present study, participants' production at a higher level of language proficiency was characterized by a lower number of special conversational p-frames and a higher number (and a more diverse repertoire) of referential p-frames. Previous studies reported the increase in noun phrases and decrease in quantifying and evaluative expressions as characteristic features of L2 learners (writers mostly) at higher levels of language proficiency (Chen and Baker 2016). Similarly, in the present study, while learners at the low intermediate level relied heavily on referential p-frames of a quantifying nature (e.g., *lot of * and, there * a lot, have many * to*), the inventory of referential expressions at the high intermediate level was more diverse and included identification, time and place reference, and specification of attributes, many of which were expressed by noun phrases (e.g., *and the * one, the * of the, the * of his, at the * of, the * for the, the * is a*).

While a series of quantitative analyses conducted in the present study revealed a number of existing differences in L2 learners' use of p-frames within a single level, a manual examination of the lists of shared p-frames in each sub-corpus provided additional evidence of the differences exhibited by the participants in their use of frequent patterns. Specifically, out of 100 most frequent patterns identified in each corpus, 12 were used in all three sub-corpora (e.g., *thank you * much, so what * you, I think * should, there * a lot*), 16 were shared between levels 1 and 2 (e.g., *I will * you, I think * you, you can * it, in my * I*), seven were shared between levels 1 and 3 (e.g., *if you * at, want to * about, I * with you*), and 11 were shared between levels 2 and 3 (e.g., *I think * is, so * do you, it's a * idea*). While it might seem that the proportion of shared p-frames identified in each corpus is rather high (from 30% in the corpus of high-intermediate learners, to 35% in the corpus of low-intermediate learners to 39% in the corpus of mid-intermediate learners), the majority of overlapping p-frames are low-variability patterns that participants generally employed to be polite, to complete the task (e.g., *to express an opinion, to identify a solution*), and to keep the conversation going. At the same time, there were several p-frames shared across the three levels that were extremely variable and included a number of fillers that were level-specific. For example, some of the most frequent fillers used across levels to complete a shared p-frame *we can * it* included *do, fix, take* in level 1, *invest, use, try, make* in level 2, and *use, say, keep* in level 3. Lastly, in addition to a set of unique variants that were identified in a number of shared p-frames, it is also important to consider how a pattern is used by the participants in each group. For example, while the p-frame *the * of the* was shared across all three participant groups, in addition to a set of specific variants identified in each corpus, it was ranked 3rd in the sub-corpus of high-intermediate learners (with a TTR value of .65), 18th in the sub-corpus of mid-intermediate learners (with an adjusted TTR value of .73), and 78th in the sub-corpus of low-intermediate learners (with an adjusted TTR value of .33), thus illustrating the usage patterns that are distinct for each participant groups – it is a more productive pattern that is frequently employed by high-intermediate learners compared to its relatively infrequent and more fixed use by low-intermediate learners.

Finally, the results of the L1-based analysis indicated that while there were differences in the preference for more or less variable p-frames between Arabic and Chinese participants, these differences were detected only for mid-intermediate learners. A quick glance at the 35 most frequent p-frames identified in Arabic mid-intermediate participants' data revealed that these learners employed a number of p-frames that performed special conversational functions in discourse, including both politeness (e.g., *a okay * you, thank you * much*) and simple inquiry (e.g., *how * you b, hi * how are*), all of which were highly fixed patterns. In terms of the functional characteristics of the p-frames, the participants in both L1 groups were consistent in their use of p-frames of the four discourse types, although Arabic participants employed more patterns serving discourse-organizing and special conversational functions. While these results are somewhat inconsistent with those reported in previous phraseology research, especially for typologically different languages (e.g., Paquot and Granger 2012; Wang 2016), findings obtained in more recent studies conducted by Römer and colleagues on verb-argument constructions illustrated that learners at the same proficiency level tended to employ similar patterns, suggesting that this phenomenon could be truly developmental.

6 Conclusion

The goal of the present study was to examine the phraseological patterns, specifically the use of p-frames, employed by L2 learners during collaborative interaction. The results of the study illustrated that a p-frame as a unit of analysis was a suitable measure to explore the differences in the use of language patterns within a single proficiency level. While not all analyses of the p-frame features captured differences among groups that were statistically significant, the overall developmental trajectory that emerged in the present study was consistent with findings obtained in previous research. Specifically, participants at higher levels of language proficiency showed higher levels of language productivity by utilizing more p-frames of a variable and highly variable nature and by expanding their repertoire of discourse functions to communicate a more diverse range of meanings. An important implication of these (and all previous) findings relates to the question of how we operationalize language development and the criteria we deem important for measuring learners' progress towards proficiency. Considering more extended phrases as a unit of linguistic analysis that recognize the interconnectedness of lexis and grammar in language use and development is not a new idea (e.g., Sinclair 2008) and a number of proposals have been articulated that focused on examining the developmental trajectory of linguistic constructions from more fixed, entrenched units to more variable, even abstract schemas (e.g., Ellis and Ferreira-Junior 2009; Eskildsen 2012). Pursuing this line of theoretical thought typically implies collecting longitudinal data and focusing on a specific construction type to trace its development in learner production, which involves labor-intensive methodology and, therefore, normally generates small-scale datasets and targets fewer participants. A corpus-based analysis focusing on the use of language patterns and, specifically, their productivity and functional use, might be a worthwhile approach to consider when investigating the development of learner constructions across various L1 groups and proficiency levels in a larger-scale study. Along the same lines, factoring in the phraseological features of oral language, especially such dimensions as evolving productivity of language patterns, in measurements and scales of L2 development could be another worthwhile attempt in the overall effort of understanding language development as a complex and dynamic process (De Bot and Larsen-Freeman 2011) which is often non-linear and does not result in native-like accuracy (also see Römer (2017) for a critical discussion of popular speaking rating scales regarding their ability to capture and reflect the phraseological nature of authentic language).

There are several limitations of the study that need to be acknowledged. To begin with, the corpora used to extract the patterns were rather limited in size and, due to this limitation, it was not possible to fully explore the effect of different L1 backgrounds on participants' production of p-frames in a sample that would be large enough to be representative. A larger corpus of oral data from L2 learners of various L1 backgrounds would be useful to explore potential effects of learners' L1 on their use of phraseological patterns at different levels of L2 proficiency. Along the same lines, it would be informative to collect a corpus of native-speaker oral data who completed the same collaborative tasks to observe the productivity and functional characteristics of their patterns and to compare them to the patterns detected for L2 learners. Furthermore, the present study is exploratory and only focused on a small set of frequent p-frames identified in each corpus, not the entire set of candidate frames. Therefore, the results of the present study are far from being conclusive and should be interpreted with caution. Despite these limitations, the study contributed to the ongoing exploration of learner spoken language and, specifically, the use of recurrent multi-word patterns in L2 oral production. It is my hope that these findings highlight the important role that phraseology plays in conceptualizing and operationalizing language development and, therefore, it should be explored in further investigations that ask additional (and more focused) research questions about L2 learners' use of language patterns.

References

Bestgen, Yves & Sylviane Granger. 2018. Tracking L2 writers' phraseological development using collgrams: Evidence from a longitudinal EFL corpus. In Sebastian Hoffmann, Andrea Sand, Sabine Arndt-Lappe & Lisa Marie Dillmann (Eds.), *Corpora and Lexis*, 277–301. Leiden & Boston: Brill/Rodopi.

Biber, Douglas. 2009. A corpus-driven approach to formulaic language in English: Multi-word patterns in speech and writing. *International Journal of Corpus Linguistics* 14. 275–311.

Biber, Douglas, Susan Conrad & Viviana Cortes. 2004. If you look at … : Lexical bundles in university teaching and textbooks. *Applied Linguistics* 25. 371–405.

Chen, Yu-Hua & Paul Baker. 2016. Investigating criterial discourse features across second language development: Lexical bundles in rated learner essays, CEFR B1, B2 and C1. *Applied Linguistics* 37(6). 849–880.

Crawford, William, Kim McDonough & Nicole Brun-Mercer. 2019. Identifying linguistic markers of collaboration in second language peer interaction: A lexico-grammatical approach. *TESOL Quarterly* 53(1). 180–207.

Cunningham, Kelly. 2017. A phraseological exploration of recent mathematics research articles through key phrase frames. *Journal of English for Academic Purposes* 25. 71–83.

De Bot, Kees & Diane Larsen-Freeman. 2011. Researching second language development from a dynamic systems theory perspective. In Marjolijn Verspoor, Kees de Bot & Wander Lowie (Eds.), *A dynamic approach to second language development: Methods and techniques*, 5–23. Amsterdam: John Benjamins.

Ellis, Nick & Fernando Ferreira-Junior. 2009. Constructions and their acquisition: Islands and the distinctiveness of their occupancy. *Annual Review of Cognitive Linguistics* 7. 188–221.

Eskildsen, Søren. 2008. Constructing another language – usage-based linguistics and second language acquisition. *Applied Linguistics* 30(3). 335–357.

Eskildsen, Søren. 2011. The L2 inventory in action: Conversation analysis and usage-based linguistics in SLA. In Gabriele Pallottii & Johannes Wagner (Eds.), *L2 learning as social practice: Conversation-analytic perspectives*, 337–373. Honolulu, HI: National Foreign Language Resource Center.

Eskildsen, Søren & Teresa Cadierno. 2007. Are recurring multi-word expressions really syntactic freezes? Second language acquisition from the perspective of usage-based linguistics. In Marja Nenonen & Sinikka Niemi (Eds.), *Collocation and idioms 1: Papers from the first Nordic Conference on syntactic freezes*, 1–14. Joensuu, Finland: Joensuu University Press.

Fletcher, William. 2002–2012. KfNgram. A free software program, available at http://www.kwicfinder.com/kfNgram/kfNgramHelp.html.

Forsyth, Richard & Łukasz Grabowski. 2015. Is there a formula for formulaic language? *Poznan Studies in Contemporary Linguistics* 51(4). 511–549.

Fuster-Márquez, Miguel. 2014. Lexical bundles and phrase frames in the language of hotel websites. *English Text Construction* 7(1). 84–121.

Fuster-Márquez, Miguel & Barry Pennock-Speck. 2015. Target frames in British hotel websites. *IJES* 15. 51–69.

Garner, James. 2016. A phrase-frame approach to investigating phraseology in learner writing across proficiency levels. *International Journal of Learner Corpus Research* 2(1). 31–68.

Gilquin, Gaëtanelle & Sylviane Granger. 2011. From EFL to ESL: Evidence from the International Corpus of Learner English. In Joybrato Mukherjee & Marianne Hundt (Eds.), *Exploring second-language varieties of English and learner Englishes: Bridging a paradigm gap*, 55–78. Amsterdam & Philadelphia: John Benjamins.

Grabowski, Łukasz. 2015. Phrase frames in English pharmaceutical discourse: A corpus-driven study of intra-disciplinary register variation. *Research in Language* 13(3). 266–291.

Granger, Sylviane & Yves Bestgen. 2014. The use of collocations by intermediate vs. advanced non-native writers: A bigram-based study. *International Review of Applied Linguistics* 52(3). 229–252.

Gray, Bethany & Douglas Biber. 2013. Lexical frames in academic prose and conversation. *International Journal of Corpus Linguistics* 18(1). 109–135.

Juknevičienė, Rita & Łukasz Grabowski. 2018. Comparing formulaicity of learner writing through phrase-frames: A corpus-driven study of Lithuanian and Polish EFL student writing. *Research in Language* 16(3). 303–323.

Laufer, Batia & Tina Waldman. 2011. Verb-noun collocations in second language writing: A corpus analysis of learners' English. *Language Learning* 61. 647–672.

Li, Peiwen, Søren Eskildsen & Teresa Cadierno. 2014. Tracing an L2 learner's motion construction over time: a usage-based classroom investigation. *The Modern Language Journal* 98(2). 612–628.

Lu, Xiaofei, Jungwan Yoon & Olesya Kisselev. 2018. A phrase-frame list for social science research article introductions. *Journal of English for Academic Purposes* 36. 76–85.

Nekrasova-Beker, Tatiana. 2016. EFL learners' use of question constructions over time: Patterns and proficiency effects. *System* 58. 82–96.

O'Donnell, Matthew, Ute Römer & Nick Ellis. 2013. The development of formulaic sequences in first and second language writing. Investigating effects of frequency, association, and native norm. *International Journal of Corpus Linguistics* 18(1). 83–108.

Paquot, Magali. 2013. Lexical bundles and L1 transfer effects. *International Journal of Corpus Linguistics* 18(3). 391–417.

Paquot, Magali & Sylviane Granger. 2012. Formulaic language in learner corpora. *Annual Review of Applied Linguistics* 32. 130–149.

Römer, Ute. 2009. English in academia: Does nativeness matter? *Anglistik: International Journal of English Studies* 20(2). 89–100.

Römer, Ute. 2010. Establishing the phraseological profile of a text type: The construction of meaning in academic book reviews. *English Text Construction* 3(1). 95–119.

Römer, Ute. 2017. Language assessment and the inseparability of lexis and grammar: Focus on the construct of speaking. *Language Testing* 34(4). 477–492.

Römer, Ute. 2019. A corpus perspective on the development of verb constructions in second language learners. *International Journal of Corpus Linguistics* 24(3). 270–292.

Römer, Ute & Jayanti Banerjee. 2017. Validating the MET speaking test through phraseological analysis: A corpus approach to language assessment. *CaMLA Working Papers* 2017-01. 1–26.

Römer, Ute & Cynthia Berger. 2019. Observing the emergence of constructional knowledge: Verb patterns in German and Spanish learners of English at different proficiency levels. *Studies in Second Language Acquisition* 41(5). 1089–1110.

Römer, Ute & James Garner. 2019. The development of verb constructions in spoken learner English: Tracing effects of usage and proficiency. *International Journal of Learner Corpus Research* 5(2). 207–230.

Römer, Ute, Matthew O'Donnell & Nick Ellis. 2014. Second language learner knowledge of verb-argument constructions: Effects of language transfer and typology. *The Modern Language Journal* 98. 952–975.

Sinclair, John. 2008. The phrase, the whole phrase, and nothing but the phrase. In Sylviane Granger & Fanny Meunier (Eds.), *Phraseology: An interdisciplinary perspective*, 407–410. Amsterdam & Philadelphia: John Benjamins.

Wang, Ying. 2016. *The idiom principle and L1 influence: A contrastive learner-corpus study of delexical Verb + Noun collocations*. Amsterdam & Philadelphia: John Benjamins.

Appendix

Most Frequent Phrase-Frames in the Three Corpora (Normalized per 100,000 words)

Rank	Group 1 P-Frames	Freq.	Group 2 P-Frames	Freq.	Group 3 P-Frames	Freq.
1	i * with you	194.8	what * you think	214.16	i * with you	116.61
2	do you * about	70.1	i agree * you	159.68	and * i think	76.79
3	i * agree with	51.2	i think * is	84.32	the * of the	73.95
4	you * with me	50.1	do you * about	64.17	do you * about	73.95
5	thank you * much	47.9	have a * of	63.43	so what * you	68.26
6	you can * it	45.6	has a * of	58.20	we can * the	65.42
7	i think * should	42.3	i * your point	53.73	i think * is	65.42
8	i think * you	33.4	so * do you	41.04	so * do you	59.73
9	if you * a	32.3	i think * should	40.29	i think * should	51.19
10	life is * than	32.3	in the * and	40.29	the * in the	45.51
11	agree with * because	28.9	i think * a	39.55	i * agree with	42.66
12	you can * a	28.9	a * of money	37.31	the * one is	36.97
13	i'm * with you	26.7	lot of * and	36.56	the * i think	34.13
14	if you * to	26.7	thank you * much	35.82	in the * the	34.13
15	i think * it's	26.7	so what * you	35.07	to * him the	31.29
16	i think * will	24.5	i think * will	34.32	we * tell him	25.60
17	you * if you	24.5	he * a lot	30.59	i think * have	25.60
18	he * go to	23.4	the * of the	29.85	the second * is	22.75
19	in my * i	23.4	the * in the	29.85	in the * so	22.75
20	you can * the	23.4	but * i think	28.36	i think * he	22.75
21	lot of * and	22.3	i * agree with	28.36	the * of his	22.75
22	if * want to	22.3	i think * have	27.61	we * tell her	22.75
23	there * a lot	21.2	want to * a	26.86	he * know the	22.75
24	i will * you	21.2	i think * need	25.37	and my * is	22.75
25	i think * can	20.0	yeah * agree with	24.62	thank you * much	22.75
26	is very * and	18.9	i think * good	24.62	and i * that	22.75
27	nice to * you	18.9	see your * but	23.13	if you * to	19.91
28	so what * you	17.8	i * to open	22.39	it's a * idea	19.91
29	it's not * for	16.7	i think * it's	21.64	but * i think	19.91
30	a * way to	16.7	think the * is	21.64	if you * at	19.91

(continued)

Rank	Group 1 P-Frames	Freq.	Group 2 P-Frames	Freq.	Group 3 P-Frames	Freq.
31	a good * for	15.6	want to * to	20.89	want to * the	19.91
32	yeah i * so	15.6	you * about the	20.89	and the * is	19.91
33	yeah i * it's	15.6	it * a lot	20.89	do you * some	19.91
34	i think * agree	15.6	long * every day	20.15	on the * and	19.91
35	a good * to	15.6	is a * student	19.40	and * will be	17.06
36	i * talk about	15.6	there * a lot	19.40	so * about you	17.06
37	you * about it	15.6	yeah * i think	19.40	of * i think	17.06
38	want to * it	15.6	it's * good idea	19.40	of the * is	17.06
39	you will * it	14.5	it's a * idea	19.40	we can * it	17.06
40	we * talk about	14.5	i * it's a	18.65	at the * of	17.06
41	do you * that	14.5	i * it's good	18.65	and the * one	17.06
42	can you * me	14.5	he * to go	18.65	i * that the	17.06
43	good for * and	14.5	i'm * with you	18.65	have to * him	17.06
44	yeah i * that	14.5	a good * to	18.65	the * will be	17.06
45	i will * about	14.5	we can * a	18.65	you think * this	17.06
46	do you * a	13.4	we * talk about	18.65	tell * about the	17.06
47	do you * the	13.4	to * a new	18.65	the * reason is	17.06
48	can * a lot	13.4	my * i think	17.91	we should * him	17.06
49	the best * to	13.4	in my * i	17.91	if he * the	17.06
50	he should * to	13.4	a i * your	17.16	think it's * to	14.22
51	i think * have	13.4	i don't * so	16.42	do you * the	14.22
52	if you * at	13.4	since * was a	16.42	will be * for	14.22
53	if you * it	13.4	think * a good	16.42	and our * is	14.22
54	want to * about	12.2	and he * to	16.42	but i * it's	14.22
55	you * buy it	12.2	she * a lot	16.42	a good * to	14.22
56	i * think it's	12.2	will be * to	16.42	but the * of	14.22
57	you can * your	12.2	a good * and	15.67	i will * him	14.22
58	you * go to	12.2	the * is the	15.67	the * for the	14.22
59	you can * with	12.2	think * is a	15.67	my * is about	14.22
60	you * like it	11.1	difficult to * the	15.67	we can * that	14.22
61	we can * a	11.1	you * about it	14.92	will be * and	14.22
62	you * make it	11.1	we will * about	14.92	want to * some	14.22
63	i * it's not	11.1	but i * the	14.92	want to * about	14.22
64	i * it's good	11.1	a * you know	14.92	and it * the	14.22
65	have a * day	11.1	a how * you	14.92	they don't * to	14.22
66	he will * to	11.1	a good * for	14.92	we can * to	14.22

(continued)

Rank	Group 1 P-Frames	Freq.	Group 2 P-Frames	Freq.	Group 3 P-Frames	Freq.
67	the * way to	11.1	you can * it	14.92	you * to say	11.38
68	it's very * and	11.1	i * what you	14.92	he will * the	11.38
69	and you * make	10.0	the * for the	14.92	he * know any	11.38
70	you don't * to	10.0	and * we can	14.92	he * go to	11.38
71	is a * way	10.0	and he * a	14.18	he * know about	11.38
72	and you * to	10.0	i * we can	14.18	is very * and	11.38
73	do you * to	10.0	he has * to	14.18	he * have a	11.38
74	if you * in	10.0	and * have a	14.18	to * about a	11.38
75	i will * to	10.0	i will * with	14.18	there * a lot	11.38
76	you have * for	8.9	we can * it	14.18	if you * the	11.38
77	because i * the	8.9	to the * and	14.18	and * want to	11.38
78	the * of the	8.9	will * a lot	13.43	and * is the	11.38
79	it's * you can	8.9	lot of * in	13.43	do you * it's	11.38
80	want to * a	8.9	is a * idea	13.43	but i * know	11.38
81	you * agree with	8.9	can you * me	13.43	but i * the	11.38
82	it's * for the	8.9	a good * but	13.43	they * have to	11.38
83	we can * it	8.9	is very * and	12.69	the * is a	11.38
84	you * do it	8.9	you * about that	12.69	the * it is	11.38
85	very * and very	8.9	we can * the	12.69	if i * a	11.38
86	i will * him	8.9	i think * you	12.69	i * that but	22.75
87	is very * for	8.9	can * a lot	12.69	i * like to	22.75
88	i agree * that	7.8	to * a lot	12.69	you should * this	22.75
89	so i * agree	7.8	so i * we	12.69	you * use it	22.75
90	i * a lot	7.8	and * want to	12.69	i don't * to	22.75
91	i would * to	7.8	we will * a	12.69	i think * better	22.75
92	for * you can	7.8	do you * the	12.69	i * use the	22.75
93	for * you know	7.8	think we * to	12.69	if you * in	25.60
94	do you * what	7.8	i will * you	12.69	and he * to	25.60
95	don't * about anything	7.8	and what * you	11.94	the second * was	22.75
96	is more * than	7.8	and it's * to	11.94	the * about the	22.75
97	have many * to	7.8	and the * is	11.94	if you * into	19.91
98	can * it in	7.8	will * with you	11.94	but * i thought	19.91
99	you will * a	7.8	the * is very	11.94	want to * this	19.91
100	to be * in	7.8	i think * are	11.94	did you * some	19.91

Kim McDonough and Pakize Uludag
Individual and Shared Assessment of ESL students' Paired Oral Test Performance: Examining Rater Judgments and Lexico-grammatical Features

1 Introduction

Reflecting the importance of interaction in second language (L2) learning and teaching, standardized proficiency tests have adopted interactive speaking tasks for assessing oral proficiency. For example, in the IELTS speaking test, candidates answer questions and discuss topics with an examiner, while the Cambridge speaking tests ask candidates to interact with an examiner as well as with another test-taker. However, questions have been raised about the extent to which examiners play a neutral role in the interaction as well as the scoring consistency across examiners (He and Young 1998; Lazaraton 2002; Morton, Wigglesworth and Williams 1997; Nakatsuhara 2008). Because an examiner leads and controls the interaction, the resulting discourse structure can be asymmetric (i.e., low equality), which reflects imbalance in the power relationship between the examiner and the candidate (Lazaraton 1996; Ross and Berwick 1992; van Lier 1989; Young and Milanovic 1992). In addition, comparisons between authentic conversations and interview tests have revealed that examiner-candidate interaction shows greater similarity to institutional talk than naturalistic conversation (van Lier 1989). Therefore, concerns have been raised about the authenticity of oral interviews with examiners commonly used for oral proficiency assessment.

Considering these potential issues with examiner-candidate interaction, there has been increased interest in asking pairs or small groups of learners to interact with each other for assessment purposes. In contrast to examiner-candidate tasks, activities in which learners interact with each other are representative of L2 classroom practices (Együd and Glover 2001; Morrison and Lee 1985; Taylor 2001). Using peer-to-peer test tasks also promotes positive washback to classroom practices encouraging the learners to perform inter-

---

Acknowledgements: We would like to thank the research assistants for their assistance with data handling, coding, and rating: Dalia Elsayed, Roza van Lieshout, Rachael Lindberg, Libing Lu, and Jie Qiu.

https://doi.org/10.1515/9781501511370-005

active tasks reflecting classroom activities (Hildson 1991; Messick 1996). Due to students' familiarity with topics and pair work activities in L2 classrooms, candidates have reported positive experiences and increased motivation with paired oral tests (Bennett 2012; Együd and Glover 2001). In addition, researchers have suggested that students experience lower levels of stress and anxiety when tested in pairs or groups (Ikeda 1998; Norton 2005; Saville and Hargreaves 1999). As a result, the conversation between learners during paired oral tests elicits more interactive and complex interactions than examiner interviews (Brooks 2009; Együd and Glover 2001; Kormos 1999; Lazaraton 1997, 2002; Taylor 2001).

Conversely, some researchers have reported that students' awareness of the assessment purpose of interactive oral tests negatively impacts the authenticity of their communication and encourages institutionalized and ritualized talk (He and Dai 2006; Luk 2010). For example, students may orient to the delivery of content information, which results in long monologic turns followed by ritualized responses (e.g., *I agree with you*) (Crawford, McDonough and Brun-Mercer 2019; Luk 2010; Nitta and Nakatsuhara 2014; Van Moere 2007). In addition to eliciting ritualized talk, paired oral test performance shows variability due to differences in the linguistic abilities of the paired candidates, which impacts both the quality and quantity of talk produced (Iwashita 1996, 1998; Norton 2005). As a result, considerable debate has occurred as to whether test performance is best interpreted as an individual or shared achievement and how individual scores from jointly-constructed interaction should be interpreted (Chalhoub-Deville 2003; McNamara 1997; McNamara and Roever 2006; O'Sullivan 2002; Swain 2001; Taylor and Wigglesworth 2009). Because the candidates' contributions are linked, it can be difficult for raters to assign an individual score (Fulcher 2003) and to ensure reliability and fairness in scoring (Ducasse and Brown 2009; May 2006, 2009, 2011).

Additional insight into individual versus shared assessment of paired oral test performance has been obtained by eliciting raters' perceptions. For example, researchers have found that IELTS raters may be influenced by the interlocutor (i.e., examiner) when assigning scores to candidates (Brown and Hill 1998; Brown 2003). Using multiple data sources, May (2009, 2011) explored raters' perceptions of interactional competence based on rater notes, stimulated verbal recalls, and rater discussions. She reported that raters attended to features outside the rating criteria and compared candidates' performance when rating. The raters also perceived some features of interaction as a mutual or shared achievement (e.g., collaboration) rather than an individual accomplishment. This body of research raises important questions about whether individual contributions to the co-constructed performance are reflected in shared scores.

Besides rater assessments, qualitative coding frameworks have also been used to explore the co-constructed nature of paired oral tests. Storch (2002) introduced the concepts of mutuality (i.e., the degree to which individuals work together for task completion) and equality (i.e., the degree to which individuals nominate and develop topics while acknowledging each other's contributions) as characteristics of collaborative interaction in her model of dyadic interactions, which also included expert-novice, dominant-passive, and dominant-dominant patterns. Also, drawing on the concepts of mutuality and equality, Galaczi (2008) identified four interaction patterns in paired oral test performance: collaborative, asymmetric (i.e., low equality), parallel (i.e., low mutuality), and blended (i.e., multiple types). Referring to this framework, researchers have revealed that collaborative and parallel interactions are more frequent than asymmetric interactions in paired oral tests (Isaacs 2013; May 2009), collaborative interactions are associated with unplanned task performance (Nitta and Nakatsuhara 2014), and collaborative interactions are associated with higher scores (Davies 2009; Galaczi 2008). Thus, the co-constructed nature of interaction between test takers seems to play a role in the assessment of their test performance.

Although prior research has investigated the co-construction of paired oral test interaction through reference to mutuality and equality, fewer studies have examined whether collaboration is associated with specific lexico-grammatical features. Despite her main focus on interactional patterns, Storch (2002) reported that pronouns were associated with low mutuality and equality. A recent study by Crawford and colleagues (Crawford et al. 2019) examined whether collaborative and noncollaborative paired oral tests had different lexico-grammatical features. Using the Corpus of Collaborative Oral Tasks (CCOT), they found that paired oral tests with high collaboration ratings contained more interpersonal lexico-grammatical features such as first and second person pronouns and *wh*-questions. In contrast, paired oral tests with low collaboration scores had characteristics of informational language use, such as nouns and nominalizations. Focusing on university classroom discourse as opposed to paired oral test performance, Barbieri (2015) found that questions, discourse markers, and linking adverbs were associated with greater student interactivity. Although limited in scope, these prior studies suggest that linguistic features are associated with co-constructed interactional patterns. However, it is unclear how the lexico-grammatical features associated with collaboration relate to shared and individual assessment of paired oral test performance.

To summarize, despite the widespread adoption of paired orals tests, questions remain as to the advantages and disadvantages of assessing test performance as an individual or joint achievement. Paired oral tests require interaction between test takers, but there can be considerable variation in the extent to which they collaborate during test performance. Even when collaboration occurs, it can be difficult for raters to attribute co-constructed achievements to individual test-takers. Furthermore, the potential relationship between lexico-grammatical features and shared rater assessments remains underexplored, especially in terms of features associated with collaborative interaction. It is also unclear whether there are differences in each individual test-taker's use of lexico-grammatical features. To shed further light on these issues, the current chapter compares shared and individual assessment of paired oral tests while also exploring whether lexico-grammatical features are related to shared ratings or differ between test-takers. The specific research questions were as follows.

1. Is there a difference in shared and individual ratings of English L2 speaker's paired oral test performance?

As prior studies have not compared individual and shared ratings of paired oral test performance, we made no predictions about the existence or directionality of differences.

2. Is there a relationship between shared ratings and the occurrence of lexico-grammatical features associated with collaboration?

Although corpus research has shown that different lexico-grammatical features are associated with high and low collaboration interactions (Crawford et al. 2019) and degree of interactivity (Barbieri 2015), studies to date have not explored whether these features are related to overall rater assessments of paired oral test performance. Therefore, we expected a positive relationship between lexico-grammatical features and collaboration scores only.

3. Are there differences in the individual speaker's production of lexico-grammatical features associated with collaboration?

Reflecting prior debate about how accurately individuals can be assessed based on co-constructed performance (e.g., O'Sullivan 2002; Taylor and Wigglesworth 2009), we explored whether the use of lexico-grammatical features within a pair differs. Insight into whether each speaker contributes equally to the "work" of collaboration can help shed light on speaker roles in a co-constructed performance. However, due to the lack of previous studies about this topic, we made no predictions.

2 Method

2.1 Paired Oral Tests

The paired oral tests (N = 77) in the CCOT were administered in an intensive English program at a regional southwestern university as part of the program's regularly-scheduled battery of achievement tests. The achievement tests targeted themes and topics discussed in the students' English classes. The speech samples included 37 paired oral tests from Level 1 students (TOEFL iBT scores ranging from 32 to 44) and 40 tests from Level 2 students (TOEFL iBT scores ranging from 45 to 56). The distribution of tests by the students' level, gender, and first language (L1) background is provided in Table 1. Most of the students were male (77%) and L1 Arabic speakers (74%).

Table 1: Biographical information by level.

	Students	Gender	L1 background
Level 1	74	61 M, 13 F	65 Arabic, 9 Chinese
Level 2	80	58 M, 22 F	49 Arabic, 29 Chinese, 1 Japanese, 1 Portuguese

Two test tasks per level were selected for inclusion in the dataset. The Level 1 tests included two decision-making tasks about the topics of spanking and simple living. Each student in a pair was given a specific position to defend. After two minutes of planning time to brainstorm ideas, the students explained the reasons for their position. For the spanking task, one student explained why spanking children should be illegal, while the other student defended the practice. For the simple living task, one student explained why simple living was advantageous while the other student argued for the benefits of modern living. After exchanging ideas, the students concluded the task by collectively deciding which position they agreed with.

The Level 2 tests were also decision-making tasks in which students were asked to select a company to invest in (restaurant or computer store) or a science project to fund (mission to Mars or space telescope). For the company task, each student had two to three minutes to review the information provided in the task materials, which listed the company's strengths, weaknesses, opportunities, and threats. After sharing information about the companies and giving reasons to invest in them, the students reached a decision about which company to support. The science project task also provided each student with information about the positive and negative aspects of one project. They had time to review the information and plan, after which they described reasons for selecting the projects.

They concluded the task by deciding which project they should fund. The paired oral tests were audio-recorded using individual digital audio-recorders as part of the assessment procedure at the intensive English program. The distribution of paired oral tests by level, topic, and test administration is provided in Table 2.

Table 2: Paired oral tests by task and test administrations.

	Number of tests	Test administrations
Level 1: Spanking	20	Fall 2010, week 15 (10)
		Spring 2011, week 15 (10)
Level 1: Simple living	17	Spring 2010, week 15 (1)
		Fall 2010, week 10 (6)
		Spring 2011, week 10 (3)
		Summer 2011, week 8 (7)
Level 2: Investing in a company	19	Fall 2011, week 15
Level 2: Investing in a science project	21	Fall 2010, week 15 (18)
		Spring 2011, week 15 (3)

2.2 Data Analysis

The audio recordings were rated by four research assistants enrolled in graduate degree programs in Education. Although the CCOT data include ratings made by instructors in the intensive English program for assessment purposes, the rubrics varied by level and task. Therefore, it was not possible to use the existing ratings. In addition, the existing criteria and scales used in individual test formats (e.g., FCE speaking exam) were not suitable for assessing the skills elicited by the tasks in this study. Therefore, a specific-purpose assessment rubric was compiled by the researchers for assessing shared and individual performances.

The rubric contained four categories that could be scored from one to four: discourse management, collaborative communication, content development, language accuracy and complexity. Discourse management descriptors were based on the FCE speaking exam criteria (University of Cambridge Local Examinations Syndicate), which describe discourse management as fluidity of language production, organization of ideas, and the use of cohesive devices and discourse markers. Collaboration was defined through reference to models of dyadic interaction (Galaczi 2008; Storch 2002), where it is characterized by equality and mutuality. Equality was operationalized in the rubric as making equal contributions to the task, while mutuality was expressed as initiating, engaging with, and responding to each other's ideas along with developing the task through collaboration and negotiation. Following Kumpulainen and Mutanen's (1999) framework, content development included informative reasoning, along with the accuracy, relevance, and innovativeness of ideas. Finally, the category of language accuracy and complexity was operationalized following the descriptors in IELTS speaking rubric, which include vocabulary range along with the appropriateness, accuracy, and complexity of grammatical structures. Although the descriptors for the shared and individual rubrics were nearly identical, there were a few differences in phrasing based on whether the raters were scoring shared performance (Appendix A) or an individual speaker's performance (Appendix B).

Whereas all four raters provided shared ratings, only two raters were assigned to an individual speaker. The raters were randomly assigned to rate shared or individual performance first to address possible ordering effects, and they were not informed that there would be a second rating session. Prior to rating, the raters participated in training sessions conducted by the second researcher. The first training session included a review and discussion of the rubric categories using paired oral tests of the same tasks that were not included in the dataset. Two raters were trained in the use of the shared rubric while two raters received training for the individual rubric. After the training session, the raters independently rated the paired oral tests. Once they submitted their first set of ratings, a second training session was held to provide information and practice about the second rating condition, either shared or individual depending on which type they had already completed. Disagreements were resolved by consensus during the training sessions. Qualitative feedback from raters indicated that the rubrics were easy to use and that the rubric categories were appropriate for assessing the speech samples. Interrater reliability was assessed using two-way mixed average measures intraclass correlation coefficients, which were .76 for shared performance, .83 for speaker A, and .73 for speaker B. As reliability reached acceptable levels, mean ratings were obtained for shared performance (four raters) and each speaker (two raters each).

As part of the creation of CCOT, the audio recordings were transcribed, verified, and deidentified by research assistants. The deidentified transcripts were analyzed for the occurrence of lexico-grammatical features associated with collaboration identified in previous research (Crawford et al. 2019): *wh*-questions, first and second person pronouns, and subordinate conjunctions. First and second person pronouns are used in oral communications to present personal opinions, (e.g., *I think*), and respond to a partner's contribution (e.g., *I agree with you*). Although Storch's (2002) qualitative analysis of pair dynamics associated these pronouns with dominant/passive interactions, in Crawford et al. (2019), high-collaborative interactions were shown to contain more personal pronouns. *Wh*-questions were also included in the analyses because they serve the functions of seeking an opinion (e.g., *what do you think about that?*) and engaging with a partner's ideas (e.g., *why do you think so?*), which are characteristics of oral discourse with high mutuality and equality. Similarly, subordinate conjunctions fulfill several functions in oral communications specifically associated with reasoning such as providing a reason for an argument (e.g., *I think it is useful because . . .*), and introducing a conditional statement (e.g., *if you agree with me, we can . . .*). Following Barbieri's (2015) research with lexico-grammatical features associated with interactivity, we also included discourse markers as indicators of collaboration. Her global category of discourse markers included lexical items, such as *well, just, okay, right, alright, oh, yeah, like* and frames that reflected a speaker's stance in terms of emotions and participation in the interaction (i.e., *I mean, I guess, you know*). Table 3 provides examples of coded features from the paired oral tests.

Table 3: Examples of coded lexico-grammatical features.

Lexico-grammatical features	Examples
1st & 2nd pronouns	*I* think *I* got what you mean.
	Actually, *I* disagree with you.
Wh-questions	*What* do you think we have to do with this five billion?
	Which company you want to invest together?
Subordinate conjunctions	*If* we see that there is some possible life, we can go there.
	Parents should never spank their children *because* it's not best way to teach children.
Discourse markers	*I mean* not all the time you should spank your children.
	I want talk to you about uh simple life *yeah* there are many advantages of living in simple life.

The lexico-grammatical features produced by each speaker were hand-coded by the researchers and a subset of the data (20%) was coded by a second coder. Interrater reliability was calculated using two-way mixed intraclass correlation coefficients, which were .97 for pronouns, .99 for *wh*-questions, .89 for subordinate conjunctions, and .96 for discourse markers.

3 Results

The first research question asked whether there was a difference between shared and individual assessment of ESL paired oral test performance. Table 4 provides the mean scores for the shared and individual ratings for both speakers.[1] Except for

---

[1] Because the overall trends in the data were similar for the two program levels (Level 1 and Level 2), we present findings based on the combined data.

collaboration, descriptively the shared ratings were slightly higher than the scores received by either individual speaker. In addition, the mean ratings for Speaker B were equal to or slightly higher than those received by Speaker A, except for collaboration. Using an adjusted alpha level of .013 for multiple comparisons (.05/4), paired samples t-tests were carried out to compare the shared ratings with Speaker B's ratings. Speaker B's ratings were selected for the comparison as the mean scores were slightly higher than those of Speaker A for three categories, thereby helping reduce the possibility of Type I error. The statistical tests indicated that the shared ratings were significantly higher for discourse management: $t(76) = 5.94$, $p = .001$, $d = .34$, although the effect size failed to reach the threshold for a small effect (.60) for within-group comparisons (Plonksy and Oswald 2014). Turning to the other categories in the rubric, there was no statistical difference in the ratings for content development [$t(76) = .55$, $p = .585$, $d = .08$], or language accuracy and complexity [$t(76) = 1.17$, $p = .247$, $d = .15$]. Because the means were identical, it is not surprising that there was no statistical difference in the collaborative communication scores: $t(76) = 0$, $p = 1.00$, $d = 0$). Thus, although the statistical tests revealed that the shared ratings were significantly higher than the individual ratings for discourse management, the effect size raises questions about the magnitude of the difference.

Table 4: Shared and individual ratings by category.

Category	Shared rating		Speaker A		Speaker B	
	M	SD	M	SD	M	SD
Discourse management	2.65	.34	2.39	.48	2.51	.37
Collaborative communication	3.12	.40	3.14	.57	3.12	.44
Content development	3.20	.22	3.16	.42	3.18	.27
Language accuracy & complexity	2.35	.38	2.26	.60	2.29	.43
Total	11.30	1.08	10.88	1.71	11.08	1.26

The second research question asked whether there was a relationship between shared ratings and the joint production of lexico-grammatical features associated with collaboration. The mean numbers of lexico-grammatical features per paired oral test are provided in Table 5. Pronouns occurred most frequently, followed by subordinate conjunctions, discourse markers, and *wh*-questions.

Table 5: Lexico-grammatical features and correlation coefficients.

Feature	M	SD	Discourse	Collaboration	Content	Language
1st & 2nd pronouns	22.40	7.78	.24*	.06	.20	.31*
wh-questions	2.05	1.73	.29*	.23*	.08	.30*
Subordinate conjunctions	5.84	3.58	.01	−.08	.16	.01
Discourse markers	4.17	3.15	.33*	.12	−.08	.26*

Note: * p < .05.

As indicated by the Pearson correlation coefficient r values, first and second person pronouns positively correlated with discourse and language while wh-questions were related to discourse, collaboration, and language. Discourse markers were positively correlated with discourse and language ratings. In contrast, subordinate conjunctions were not related to any of the shared ratings. The r values for all of the statistically significant correlations were in the range of the small to medium benchmarks (.25 to .40; Plonksy and Oswald 2014). Thus, the correlation results provide some evidence for a positive relationship between shared ratings and the joint production of lexico-grammatical features associated with collaboration.

Turning to the final research question, which asked whether there were differences in individual speakers' production of lexico-grammatical features associated with collaboration, Table 6 provides the descriptive statistics for the features related to collaboration and interactivity by speaker. Descriptively, the mean numbers of lexico-grammatical features were higher for speaker A than speaker B in all five categories. However, paired-samples t-tests using an adjusted alpha level of .013 (.05/4) indicated that the difference reached statistical significance for wh-questions, first and second person pronouns, and subordinate conjunctions only. The effect sizes for wh-questions and subordinate conjunctions failed to reach the small benchmark, while the effect size for pronouns was in the range of small to medium. Thus, the analysis of lexico-grammatical features showed some divergence in the individual speaker's production, at least for the features associated with collaboration.

Table 6: Lexico-grammatical features by speaker.

Feature	Speaker A		Speaker B		Comparison		
	M	SD	M	SD	t	p	d
wh-questions	1.26	1.16	.79	1.10	2.80	.006	.42
1st & 2nd pronouns	13.23	5.87	9.17	3.90	5.73	.001	.81
Subordinate conjunctions	3.39	2.70	2.45	1.81	2.84	.006	.41
Discourse markers	2.34	1.91	1.83	2.14	1.74	.086	.25

4 Discussion

To summarize the main findings, there were few differences in the shared and individual ratings of these English L2 speakers' paired oral test performance. The shared ratings of discourse management were slightly higher than individual ratings, but the effect size was marginal. Although researchers have questioned whether paired oral tests should be evaluated individually or jointly (McNamara 1997; O'Sullivan 2002; Swain 2001; Taylor and Wigglesworth 2009), our results indicated that raters provided consistent ratings when considering individual or shared performance. Furthermore, the ratings received by each student in a pair were very similar without any significant differences. Taken together, these findings provide support for both types of assessment as there were no meaningful differences in these ESL students' shared and individual ratings.

Turning to the analysis of lexico-grammatical features, the findings revealed a positive association between a pair's language ratings and discourse management ratings and their production of three lexico-grammatical features: *wh*-questions, first and second person pronouns, and discourse markers. It is not surprising that the production of discourse markers was associated with discourse management ratings because the rubric mentioned the use of cohesive devices and discourse markers. Furthermore, the positive association between language ratings and lexico-grammatical feature is unsurprising as the rubric mentions the appropriate and accurate use of language structures and vocabulary. Whereas Crawford et al. (2019) found an association between high collaboration scores and *wh*-questions, pronouns, and subordination, only *wh*-questions were significantly correlated with collaboration ratings in the current dataset. The failure to confirm their findings may be due to differences in the rubric. The raters in Crawford et al. (2019) used the intensive English program's rubric, which consisted of three criteria (collaboration, task accomplishment, style) whereas our rubric included separate categories for discourse management and collaborative communication. It is possible that some elements of collaboration were captured by the discourse management ratings, which had more significant correlations with the lexico-grammatical features. There was a strong correlation between the raters' discourse management and collaborative communication ratings ($r = .82$), which suggests that these categories may share underlying features. Future research is needed to validate discourse and collaboration criteria and explore which lexico-grammatical features are associated with each dimension.

For the comparison of lexico-grammatical features by speakers within a pair, Speaker A produced significantly more *wh*-questions, first and second person pronouns, and subordinate conjunctions than Speaker B. Even though their production of lexico-grammatical features associated with collaboration diverged, their mean collaborative communication ratings were similar (3.14 and 3.12, respectively), which suggests that raters may not have attended to these features when rating. It appears that the student who spoke first, and was thus labeled Speaker A, took on greater responsibility for eliciting information, such as by asking more *wh*-questions. Example (1) illustrates this pattern, with Speaker A asking five *wh*-questions to elicit information about Speaker B's company (questions in italics). In contrast, although Speaker B responds to the questions by delivering content information, she does not ask Speaker A any questions about his company.

(1) Greater use of *wh*-questions by Speaker A[2]
    A: Okay, I think my company is better than yours because of many reasons. That's what I will tell you. My first strength is you get unique help for each customer. *What about your restaurant?*
    B: I disagree with you but my restaurant have international food, and free dishes and inexpensive.
    A: Okay, I have a weakness in my computer store that it's uh expensive, and it takes more time, more longer time. *What about your weaknesses?*
    B: And my weak is difficult to find. A new weakness in my restaurant, also location.
    A: Okay. Uh, I actually agree with you. And uh I think drive-thru restaurant is a good idea. But listen, *what about your opportunities?* I don't have any competing businesses nearby.
    B: Yeah, my opportunity large international population, and you can to find what you want easy yeah, yeah.
    A: Yeah, so I think it's very good idea that you have international food. And any food you want, you can find it in your restaurant. *What about the threat?* I have a threat the online shopping trend, that there is another companies you can shop online. *What about your threat?*
    B: I have to some threat, high to tax for this kind business and also to have –
    A: – Okay, so I think it's a really good idea, and I agree with your restaurant, cause it's international. Thank you.

This finding should be interpreted cautiously however, as the current study was not designed to investigate differences in lexico-grammatical features based

---

[2] To facilitate reading ease, the transcripts were edited by removing dysfluencies (filled and unfilled pauses, false starts, repetitions) and adding writing conventions such as capitalization and punctuation.

on speaker order. Future studies can explore this possibility more rigorously by adopting a within-groups design where students carry out two tasks but reverse their speaking order. A within-groups design would help rule out other possible explanations (e.g., proficiency, personality, willingness to communicate) for Speaker A's greater use of these lexico-grammatical features associated with collaboration.

As mentioned in the literature review, some researchers have questioned whether the students' awareness of the testing context negatively impacts the naturalness of their interaction (He and Dai 2006; Luk 2010). Also using the CCOT data, Crawford et al. (2019) found that some pairs accomplished the task by taking long turns to deliver their own content information with little engagement with each other's ideas, which researchers have classified as low mutuality interactions such as dominant/dominant (Storch 2002) or parallel (Galaczi 2008). Our data provide further evidence that some students may perform paired oral tests by delivering content along with minimal or routinized responses for task accomplishment (i.e., agreeing and reaching consensus). This pattern is illustrated in (2), where each speaker delivers key information from their task handouts about the strengths, weaknesses, opportunities, and threats associated with opening a new business. However, there is little engagement with each other's ideas and the task is accomplished (i.e., they select which business to support) through Speaker A's unilateral decision "so I agree with you" after which he declares "that's all", signalling that they have achieved the task's communicative goal.

(2) Content delivery with minimal responses
    A: I want to open Amazing Computer Store. My strength is it can help every people in this daily life. But, the computer is so expensive and maybe it's take a lot of time to buy it. So, what about you?
    B: I want to open a Super Amazing International Drive-Thru Restaurant. To open this restaurant, it's uh delicious, but it is expensive international food. And this is disadvantage, it's difficult to find a location with enough space.
    A: So what's your opportunities and threat?
    B: There's an opportunity is a large international population. People like to eat this food so it have many chance can earn many money.
    A: Oh, uh you have uh great opportunities but I'm opportunities is I don't have the competing business nearby. But I have a lot of competing on the Internet. So I think I have a great challenge than you. So I agree with you to open a restaurant. That's all.

It was beyond the scope of the current paper to adopt a micro-analytic analysis of the students' interaction, but future studies should further explore the extent to which students use naturalistic or authentic conversational frames when carrying out key elements of the task (e.g., agreeing, disagreeing, proposing and accepting solutions).

Our focus here was on how to best assess paired oral tests performance, either by giving each student a separate score or by evaluating their co-constructed performance. The lack of major differences between the two assessment options may help instructors and program directors make decisions based on which type of evaluation is more feasible in their context. However, this study does not provide insight into how to implement paired oral tests in ways that maximize student performance. Prior studies have shown that a student's score can be affected by interlocutor variables such as proficiency (Bennett 2012; Davis 2009; Lazaraton and Davis 2008; Iwashita 1996)), gender (Brown and McNamara 2004; O'Sullivan 2000), personality (Berry 2007; Nakatsuhara 2011; Ockey 2009), and familiarity (Katona 1998; O'Sullivan 2002). An interesting question is whether shared and individual assessment would be similar across these interlocutor variables. The students here self-selected partners, presumably selecting a peer with whom they felt comfortable interacting. This may not be the case in all testing situations, so future studies should examine shared versus individual assessment under more diverse test implementation conditions.

Although this study provides some positive evidence about the comparability of shared and individual assessment of paired oral tests, there are some issues that may limit its generalizability. To reduce possible task effects, we included decision-making tasks which required students to share information and then reach consensus. It is unclear whether the results would be similar for other task types, such as opinion-exchange, role-plays, or interviews. In addition, although we included data from two levels of pre-academic ESL students, we did not sample paired oral test interaction from the highest level in the intensive English program due to task type differences. An important issue for future research is to determine whether the findings extend to higher proficiency students including those in both pre-academic and university programs.

To assess individual and shared performance, we compiled an evidence-based rubric by drawing predominantly on existing scales and qualitative coding frameworks. Although the raters implemented the rubric with an acceptable level of reliability, the rubric needs to be empirically validated using PCA or Rasch analysis. An important next step is to elicit raters' perceptions about their experiences using the rubric, when evaluating both individual and shared performance. Their experiences might provide insight into what aspects of performance underlie their ratings and what linguistic features they orient to when rating. Such data might help explain the strong correlation between discourse management and collaboration ratings and clarify how speakers with different levels of production of lexico-grammatical features receive similar ratings. Finally, due to our focus on the co-construction of paired oral test performance, our lexico-grammatical analysis focused narrowly on features associated with collaboration. Future studies might take a broader perspective to determine how linguistic features are related to ratings in all the sub-categories, especially those for language use.

In conclusion, although our findings have illuminated few substantial differences between shared versus individual assessment of paired oral test performance, future research is needed to determine under what conditions it may be beneficial to assess students individually as opposed to collectively. While the raters did not differentiate much between individual and shared assessment, the linguistic analysis revealed differences between speakers in terms of the quantity of lexico-grammatical features associated with collaboration they produced. Additional linguistic analyses are needed to explore the extent to which raters draw upon linguistic features when assessing test performance. Including both human judgments and linguistic analysis when evaluating students' performance, paired oral tests may provide a more complete picture of their abilities. Our future research aims to explore these issues in more detail and with greater methodological rigor.

Funding statement: Funding for this study was provided by a grant provided to the first author by the Canada Research Chairs program (Grant number 950-231218).

References

Barbieri, Federica. 2015. Involvement in university classroom discourse: Register variation and interactivity. *Applied Linguistics* 36(2). 151–173.

Bennett, Rita. 2011. Is linguistic ability variation in paired oral language testing problematic? *ELT Journal* 66(3). 337–346.

Berry, Vivien. 2007. *Personality differences and oral test performance*. Frankfurt am Main: Peter Lang.

Brooks, Lindsay. 2009. Interacting in pairs in a test of oral proficiency: Co-constructing a better performance. *Language Testing* 26(3). 341–366.

Brown, Annie & Tim McNamara. 2004. 'The devil is in the detail': Researching gender issues in language assessment. *TESOL Quarterly* 38(3). 524–538.

Brown, Annie. 2003. Interviewer variation and the co-construction of speaking proficiency. *Language Testing* 20(1). 1–25.

Chalhoub-Deville, Micheline. 2003. Second language interaction: current perspectives and future trends. *Language Testing* 20(4). 369–383.

Crawford, William J., Kim McDonough & Nicole Brun-Mercer. 2019. Identifying linguistic markers of collaboration in second language peer interaction: A lexico-grammatical approach. *TESOL Quarterly* 53(1). 180–207.

Davis, Larry. 2009. The influence of interlocutor proficiency in a paired oral assessment. *Language Testing* 26(3). 367–396.

Ducasse, Ana Maria. & Annie Brown. 2009. Assessing paired orals: Raters' orientation to interaction. *Language Testing* 26(3). 423–443.

Együd, Györgyi & Philip Glover. 2001. Oral testing in pairs – a secondary school perspective. *ELT Journal* 55(1). 70–76.

Fulcher, Glenn. 2003. *Testing second language speaking*. Harlow: Pearson.

Galaczi, Evelina D. 2008. Peer-peer interaction in a speaking test: The case of the First Certificate in English examination. *Language Assessment Quarterly* 5(2). 89–119.

He, Lianzhen & Ying Dai. 2006. A corpus-based investigation into the validity of the CET-SET group discussion. *Language Testing* 23(3). 370–401.

He, Agnes Weiyun & Richard Young. 1998. Language proficiency interviews: A discourse approach. In Richard Young & Agnes Weiyun He (Eds.), *Talking and testing: Discourse approaches to the assessment of oral proficiency*, 1–24. Amsterdam: John Benjamins.

Hildson, J. 1991. The group oral exam: Advantages and limitations. In J. Charles Alderson & Brian North (eds.), *Language testing in the 90's: The communicative legacy*, 189–197. London: Modern English Publications and the British Council.

Ikeda, Ken. 1998. The paired learner interview: A preliminary investigation applying Vygotskyan insights. *Language, Culture and Curriculum* 11(1). 71–96.

Isaacs, Talia. 2013. International engineering graduate students' interactional patterns on a paired speaking test: Interlocutors' perspectives. In Kim McDonough & Alison Mackey (Eds.) *Second Language interaction in diverse educational contexts*, 227–245. Amsterdam: John Benjamins.

Iwashita, Noriko. 1996. The validity of the paired interview format in oral performance assessment. *Melbourne Papers in Language Testing* 5(2). 51–65.

Iwashita, Noriko. 1998. The validity of the paired interview in oral performance assessment. *Melbourne Papers in Language Testing* 5(2). 51–65.

Katona, Lucy. 1998. Meaning negotiation in the Hungarian oral proficiency examination of English. In Richard Young & Agnes Weiyun He (Eds.), *Talking and testing: Discourse approaches to the assessment of oral proficiency*, 239–267. Philadelphia, PA: John Benjamins.

Kumpulainen, Kristiina & Mika Mutanen. 1999. The situated dynamics of peer group interaction: An introduction to an analytic framework. *Learning and Instruction* 9(5). 449–473.

Kormos, Judit. 1999. Simulating conversations in oral proficiency assessment: A conversation analysis of role plays and non-scripted interviews in language exams. *Language Testing* 16(2). 163–188.

Lazaraton, Anne. 1996. Interlocutor support in oral proficiency interviews: The case of CASE. *Language Testing* 13(2). 151–172.

Lazaraton, Anne. 1997. Preference organization in oral proficiency interviews. *Research on Language and Social Interaction* 30. 53–72.

Lazaraton, Anne. 2002. *A qualitative approach to the validation of oral language tests*. Cambridge: UCLES/Cambridge University Press.

Lazaraton, Anne & Larry Davis. 2008. A microanalytic perspective on discourse, proficiency, and identity in paired oral assessment. *Language Assessment Quarterly* 5(4). 313–335.

Luk, Jasmine. 2010. Talking to score: Impression management in L2 oral assessment and the co-construction of a test discourse genre. *Language Assessment Quarterly* 7(1). 25–53.

May, Lyn. 2006. An examination of rater orientations on a paired candidate discussion task through stimulated recall. *Melbourne Papers in Language Testing* 11(1). 29–51.

May, Lyn. 2009. Co-constructed interaction in a paired speaking test: The rater's perspective. *Language Testing* 26(3). 397–421.

May, Lyn. 2011. Interactional competence in a paired speaking test: Features salient to raters. *Language Assessment Quarterly* 8(2). 127–145.

McNamara, Tim. 1997. 'Interaction' in second language performance assessment: Whose performance? *Applied Linguistics* 18(4). 446–466.

McNamara, Tim & Carsten Roever. 2006. *Language testing: The social dimension*. Malden, MA: Blackwell.

Messick, Samuel. 1996. Validity and washback in language testing. *Language Testing* 13(3). 241–256.

Morrison, D. M., & Lee, N. 1985. Simulating an academic tutorial: A test validation study. In Y. P. Lee, Angela C. Y. Y. Fok, Robert Lord & Graham Low (Eds.), *New directions in language testing*, 85–92. Oxford: Pergamon Institute of English.

Morton, Janne, Gillian Wigglesworth & Donna Williams. 1997. Approaches to validation: evaluating interviewer performance in oral interaction tests. In Geoff Brindley & Gillian Wigglesworth (Eds.), *Access: Issues in language test design and delivery*, 175–196. Sydney: NCELTR.

Nakatsuhara, Fumiyo. 2008. Inter-interviewer variation in oral interview tests. *ELT Journal* 62(3). 266–275.

Nakatsuhara, Fumiyo. 2011. Effects of test-taker characteristics and the number of participants in group oral tests. *Language Testing* 28(4). 483–508.

Nitta, Ryo & Fumiyo Nakatsuhara. 2014. A multifaceted approach to investigating pre-task planning effects on paired oral test performance. *Language Testing Research* 31(2). 147–175.

Norton, Julie. 2005. The paired format in the Cambridge Speaking Tests. *ELT Journal* 59(4). 287–297.

Ockey, Gary J. 2009. The effects of group members' personalities on a test taker's L2 group oral discussion test scores. *Language Testing* 29(2). 161–186.

O'Sullivan, Barry. 2000. Exploring gender and oral proficiency interview performance. *System* 28(3). 373–386.

O'Sullivan, Barry. 2002. Learner acquaintanceship and oral proficiency test pair-task performance. *Language Testing* 19(3). 277–295.

Plonsky, Luke & Frederick L. Oswald. 2014. How big is "Big"? Interpreting effect sizes in L2 research. *Language Learning* 64(4). 878–912.

Ross, Steven & Richard Berwick. 1992. The discourse of accommodation in oral proficiency interviews. *Studies in Second Language Acquisition* 14(2). 159–176.

Saville, Nick & Peter Hargreaves. 1999. Assessing speaking in the revised FCE. *ELT Journal* 53(1). 42–51.

Storch, Neomy. 2002. Patterns of interaction in ESL pair work. *Language Learning* 52(1). 119–58.

Swain, Merrill. 2001. Examining dialogue: Another approach to content specification and to validating inferences drawn from test scores. *Language Testing* 18(3). 275–302.

Taylor, Lynda. 2001. The paired speaking test format: Recent studies. *Cambridge ESOL Research Notes* 6. 15–17.

Taylor, Lynda & Gillian Wigglesworth. 2009. Are two heads better than one? Pair work in L2 assessment contexts. *Language Testing* 26(3). 325–339.

van Lier, Leo. 1989. Reeling, writhing, drawling, stretching and fainting in coils: Oral proficiency interviews as conversations. *TESOL Quarterly* 23(3). 489–508.

Young, Richard & Michael Milanovic. 1992. Discourse variation in oral proficiency interviews. *Studies in Second Language Acquisition* 14(4). 403–424.

Appendix A: Shared Rubric

Score	Discourse Management	Collaborative Communication	Content Development	Language Accuracy & Complexity
4	– They produce extended stretches of language with no hesitation – There is a clear organization of ideas – They use full range of cohesive devices and discourse markers	– They initiate, respond, and engage with each other's ideas consistently – They make equal contributions to the task – They develop the topic through constant collaboration and negotiation	– They deliver the content accurately – They provide reasoning for their arguments consistently – Contributions are relevant and innovative	– They use a wide range of vocabulary accurately – They use structures appropriately – They produce consistently accurate and complex structures
3	– They produce stretches of language with little hesitation – Organization of ideas is mostly clear – They use cohesive devices and discourse markers	– They respond and engage with each other's ideas adequately – They contribute to the task mostly equally – They develop the topic through collaboration and negotiation	– They deliver the content mostly accurately – They provide reasoning for their arguments – Contributions are mostly relevant and innovative	– They use an appropriate range of vocabulary mostly accurately – They use most structures appropriately – They produce mostly accurate and complex structures

(continued)

Score	Discourse Management	Collaborative Communication	Content Development	Language Accuracy & Complexity
2	– They produce stretches of language with some hesitation – They organize ideas with some clarity – They use a limited range of cohesive devices and discourse markers	– They engage with each other's ideas sometimes – They contribute to the task somewhat equally – They develop the topic through limited collaboration and negotiation	– They deliver the content with some accuracy – They provide some reasoning for their arguments – Contributions may not be relevant innovative	– They use a range of vocabulary with some accuracy – They use some structures appropriately – They produce structures with some accuracy and complexity
1	– They produce responses with short phrases and there is much hesitation – Organization of ideas is unclear – They rarely use cohesive devices and discourse markers	– They do not engage with each other's ideas – They do not make equal contributions to the task – They develop the topic without much collaboration	– They deliver some inaccurate content – They rarely provide reasoning for their arguments – Contributions are rarely relevant and innovative	– They use a limited range of vocabulary with some accuracy – They use most structures inappropriately – They rarely produce accurate and complex structures

Appendix B: Individual Rubric

Score	Discourse Management	Collaborative Communication	Content Development	Language Accuracy & Complexity
4	– Produces extended stretches of language with no hesitation – There is a clear organization of ideas – Uses full range of cohesive devices and discourse markers	– Initiates, responds, and engages with partners' ideas consistently – Makes equal contributions to the task – Develops the topic through constant collaboration and negotiation	– Delivers the content accurately – Provides reasoning for the arguments consistently – Contributions are relevant and innovative	– Uses a wide range of vocabulary accurately – Uses structures appropriately – Produces consistently accurate and complex structures
3	– Produces stretches of language with little hesitation – Organization of ideas is mostly clear – Uses cohesive devices and discourse markers	– Initiates, responds, and engages with partners' ideas adequately – Makes mostly equal contributions to the task – Develops the topic through collaboration and negotiation	– Delivers the content mostly accurately – Provides reasoning for the arguments – Contributions are mostly relevant and innovative	– Uses an appropriate range of vocabulary accurately – Uses most structures appropriately – Produces mostly accurate and complex structures

(continued)

Score	Discourse Management	Collaborative Communication	Content Development	Language Accuracy & Complexity
2	– Produces short stretches of language with some hesitation – Organizes ideas with some clarity – Uses a limited range of cohesive devices and discourse markers	– Engages with partners' ideas only sometimes – Contributes to the task somewhat equally – Develops the topic with limited collaboration and negotiation	– Delivers the content with some accuracy – Provides some reasoning for the arguments – Contributions may not be relevant and innovative	– Uses a range of vocabulary with some accuracy – Uses some structures appropriately – Produces structures with some accuracy and complexity
1	– Produces responses with short phrases and there is much hesitation – Organization of ideas is unclear – Uses cohesive devices and discourse markers rarely	– Shows no engagement with partners' ideas – Makes no equal contributions to the task – Develops the topic without much collaboration	– Delivers some inaccurate content – Provides only limited reasoning for the arguments – Contributions are rarely relevant and innovative	– Uses a limited range of vocabulary with little accuracy – Uses most structures inappropriately – Produces accurate and complex structures rarely

Anthony Becker
Exploring Multiple Profiles of Highly Collaborative Paired Oral Tasks in an L2 Speaking Test of English

1 Introduction

In their 2019 article published in *TESOL Quarterly*, Crawford, McDonough, and Brun-Mercer sought to identify linguistic markers of collaboration in second language (L2) peer interaction. Implementing a key feature analysis (Biber and Egbert 2018), the authors focused on the co-occurrence of 58 lexico-grammatical features identified in paired oral discourse. The purpose of their study was to determine if there were particular lexico-grammatical features that were closely associated with high- and low-collaboration peer interaction. While Crawford et al. (2019) acknowledge that previous L2 assessment research related to collaboration has focused largely on rater judgments of collaboration and qualitative coding of interactional patterns, they note that studies showing any sort of relationship between linguistic features and quality of peer interactions were relatively non-existent. Therefore, their study was an exploratory investigation that sought to address this perceived gap in the current L2 speaking assessment literature, primarily the lack of research concerning the characteristic linguistic features of collaboration in peer-to-peer oral interactions. Given the dearth of research on this particular topic, as well as the prominence of peer-to-peer interaction in many L2 learning and assessment settings (Taylor and Wigglesworth 2009), this paper serves to build upon the work carried out in Crawford et al.'s (2019) study. It does so by comparing the linguistic features associated with paired oral tasks produced by non-native speakers of English that were rated as being highly collaborative. The samples of oral tasks were taken from the Corpus of Collaborative Oral Tasks (hereafter CCOT)[1] and analyzed using Cluster Analysis.

This study begins by reviewing research that outlines the benefits of peer-to-peer interaction, as well as research that explores how collaboration in peer-to-peer interaction has been researched in L2 assessment, with an emphasis on studies that have investigated paired oral tasks. This is followed by an overview of research that has explored the relationship between distributions of various

---

[1] For a detailed description of the CCOT, refer to Crawford and McDonough (this volume).

linguistic features and the quality of collaboration in paired oral tasks, as well as a brief discussion of statistical Cluster Analysis and its application to linguistic features tagged in the CCOT. The results for two sets of data from the corpus are then presented and discussed.

2 Review of Literature

2.1 Benefits of Peer-to-peer Interaction

Collaboration, defined as a situation in which two or more people capitalize on one another's resources and skills in an attempt to learn something or accomplish a task together (Dillenbourg 1999), has been a prominent topic of discussion in L2 research for nearly two decades. Collaboration that takes place during pair work formats has been a particular point of interest, as it is believed that pair work, which is typically used to elicit peer-to-peer interactions, facilitates collaboration among L2 learners. That is, pair work is thought to help mediate the effectiveness of collaboration, since tasks involving pair work help to promote a process of discovery and problem-solving that can only be achieved through the creation of conversation and cooperation within small groups. Furthermore, peer-to-peer interactions involving pair work also provide meaningful opportunities for L2 students to actively use both their receptive and productive language skills, as well as receive timely feedback from their peers (Taylor and Wigglesworth 2009). For these reasons (and more), it is believed that collaborative peer-to-peer interactions, including tasks that incorporate elements of pair work, can be beneficial for assessing student learning (Lai 2011).

Speaking tasks involving peer-to-peer interaction are increasingly being incorporated into language proficiency assessments (Ducasse and Brown 2009). This increase has largely been a response to the perceived need for a broader range of test tasks that would elicit different aspects of L2 speaking proficiency and would provide more opportunities for demonstrating interactive skills than has been found in more traditional testing formats, such as the one-to-one proficiency interview, which involves a single test-taker with an examiner. As Ducasse and Brown (2009) explain, interview tests are often limited by the realization that the test-taker acts as an interviewee responding to questions, rather than someone who can demonstrate their ability to collaborate and support their interactional partner to co-construct a spoken performance. In contrast, speaking tasks that promote peer-to-peer interaction have greater potential to "enable a wider range of language functions and roles to be engineered to provide a better basis for oral language sampling with less asymmetry between participants" (Skehan 2001: 169). In this sense, test-takers have more control to co-construct conversations in ways that they see fit, thus promoting their interactional competence (Galaczi 2014). Furthermore, because of their interactive and performance-based nature, peer-oriented speaking tasks (e.g., paired oral tasks) prompt participants to modify the input that is made available to them so as to increase the comprehensibility of utterances and actively notice potential gaps in their (or others') linguistic knowledge, while also providing opportunities for test-takers to produce output that can contribute to noticing, as well as the co-construction and negotiation of knowledge (Crosthwaite and Raquel 2019; Kasper 2013; Philp, Adams and Iwashita 2014).

2.2 Assessing Paired Oral Tasks

A major reason for the adoption of paired oral assessments is the co-constructed nature of peer-to-peer interaction involved, as co-participants engage in dialogue and navigate through a performance together. However, the co-constructed nature of paired oral tasks in L2 speaking assessment also presents challenges, such as how interactional competency fits into the construct of speaking (construct validity), whether raters should assign individual and/or collective scores to the participants (reliability), and how to assign pairings to ensure equitable interactions (fairness). To gain a better understanding of these challenges, several lines of research have been pursued in L2 speaking assessment, including studies that concern the effects of the test examiner (Brooks 2009; Brown 2003), as well as the characteristics of the interlocutor, such as personality (Berry 2007; Bonk and Van Moere 2004), proficiency level (Davis 2009; Nakatsuhara 2006), and gender (Brown and McNamara 2004). Overall, these studies highlight the complex nature of using paired oral tasks to assess learners' L2 speaking proficiency.

A smaller number of studies have focused on identifying and describing patterns of discourse that are produced by participants during peer-to-peer interactions, including paired oral tasks (e.g., Brooks 2009; Galaczi 2008; Lazaraton and Davis 2008; Storch 2002). These studies, which have mainly adopted a Conversation Analysis (CA) approach, have shed light on the types of patterns of interaction that are observed in actual samples of paired oral discourse. For instance, Galaczi (2008) examined the discourse produced by test-takers in the paired oral tasks used in the *First Certificate in English* speaking tests. Through the examination of 30 paired dyads, she identified three global patterns of peer-to-peer interaction: (a) collaborative, (b) parallel, and (c) asymmetrical. According to the author, collaborative interactions exhibited high mutuality and high equality; that is, interactions that are rich in reciprocal feedback and a sharing of ideas, as well as rich in instances where both participants take directions from each other (Storch 2002). In addition, Galaczi (2008) found that parallel interactions resembled two 'solo' paths of conversation, in which "both speakers initiated and developed topics (high equality) but engaged little with each other's ideas (low mutuality)" (102), while asymmetric interactions, or dyads in which the interlocutors took on different discourse roles (e.g., one dominant and one passive), were also identified. These findings closely reflect the patterns of dyadic interaction found in Storch's (2002) study, which identified four distinct patterns: (a) collaborative, (b) dominant/dominant, (c) dominant/passive, and (d) expert/novice. Taken together, the findings from these two studies highlight the different patterns of peer-to-peer interaction that are typical in many dyadic interactions such as paired oral tasks.

Furthermore, Galaczi (2008) found a close relationship between the above-mentioned patterns of interaction and interactive communication (IC) scores awarded for FCE. Specifically, she found that dyads with collaborative interaction received higher scores on average than did the other two interaction types (i.e., parallel and asymmetric), which, as the author notes, provided evidence of validity for the test scores. Although Galaczi (2008) does not specify the criteria used to assign IC scores in her study, a review of the *Cambridge ESOL* website[2] reveals that IC scores are based on a candidate's ability to listen to a partner and respond to what they are saying, initiate ideas, and work towards an outcome. These same descriptors, or at least similar manifestations of these descriptors, are also used to describe the construct of collaboration in scoring rubrics from several other studies concerning group and/or paired oral tests (e.g., Ahmadi and Sedeghi 2016; Winke 2013). It is worth noting that similar criteria for describing collaboration are included in the analytic scoring rubric (described in the method section) used to score the two paired oral tasks for the present study.

2.3 The Relationship between Linguistic Features and Collaboration in Paired Oral Tasks

Very few studies concerning peer-to-peer interaction in paired oral tasks to date have sought to identify the linguistic features of collaboration. While studies like Storch (2002) and Galaczi (2008) touch upon a few isolated linguistic markers

---

[2] Information about FCE is available on the Cambridge English website (http://www.cambridgeESOL.org).

of collaboration (e.g., first, second, and third person pronouns to maintain syntactic cohesion; questions to generate involvement; mental verbs to emphasize and/or state an opinion), there is very little discussion of how specific linguistic features of peer-to-peer interaction relate to the dyadic interactions observed in those studies. Since the linguistic features incorporated during peer-to-peer interactions in paired oral tests can be numerous, there is clearly a need to identify if there are any salient linguistic features, as these might be ostensibly attended to by raters when making scoring judgments.

To address this issue, Crawford et al. (2019) looked at the presence and/or absence of lexico-grammatical features associated with high- and low-collaboration interactions, including lexical, phrasal, and clausal features (e.g., *adjectives, conjunctions, nouns, passive voice constructions, relative clauses, wh- questions*). Looking at the transcribed samples of students' (n = 80) performance on a paired oral task from the CCOT, they conducted a key feature analysis (see Biber and Egbert 2018), whereby they sought to determine the extent to which lexico-grammatical features differentiate interactions that were deemed to be high and low in collaboration. Overall, 28 lexico-grammatical features were found to be associated with high-collaboration interactions and 30 lexico-grammatical features associated with low-collaboration interactions, for a total of 58 salient features. However, only 14 of the 58 features were identified as being *strongly* associated with high- or low-collaboration interactions, defined by the authors as having a Cohen's *d* value of ±.40 (Crawford et al. 2019: 188); that is, six features were strongly associated with high-collaboration interactions (i.e., *first person pronouns, second person pronouns, all pronouns, wh-questions, 'that' deletion, subordinating conjunctions*), while eight features were strongly associated with low-collaboration interactions (i.e., *compound nouns, emphatics, nominalizations, contractions, all nouns, definite articles, verb 'be', attributive adjectives*). The authors emphasized that "the lexico-grammatical features associated with high- and low-collaboration interactions revealed that high-collaboration interactions contain more involved and interpersonal linguistic features characteristic of spoken interaction," while the low-collaboration interactions shared features which are "characteristic of informational language as opposed to involved language" (Crawford et al. 2019: 191–192). They added that it is important to consider how features associated with high- and low-collaboration interactions might vary when other types of tasks are performed, including different information-exchange activities.

While Crawford et al.'s (2019) study successfully demonstrated that there are distinct linguistic features that distinguish paired oral tasks with high-collaboration from low-collaboration interactions, the results of their study do not paint the entire picture of linguistic features found in collaborative interactions with paired oral tasks. Just as there are different linguistic features associated with high and low collaboration, as found in their study, it stands to reason that different profiles of highly collaborative interactions also likely exist, with varying combinations of linguistic features co-occurring with those profiles. However, L2 research that identifies possible profiles of linguistic features in paired oral tasks has not yet been pursued.

In L2 writing research, two such studies have already taken up this approach, investigating the linguistic profiles of highly rated texts written by NNS English students (see Friginal, Li and Weigle 2014; Jarvis, Grant, Bikwoski and Ferris 2003). Using Cluster Analysis, a multivariate statistical technique that can be used to classify and categorize individuals, objects (such as linguistic features), or observations into specific groups based on cumulative values from a set of predictor variables (Tabachnick and Fidell 2001; as cited in Friginal et al. 2014: 1), these two studies analyzed a set of similar linguistic features that were identified as being salient in highly rated essays from different L2 learner corpora. Both studies showed that highly rated essays could be classified into different clusters (i.e., profiles) of texts using the targeted linguistic features, some of which belonged only to one given cluster and some of which overlapped with other clusters. Although the two abovementioned studies focus on L2 writing, the present study adopts the "profile" approach used in both studies.

3 The Present Study

As Crosthwaite and Raquel (2019: 2) argue, more research in L2 assessment that uses a bottom-up approach of the linguistic features involved in group/pair discussion tasks is needed, as this type of analysis "may serve to augment ratings of student performance on a given assessment and may help in "compiling evidence of the bottom-up linguistic features involved in raters' decisions to award certain grades across the rating scale," both of which concern the construct validity of such scales. This paper serves to extend the bottom-up approach utilized in Crawford et al. (2019) by: (1) using two similar (albeit different) speaking prompts; (2) focusing only on paired oral tasks identified as being highly collaborative; and (3) adopting a Cluster Analysis approach used in Jarvis et al. (2003). The primary purpose of the present study was not to explore differences between highly rated and lower rated oral texts, as was the case in Crawford et al. (2019), but rather to determine whether speaking samples from test-takers' paired oral test interactions that were highly rated for collaboration produce similar (or different) patterns of linguistically co-occurring features.

4 Method

4.1 Description of Data

Data for the present study were obtained from two paired oral test interactions taken from the CCOT (for a description of the CCOT, see Crawford and McDonough, this volume). The dyadic interactions included in the CCOT are derived from international undergraduate students who studied full-time at an intensive English program (IEP) from 2009–2012. The corpus was annotated for part-of-speech (POS) and semantic categories using the Biber Tagger (1988, 2006). The Biber tagger, which incorporates an extended version of the tagset from Constituent Likelihood Automatic Word-Tagging System (CLAWS), is "a computer program created and developed over more than a 10-year period and designed to identify a large number of linguistic features from basic POS tags (e.g., nouns, adjectives), semantic tags (e.g., private verb, concrete noun), and clausal tags (e.g., that-complement clause)" (Friginal et al. 2014: 4). The Biber Tagger has demonstrated extremely high rates of tag accuracy for spoken language data (see Biber and Gray 2013; Thirakunkovit, Rodriguez-Fuentes, Park and Staples 2019).

The spoken interactions are derived from two comparable information-exchange speaking tasks in the CCOT and are reported in the present study as two separate sets of data. The first data set (i.e., Data Set 1) consists of 22 dyadic interactions performed by 44 international students. For this data set, students' interactions for three versions of the same oral test task administered over the course of five different academic semesters were included. The test task, which is provided in Appendix A (including its variants), is the same task outlined in Crawford et al. (2019: 184):

> [T]he students adopted the perspective of a nutritionist to decide which patient should be admitted to a weight loss clinic. Each student in a pair received different information about two potential patients. For example, one student received information about a professor who sleeps only 4 hours per week, has cardiovascular disease, and frequently eats at McDonald's, whereas the other student was given information about a bank manager who recently gained 20 pounds and often eats food from vending machines. They were asked to share information about the patients and reach consensus about which one would benefit most from attending the health clinic.

The second data set (i.e., Data Set 2) consists of 26 dyadic interactions performed by 52 international students. For this data set, students' interactions for one version of an oral test task administered over the course of three different academic semesters were included (see Appendix B for the actual task). The task required students to pretend that they were business partners looking to open a new store at a local mall. Each student in a pair was first asked to spend some time considering their own idea for the type of store to open. Then, the students were asked to discuss each other's ideas and reach consensus on the type of store they wanted to open. Students were encouraged to develop and organize their ideas using a SWOT Analysis matrix, whereby the strengths, weaknesses, opportunities, and threats of a business venture are considered.

At least two trained teacher-raters working at the IEP scored all dyadic interactions in the CCOT using established scoring rubrics. For the present study, teacher-raters scored each of the paired oral tasks using the same analytic rubric (see Appendix C). The rubric consisted of three categories: task completion, style, and collaboration. Crawford et al. (2019: 185) note the following about the rubric and its use:

> Each of the three rubric categories could be scored from 0 (low) to 4 (high), with half-points allowed, resulting in a total possible score of 12. The raters first received training that consisted of a review of the rubric categories followed by rating and discussion of sample tests from previous semesters. Following training, the raters then independently scored the paired oral tests. The raters' scores were combined and an average was obtained.

Only paired oral samples that received a collaboration score of 4 from both raters were selected for analysis in this present study. The students who provided these paired oral samples represented various L1 backgrounds, as shown in Table 1.

Table 1: First language backgrounds of NNS participants in both data sets.

Data set	Native language	Gender	N
1	Arabic	F = 15 / M = 16	31
	Chinese	F = 4 / M = 6	10
	Japanese	F = 0 / M = 2	2
	Korean	F = 0 / M = 1	1
TOTAL			44
2	Arabic	F = 12 / M = 23	35
	Chinese	F = 5 / M = 9	14
	Korean	F = 1 / M = 1	2
	Pashto	F = 0 / M = 1	1
TOTAL			52

Although the paired oral samples were not all collected during the same semester at the IEP – the students were enrolled across eight different semesters – they were collected from students who all placed at an intermediate level of English language proficiency (i.e., Level 4 of the IEP), which is roughly equivalent to TOEFL iBT scores 45–56. Placement scores were determined using an in-house (four-skills) proficiency exam[3] which was administered at the beginning of the semester in which students performed the speaking tasks included in the study.

To confirm that students in the two groups (i.e., students belonging to the two data sets) had similar English language proficiency, scores collected from students' placement exams were compared within and between the two groups of students. The results of the Kruskal-Wallis tests showed that there were no significant differences in overall proficiency test scores across the five semesters of the first data set ($X^2(4) = 2.71$, $p = .29$), nor across the three semesters of the second data set ($X^2(2) = 1.98$, $p = .38$). In addition, students' overall compensatory scores and combined speaking scores from the placement exams were considered across the two data sets. One-way analysis of variance (ANOVA) showed no significant differences in the students' overall English language proficiency [$F(7,92) = 1.374$, $p = .45$], nor their speaking ability [$F(7,92) = 1.091$, $p = .28$]. Therefore, students' English language proficiency was assumed to be relatively similar within and between the groups included in each data set.

4.2 Targeted Linguistic Features

Twenty-nine (29) linguistic features from Crawford et al. (2019) were included in the present study (i.e., features that were associated with high-collaboration interactions). In Crawford et al., all pronouns that were not first- and second-person pronouns were included under one feature (i.e., All pronouns). However, in this study, third-person pronouns (excluding impersonal pronoun *it*) were treated as a separate category (i.e., Third person pronouns), while all other pronouns such as indefinite pronouns (all, some, anybody), demonstrative pronouns (this, that, these) and impersonal pronoun *it* were included in a separate category (i.e., Other pronouns). The 29 linguistic features included in the Cluster Analysis were:
1. First person pronouns – including possessives (e.g., *I*, *my*, *our*)
2. Second person pronouns – including possessives (e.g., *you*, *your*)

---

[3] Two forms of the exam were administered across the eight semesters (i.e., Form A and Form B). The parallel forms reliability coefficient ($r = 0.89$) suggests that the two forms were more or less equivalent.

3. Third person pronouns – excluding *it* (e.g., *his, their*)
4. Other pronouns (e.g., *it, none, some*)
5. *Wh*-questions (e.g., *What are you doing here?*)
6. *That* deletion (e.g., I see *[that]* you are hiding from me.)
7. Subordinating conjunctions (e.g., *because, if, unless*)
8. Adverbial downtoners (e.g., *only, maybe*)
9. *Wh* complement clause controlled by mental verbs (e.g., I **know** *what you mean.*)
10. *Wh* relative clause in subject position (e.g., I like the neighbor *who lives next door.*)
11. Necessity modal verb (e.g., *must, have to*)
12. Subordinating conjunction, phrasal (e.g., *as soon as, even though*)
13. Verb *have* (e.g., *have, had*)
14. Attributive adjectives, all (e.g., *sad* film, *big* man)
15. Present tense verbs (e.g., *drive, drives*)
16. Proper nouns (e.g., *Microsoft, Donald Miller*)
17. Passive voice, all (e.g., *is measured by*)
18. Passive voice, no *by* phrase (e.g., *were given*)
19. All verbs – excluding verb *have* and present tense verbs
20. *That* relative clauses (e.g., There is the car *that I was talking about yesterday.*)
21. *Wh* complement clause controlled by communication verbs (e.g., Let me **explain** *what I mean now.*)
22. Place adverbs (e.g., She took the child *outside.*, *Here* they are!)
23. All prepositions (e.g., *in, on, behind*)
24. Predicative adjectives, epistemic (e.g., It is *obvious.*, That is *impossible!*)
25. Conjunctions, all (e.g., *and, but, or*)
26. Adjectives, all – including attributive and predicative
27. Complement clause controlled by likelihood verb (e.g., It **seems** *that you are correct.*)
28. Possibility modal (e.g., *may, might*)
29. *That* complement clause controlled by verbs (e.g., I **argue** *that it is wrong.*)

4.3 Statistical Analysis

To identify the linguistic profiles of dyadic interactions that were highly rated in collaboration for two paired oral tests, the method of analysis was the same for both data sets. In both cases, Cluster Analysis was used to examine the distributions of the 29 linguistic features under investigation. The Cluster Analysis procedure produces a statistical grouping of these linguistic features based on their cumulative values obtained from the tagging process (Friginal et al. 2014). To perform Cluster Analysis, raw counts of the 29 features were first obtained for each text and then normalized to reflect the relative frequencies of each linguistic feature rather than their raw (non-normalized) frequencies. Following Crawford et al. (2019), all 29 of the linguistic features within each text were normalized to a count of 1000 words. Next, the normalized counts for each text were subjected to an agglomerative hierarchical Cluster Analysis with between-groups linkage and squared Euclidean distance measure in SPSS. Finally, to explore whether the patterns of linguistic features found in the clusters of highly collaborative interactions were comparable across clusters and the two data sets, mean Z scores were calculated for all paired oral tests in both data sets. As Jarvis et al. (2003: 387) note, "one can characterize the profiles of the clusters in terms of their noteworthy high (Z > .50) and low (Z < –.50) use of various linguistic features," thus helping to shed light on whether a particular feature signifies strong cluster membership.

5 Findings

As indicated above, a separate Cluster Analysis was performed on each data set. For both data sets, a solution of three clusters was found to be optimal. Each cluster was presumed to represent a different profile of linguistic features for highly collaborative paired oral interactions. Overall, the majority of the paired oral interactions were grouped into Cluster 1 for both data sets: 14 out of 22 interactions for Data Set 1, and 17 out of 26 interactions for Data Set 2 (see Table 2). The detailed results of each Cluster Analysis for both data sets are presented below.

Table 2: Composition of high-collaboration paired oral interactions in both data sets.

Data set	Cluster 1	Cluster 2	Cluster 3	Total
1	14	3	5	22
2	17	6	3	26
Total	31	9	8	48

5.1 Data Set 1

The mean Z scores of the normed frequencies for each of the 29 linguistic features are provided in Table 3. As can be seen in this table, the mean Z scores for three features were positive across all three clusters: Feature 1 (first person pronouns), Feature 7 (subordinating conjunctions), and Feature 16 (proper nouns). However, it should be noted that only one of these three features had mean Z scores above 0.50 across all three clusters (i.e., Feature 7 – subordinating conjunctions). Meanwhile, the mean Z scores for four features were negative across all three clusters: Feature 10 (*wh* relative clause in subject position), Feature 18 (passive voice, no *by* phrase), Feature 21 (*wh* complement clause controlled by communication verbs), and Feature 22 (place adverbs). None of these four features had mean Z scores less than –0.50 across the three clusters. For the other 22 linguistic features, the positive and negative mean Z scores varied considerably across the three clusters. The profiles of each cluster in terms of their mean Z scores for each linguistic feature are illustrated in Figures 1–3 (see Appendix D).

Table 3: Mean Z scores for the 29 linguistic features of the 3 clusters in Data Set 1.

Features	Cluster 1	Cluster 2	Cluster 3
First person pronouns	0.93	1.98	0.44
Second person pronouns	−1.32	1.27	−1.02
Third person pronouns (excl. it)	0.15	−1.46	0.86
Other pronouns	0.55	−0.27	−0.18
Wh-questions	−1.33	0.17	−0.95
That deletion	−0.89	1.31	1.21
Subordinating conjunctions	2.30	0.52	0.58
Adverbial downtoners (e.g., only)	−0.15	−0.29	0.41
Wh complement clause controlled by mental verbs (e.g., know)	−0.42	0.30	−0.42
Wh relative clause in subject position	−0.53	−0.13	−0.53
Necessity modal verb (must)	−0.85	1.05	−0.64
Subordinating conjunction, phrasal	2.21	−0.36	−0.36
Verb have	−0.99	1.27	0.05
Attributive adjectives, all	1.72	−1.11	−0.44
Present tense verbs	−0.56	0.91	0.95
Proper nouns	0.34	0.21	1.51
Passive voice, all	−0.27	−0.27	1.41
Passive voice, no by phrase	−0.72	−0.72	−0.03
All verbs	0.77	−1.44	−0.26

Table 3 (continued)

Features	Cluster 1	Cluster 2	Cluster 3
That relative clauses	1.66	−0.55	0.20
Wh complement clause controlled by communication verbs (e.g., say)	−0.31	−0.31	−0.31
Place adverbs	−0.38	−0.38	−0.38
All prepositions	0.27	−0.81	−0.79
Predicative adjectives, epistemic	−0.55	−0.55	1.21
Conjunctions, all	1.31	−0.13	1.12
Adjectives, all	1.48	−0.03	1.17
Complement clause controlled by likelihood verb (e.g., seem)	−0.35	0.91	−0.35
Possibility modal (e.g., may)	−0.83	1.53	0.11
That complement clause controlled by verbs	−0.72	−0.24	0.74

As shown in Table 4 below, each of the three clusters demonstrated a relatively unique combination of mean Z scores above 0.50 ("+") and below −0.50 ("-"), representing noteworthy departures from the central tendency of the distribution for each cluster. In order to investigate the uniqueness of the three clusters, a series of non-parametric Kruskal-Wallis tests were performed; the Kruskal-Wallis tests were preferred (instead of one-way ANOVAs) because several linguistic features had slight violations of the assumption of normality. To avoid inflating the possibility of making a Type-I error when making multiple comparisons with the same data, a Bonferroni adjustment was applied; therefore, the adjusted alpha was set at 0.017 (i.e., .05/3 = 0.017). Each linguistic feature served as the dependent variable and cluster membership served as the fixed factor. Overall, the results of the Kruskal-Wallis tests revealed significant differences across the three clusters for the following seven linguistic features:

- First person pronouns (Feature 1) ($\chi^2(2) = 11.081, p < .001$),
- Third person pronouns (Feature 3) ($\chi^2(2) = 4.579, p = 0.010$),
- *Wh* complement clause controlled by mental verbs (Feature 9) ($\chi^2(2) = 18.330, p < .001$),
- Subordinating conjunctions, phrasal (Feature 12) ($\chi^2(2) = 28.623, p < .001$),
- Proper nouns (Feature 16) ($\chi^2(2) = 8.144, p = 0.004$),
- Passive voice (Feature 17) ($\chi^2(2) = 13.969, p < .001$),
- Possibility modal (Feature 28) ($\chi^2(2) = 4.522, p = 0.014$).

Table 4: Profiles of the 3 clusters in terms of high (+) and low (−) use of the linguistic features.

Features	Cluster 1	Cluster 2	Cluster 3
First person pronouns	+	+	
Second person pronouns	−	+	−
Third person pronouns (excl. it)		−	+
Other pronouns	+		
Wh-questions	−		−
That deletion	−	+	+
Subordinating conjunctions	+	+	+
Adverbial downtoners (e.g., only)			
Wh complement clause controlled by mental verbs (e.g., know)			
Wh relative clause in subject position	−		−
Necessity modal verb (must)	−	+	−
Subordinating conjunction, phrasal	+		
Verb have	−	+	
Attributive adjectives, all	+	−	
Present tense verbs	+	+	+
Proper nouns			+
Passive voice, all			+
Passive voice, no by phrase	−	−	
All verbs	+	−	
That relative clauses	+	−	
Wh complement clause controlled by communication verbs (e.g., say)			
Place adverbs			
All prepositions		−	−
Predicative adjectives, epistemic	−	−	+
Conjunctions, all	+		+
Adjectives, all	+		+
Complement clause controlled by likelihood verb (e.g., seem)		+	
Possibility modal (e.g., may)	−	+	
That complement clause controlled by verbs	−		+

5.2 Data Set 2

Similar to the previous data set, the mean Z scores for each of the 29 linguistic features were evaluated across the three clusters identified for the second data set. As can be seen in Table 5, the mean Z scores for four features were positive across all three clusters: Feature 3 (third person pronouns, excl. *it*), Feature 10 (*wh* relative clause in subject position), Feature 20 (*that* relative clauses), and Feature 29 (*that* complement clause controlled by verbs). However, it should be noted that only two of these features had mean Z scores above 0.50 across all three clusters (i.e., third person pronouns, excl. *it* and *that* relative clauses). Meanwhile, the mean Z scores for three features were negative across all three clusters: Feature 9 (*wh* complement clause controlled by mental verbs), Feature 14 (attributive adjectives, all), and Feature 23 (all prepositions). None of these three features had mean Z scores less than −0.50 across the three clusters. As demonstrated by the cluster profiles in Figures 4–6 (see Appendix E), there was considerable variation among the positive and negative mean Z scores for the 22 remaining linguistic features.

Table 5: Mean Z scores for the 29 linguistic features of the 3 clusters in Data Set 2.

Features	Cluster 1	Cluster 2	Cluster 3
First person pronouns	−0.48	−0.48	0.29
Second person pronouns	−0.48	1.39	0.23
Third person pronouns (excl. it)	0.70	0.51	1.28
Other pronouns	−1.01	0.33	−0.87
Wh-questions	−0.56	−0.08	2.27
That deletion	1.18	1.12	−0.47
Subordinating conjunctions	1.73	0.20	−0.98
Adverbial downtoners (e.g., only)	−0.63	0.39	−0.90
Wh complement clause controlled by mental verbs (e.g., know)	−0.12	−0.12	−0.57
Wh relative clause in subject position	2.14	0.30	1.07
Necessity modal verb (must)	0.91	−0.66	−0.66
Subordinating conjunction, phrasal	−0.53	−0.53	1.54
Verb have	0.39	−0.13	−0.89
Attributive adjectives, all	−0.09	−0.12	−0.36
Present tense verbs	0.61	−0.25	1.18
Proper nouns	−0.37	2.04	−0.63
Passive voice, all	−0.26	1.70	−0.26

Table 5 (continued)

Features	Cluster 1	Cluster 2	Cluster 3
Passive voice, no by phrase	−0.26	2.27	−0.26
All verbs	−0.38	−0.10	0.26
That relative clauses	0.76	1.34	2.30
Wh complement clause controlled by communication verbs (e.g., say)	2.21	−0.32	−0.32
Place adverbs	−0.03	0.34	0.46
All prepositions	−0.62	−0.57	−0.08
Predicative adjectives, epistemic	−0.38	−0.38	1.13
Conjunctions, all	−1.10	−0.18	1.10
Adjectives, all	−1.24	1.64	0.02
Complement clause controlled by likelihood verb (e.g., seem)	1.45	−0.36	−0.36
Possibility modal (e.g., may)	0.25	−0.50	2.41
That complement clause controlled by verbs	1.61	1.57	0.10

Similar to the cluster profiles outlined in the first data set, each of the three clusters in the second data set demonstrated a relatively unique combination of high ($Z > 0.50$) and low ($Z < -0.50$) use of the 29 linguistic features included in the study; the distinguishing characteristics of the three cluster profiles are summarized in Table 6 below. Again, Kruskal-Wallis tests were conducted to investigate the uniqueness of the three clusters in this data set, with the adjusted alpha set at 0.017. The results of the Kruskal-Wallis tests revealed significant differences across the three clusters for the following eight linguistic features:

- *Wh* questions (Feature 5) ($\chi^2(2) = 6.473$, $p = .010$),
- *Wh* complement clause controlled by mental verbs ($\chi^2(2) = 9.224$, $p < .001$),
- Necessity modal verb (Feature 11) ($\chi^2(2) = 4.983$, $p = .016$),
- Proper nouns (Feature 16) ($\chi^2(2) = 13.099$, $p < .001$),
- Passive voice, no *by* phrase (Feature 18) ($\chi^2(2) = 11.167$, $p < .001$),
- *That* relative clauses (Feature 20) ($\chi^2(2) = 5.570$, $p = .012$),
- Complement clause controlled by likelihood verb (Feature 27) ($\chi^2(2) = 8.702$, $p = .006$),
- Possibility modal (Feature 28) ($\chi^2(2) = 17.431$, $p < .001$).

Table 6: Profiles of the 3 clusters in terms of high (+) and low (−) use of the linguistic features.

Features	Cluster 1	Cluster 2	Cluster 3
First person pronouns			
Second person pronouns		+	
Third person pronouns (excl. it)	+	+	+
Other pronouns	−		−
Wh-questions	−		+
That deletion	+	+	
Subordinating conjunctions	+		−
Adverbial downtoners (e.g., only)	−		−
Wh complement clause controlled by mental verbs (e.g., know)			−
Wh relative clause in subject position	+		+
Necessity modal verb (must)	+	−	−
Subordinating conjunction, phrasal	−	−	+
Verb have			−
Attributive adjectives, all			
Present tense verbs	+		+
Proper nouns		+	−
Passive voice, all		+	
Passive voice, no by phrase		+	
All verbs			
That relative clauses	+	+	+
Wh complement clause controlled by communication verbs (e.g., say)	+		
Place adverbs			
All prepositions	−	−	
Predicative adjectives, epistemic			+
Conjunctions, all	−		+
Adjectives, all	−	+	
Complement clause controlled by likelihood verb (e.g., seem)	+		
Possibility modal (e.g., may)		−	+
That complement clause controlled by verbs	+	+	

5.3 Insights from Student-student Dialogues

As demonstrated in Tables 4 and 6 above, although the clusters did share some similar linguistic features, three rather unique clusters were identified in both data sets. For instance, in Examples (1) and (2) (see below), which illustrate representative high-collaboration interactions, both samples are marked by interactive turns that are relatively equal across the two speakers involved.[4] Furthermore, both samples make similar (frequent) use of subordinating conjunctions (mainly *because*) and present tense verbs (e.g., *think*, *has*, *is*), which demonstrate the involved and interpersonal nature of many unrehearsed spoken interactions (Biber 1988).

(1) Sample of paired oral task from Cluster 2 (Data Set 1)
    1B: Uh I *have* uh a patient who *has* problem with **his** weight. ***He is*** a graduate student si-*and* since **he** was a boy **he he** always *have* twenty five pounds overweight.
    2A: Really?
    3B: Yeah. What about **your** patient?
    4A: I *have* Anne. **She** *has* gained uh fifteen pounds *and* **she** *is* in class from eight a.m. *and* until seven p.m. I *think* **she**--
    5B: --*Excuse* **me** *excuse* me *but* we *have* uh the **we we** *have* to just accept one uh of the patient **mine** *or or* **yours**.
    6A: I *know* but **you** --
    7B: -- So **you** *know*, I *think* it'*s* **my my** patient *is* deserve to to ha--to *has* to come to **our** room *because* **he** always *has* twenty five overweight *and* **he** also worried about **his** diabetes maybe **he** *gets* diabetes *and* **he** never *work or* **he** less *work* uh *because* **he he** always *sit* at at **his** desk for long hours so **he** *has* uh less work.
    8A: I *know* it'*s* a big problem *but* **we** should *see* Anne *because* **she** also *has* a big problem. **She** had fifteen pounds *and* sh-**she** *take* more classes how can **she** *know* about uh the times *and* about the weight I *think* it'*s* difficult for **her**. What do **you** *think*?
    9B: I *understand* **your** opinion *but* I *think* uh **my** patient *is* more need to help than **your** patient *because as* I said **he**... **he** uh *has* twenty five pounds from from many years I mean over-overweight twenty five pounds overweight from many years *and* **he**... *need* **he** worried about **his** diabetes *and* I *think* diabetes it'*s* a dangerous disease so *that* I *think* **he** *is* deserve to come first.

---

[4] The examples are also similar in terms of length (about 350 words) and turns (12 and 11), respectively.

10A: **You** _know_ I I _think_ I _agree_ with **you** because... **your** student **your** man uh _has_ twenty five pounds more than Anne because Anne _has_ fifteen pounds I _think_ I'm _agree_ with **you**.
11B: Thank **you** that's _make_ uh _make_ it good. So _let_**'s** _take_ Joe.
12A: Okay thank **you** for **your** opinion.

Note: The following formatting features are used to highlight the linguistic markers in the example – **1st person pronouns**; **2nd person pronouns**; 3rd person pronouns; subordinating conjunctions; coordinating conjunctions; _present tense verbs_.

(2) Sample of paired oral task from Cluster 3 (Data Set 1)
1A: Uh **my**... **my** patient _is_ his na-her name K-uh Cindy. She _work_ at Wells Fargo Bank and she every day _runs_ in her family and she _work_ at Wells Fargo Bank and she _has_-and she _work_ from seven until five p.m. and she _have_ time after five and she can _sleep_ early and she _work_ and she woke up early to go to her work and she _has_ gained twenty pounds and she _eats_ vending machine every day. And I _think_ it'_s_ good to for /---/ at health centre. I _think_ it'_s_ good for her to go to health centre.
2B: Uh **my** patient uh person name _is_ Lou. Uh I _think_ he _needs_ to go to health centre because he'_s_ a professor is _means_ he'_s_ very busy man so sometimes he _has_ no time he so he _goes_ to eat at McDonald's /---/ time week. He also-he also _sit_ his desk for a long time every day and uh he uh _has_ cardiv-cardi disease _run-runs_ in his family and he _is_ very worried his health. I _think_ he _needs_ help.
3A: No I _think_ uh Cindy _has_ a lot of time after five and she can _go_ to health centre and she not busy every time and she _sleep_ early.
4B: I _think_ Lou is very uh busy busy too because she just _sleep_ only four hours at night.
5A: Yeah that'_s_ not good for him because he _sleep_ four hours and he worried about his hea-his health but he _have_ disease and he _sit_ long time in his desk and so that'_s_ not good for him. So I _think_ Cindy _has_ a lot of time and he _work_ at Wells Fargo Bank and and he _runs_ every day so that'_s_ okay for %for her and% she
6B: %Okay I will /---/% because she _is_ gained uh t-twenty pounds so I _think_ she _need_ more help. Okay
7A: %Yeah%

8A: %*Stop*%
9A: So *let's* go to--
10B: --*Stop stop stop. Stop.*
11A: Thank you.

Note: The following formatting features are used to highlight the linguistic markers in the example – **1st person pronouns**; **2nd person pronouns**; *3rd person pronouns*; subordinating conjunctions; coordinating conjunctions; *present tense verbs*.

At the same time, the distribution of personal pronouns across the two samples is quite different. For instance, Example (1) demonstrates far greater use of first and second person pronouns than Example (2) (29 instances vs. 12 instances and 12 instances vs. 0 instances, respectively), while Example (2) demonstrates far greater use of third person pronouns than Example (1) (49 instances vs. 29 instances). Furthermore, while first person pronouns are used in both samples to describe participant perspectives (*I think*), there are more varied uses of these pronouns in Example (1): to interrupt (*Excuse me*); to show agreement (*I agree*); to confirm understanding (*I understand*; *I know*); and to express necessity (*we have to*). In contrast, third person pronouns appear much more frequently in Example (2), as well as across all three clusters in Data Set 2, suggesting a narrative-like element to the interactions elicited by the two tasks examined in this study (Biber 1988).

The distributions of coordinating conjunctions across the same two examples also helps to illustrate some of the stylistic differences among high-collaboration interactions. For instance, in Cluster 3 (Example (2) here), coordinating conjunctions are a strong indicator of cluster membership, while they are not in Cluster 2 (Example (1) here); there are 25 occurrences in Example (2) and 15 occurrences in Example (1). Furthermore, the participants in Example (2) rely almost exclusively on the coordinator *and* (24 out of 25 occurrences), as they appear to use *and* to "stack" patient information (about Cindy and Lou) at the beginning of the conversation–13 of the 24 occurrences appear within the first two turns. In contrast, three different coordinators are used in Example (1): *and* (9 times); *but* (4 times); and *or* (2 times). Interestingly, the coordinator *but* is used almost exclusively after a mental-state verb to preface a rebuttal and/or express disagreement (e.g., I know but . . ., I understand your opinion but . . .), enabling both speakers in Example (1) to express her/his stance.

6 Discussion

Overall, the results of the present study suggest that there are multiple profiles of linguistic features associated with highly collaborative peer-to-peer interaction. While interacting in pairs, test-takers seemed to draw on a broad range of linguistic features to complete the two speaking tasks, from personal pronouns to *wh* questions to subordinating clauses, which led to considerable variation in the linguistic makeup associated with the different clusters identified in the present study. Reflective of this was the finding that, although there was some overlap, the clusters identified in each data set appeared to consist of rather unique combinations of high and low use of linguistic features. The findings from the cluster analyses (specifically, Tables 4 and 6 above), coupled with the qualitative data from the student-student dialogues, demonstrate the unique combinations of linguistic features that were utilized by test-takers during peer-to-peer interactions.

While a number of linguistic features appeared to contribute to the overall quality of the spoken performances, high levels of some features seemed to bring about lower levels of other features. That is, many of the linguistic features identified within the clusters appeared to be in complimentary distribution (Jarvis et al. 2003). For example, for the *Business Venture* task in the present study (i.e., Data Set 2), it was found that Clusters 1 and 2 exhibited greater instances of *that*-deletion accompanied by a low use of prepositions. Whereas prepositional phrases occur far more frequently in academic writing than in speech and are more closely associated with conveying information (Biber and Gray 2013), *that*-deletion occurs much more frequently in (involved) conversation since the omission of *that* favors the reduction or omission of constituents that are not seen as being necessary (Biber 2006). Similar patterns were also identified for the *Nutritionist* task in the present study (i.e., Data Set 1), particularly the juxtaposition of test-takers' use of coordination versus dependent clauses (e.g., relative clauses). That is, for the *Nutritionist* task, when test-takers make frequent use of coordinators in their discourse, typically as an "add-on strategy" to extend turns and elaborate conversation (Biber, Johansson, Leech, Conrad and Finegan 1999: 1078), this is systematically accompanied by rather infrequent use of dependent clauses. While there are other additional examples of this phenomenon of complimentary distribution in the present study, all of these occurrences taken together signify "important constraints on the degree to which different linguistic features can co-occur in a text" (Jarvis et al. 2003: 399).

Despite the variability of linguistic features utilized across the clusters, there also appeared to be constraints on the differences that existed between the multiple profiles of paired oral samples that were rated as being highly collaborative. As mentioned earlier, significant differences were found for 15 linguistic features across the two data sets. However, of those 15 features, only three of them were in fact the same across the two data sets: *wh*-complement clauses controlled by mental verbs; proper nouns; and possibility modals. In other words, the six profiles of (highly collaborative) paired oral tasks appeared to differ more prominently from one another in relation to these three features. Conversely, it seems that there was less variation for the other 12 linguistic features that were identified as being significantly different across clusters (e.g., *that* relative clauses, necessity modal verb, *wh* questions), suggesting that the profiles identified here may actually be more alike than they initially appeared. As Jarvis et al. (2003: 400–401) explain, this "suggests that a high rating on a given task may require a rather specific level of use of certain linguistic features, even while allowing texts to vary more or less freely with respect to other features." However, although the findings for the present study provide tentative evidence to support that highly collaborative peer-to-peer interactions consist of distinguishable linguistic profiles, it is unclear whether clusters of linguistic features would also be identifiable at the middle or lower ends of the same rating scale (for the same intermediate-level test-takers). Future studies concerning paired oral assessment would do well to collect more data, particularly at the lower and middle segments of a (similar) rating scale, to determine if there are distinguishable profiles of linguistic features across the different scoring categories of the rating scale. Additionally, in order to compare and contrast test-takers at different levels of language proficiency, future studies could investigate the extent to which different profiles of linguistic features are identifiable across advanced, intermediate, and novice levels.

In this study, it is clear that the rating scale does not fully capture the variability of performances co-constructed in the paired speaking tasks. For example, although the rating scale does include criteria related to "narration techniques" and "stating an opinion" within the *Style* category, the descriptors do not specify the features of effective narration techniques or how test-takers should structure an opinion when they are co-constructing a performance. While it may be desirable to include more specific descriptions of linguistic features within the rating scale itself and an expanded construct, such rich, detailed descriptions of performance could potentially overwhelm the raters, introducing threats to reliability and practicality (Bachman and Palmer 2010). As an alternative, richer descriptions of the various (sub-)constructs included within a rating scale (e.g., collaboration, task completion, style) can be discussed alongside samples of different profiles of (similarly effective) performance during rater training sessions. For instance, in the present study, test-takers' differing uses of personal pronouns in highly collaborative paired oral tasks could be discussed during rater training, such as the use of first person pronouns to state an opinion and/or express disagreement (Crosthwaite and Raquel 2019; Gan 2010) and the use of third person pronouns to establish grammatical cohesion through referential links (Biber 1988). Greater consideration of linguistic features that complement collaboration may serve to inform raters' interpretation and operationalization of peer-to-peer interaction (Ducasse and Brown 2009).

7 Conclusion

Throughout the past two decades, identifying patterns of behavior that enable us to better understand how interlocutors collaborate during peer-to-peer interaction has been the subject of extensive investigation, with a number of studies investigating various issues concerning the use of paired oral tasks in L2 speaking assessment (e.g., Brooks 2009; Ducasse and Brown 2009; Galaczi 2014; Lazaraton and Davis 2008). More recently, the focus has been on analyzing the linguistic features of peer-to-peer interaction with a view towards considering how co-occurring features work in scoring collaboration (e.g., Crawford et al. 2019). However, at the time of the present study, no studies have been conducted to determine the extent to which test-takers' paired oral test interactions that were highly rated for collaboration produce similar (or different) profiles of linguistic features. The current study, while exploratory in nature, incorporates a unique methodology for examining profiles of test-taker performance in peer-to-peer interactions.

In the current study, the speech samples of 48 paired oral test tasks were analyzed using 29 linguistic features identified in Crawford et al., (2019). Cluster Analysis was carried out to address the research topic under investigation. The results demonstrated that, first, three clusters emerged across both data sets included in the study, for a total of six clusters; second, only three of the linguistic features (i.e., possibility modals; proper nouns; and *wh*-complement clauses controlled by mental verbs) included in the Cluster Analysis demonstrated significant differences across the three clusters in both data sets. Building on Crawford et al.'s (2019) work, the findings from the current study support that there is not just one set of linguistic features that characterize collaborative peer-to-peer interaction.

In conducting this research, there are potential limitations that must be acknowledged. First, while the linguistic features used in the present study were previously identified in Crawford et al. (2019) as being strongly associated with high-collaboration interactions, it is not possible to characterize the notion of collaboration in terms of only 29 linguistic features. Future research would do well to combine additional linguistic features associated with conversational discourse (e.g., see Biber et al. 1999). In addition, the data included in the present study was selected as a matter of convenience, taken from the CCOT, which was compiled from classroom-based speaking tests. As a result, a number of factors which might have impacted the results of this study could not be controlled (e.g., proficiency, task pairing, task type). Therefore, caution must be taken when interpreting the results of this study.

References

Ahmadi, Alireza & Elham Sadeghi. 2016. Assessing English language learners' oral performance: A comparison of monologue, interview, and group oral test. *Language Assessment Quarterly* 13(4). 341–358.

Bachman, Lyle & Adrian Palmer. 2010. *Language assessment in practice*. Oxford: Oxford University Press.

Berry, Vivien. 2007. *Personality differences and oral test performance*. Frankfurt: Peter Lang.

Biber, Douglas. 1988. *Variation across speech and writing*. Cambridge: Cambridge University Press.

Biber, Douglas. 2006. *University language: A corpus-based study of spoken and written registers*. Amsterdam: John Benjamins Publishing.

Biber, Douglas, Stig Johansson, Geoffrey Leech, Susan Conrad & Edward Finegan. 1999. *Longman grammar of spoken and written English*. Essex: Pearson Education.

Biber, Douglas & Bethany Gray. 2013. Discourse characteristics of writing and speaking task types on the TOEFL-iBT test: A lexico-grammatical analysis. *ETS Research Report Series* (1). i–128. Princeton: Educational Testing Service.

Biber, Douglas & Jesse Egbert. 2018. *Register variation online*. Cambridge: Cambridge University Press.

Bonk, William & Alistair Van Moere. 2004. L2 group oral testing: The influence of shyness/outgoingness, match of interlocutor's proficiency level, and gender on individual scores. Paper presented at the Language Testing Research Colloquium, Temecula, 24–28 March.

Brooks, Lindsay. 2009. Interacting in pairs in a test of oral proficiency: Co-constructing a better performance. *Language Testing* 26(3). 341–366.

Brown, Annie. 2003. Interviewer variation and the co-construction of speaking proficiency. *Language Testing* 20(1). 1–25.

Brown, Annie & Tim McNamara. 2004. "The devil is in the detail": Researching gender issues in language assessment. *TESOL Quarterly* 38(3). 524–538.

Crawford, William, Kim McDonough & Nicole Brun-Mercer. 2019. Identifying linguistic markers of collaboration in second language peer interaction: A lexico-grammatical approach. *TESOL Quarterly* 53(1). 180–207.

Crosthwaite, Peter & Michelle Raquel. 2019. Validating an L2 academic group oral assessment: Insights from a spoken learner corpus. *Language Assessment Quarterly* 16(1). 39–63.

Davis, Larry. 2009. The influence of interlocutor proficiency in paired oral assessment. *Language Testing* 26(3). 367–396.

Dillenbourg, Pierre. 1999. What do you mean by collaborative learning? In Pierre Dillenbourg (Ed.), *Collaborative learning: Cognitive and computational approaches*, 1–19. Oxford: Elsevier.
Ducasse, Ana Maria & Annie Brown. 2009. Assessing paired orals: Raters' orientation to interaction. *Language Testing* 26(3). 423–443.
Friginal, Eric, Man Li & Sara Weigle. 2014. Revisiting multiple profiles of learner compositions: A comparison of highly rated NS and NNS essays. *Journal of Second Language Writing* 23. 1–16.
Galaczi, Evelina. 2008. Peer-peer interaction in a speaking test: The case of the First Certificate in English examination. *Language Assessment Quarterly* 5(2). 89–119.
Galaczi, Evelina. 2014. Interactional competence across proficiency levels: How do learners manage interaction in paired speaking tests? *Applied Linguistics* 35(5). 553–574.
Gan, Zhengdong. 2010. Interaction in group oral assessment: A case study of higher- and lower- scoring students. *Language Testing* 27(4). 585–602.
Jarvis, Scott, Leslie Grant, Dawn Bikowski & Dana Ferris, D. 2003. Exploring multiple profiles of highly rated learner compositions. *Journal of Second Language Writing* 12. 377–403.
Kasper, Gabriele. 2013. Managing task uptake in oral proficiency interviews. In Steven Ross & Gabriele Kasper (Eds.), *Assessing second language pragmatics*, 258–287. New York: Palgrave Macmillan.
Lai, Emily. 2011. *Collaboration: A literature review*. Research Report. New York: Pearson. http://images.pearsonassessments.com/images/tmrs/Collaboration-Review.pdf (accessed 18 June 2019).
Lazaraton, Anne & Larry Davis. 2008. A microanalytic perspective on discourse, proficiency, and identity in paired oral assessment. *Language Assessment Quarterly* 5(4). 313–335.
Nakatsuhara, Fumiyo. 2006. The impact of proficiency level on conversational styles in paired speaking tests. *University of Cambridge ESOL Examinations Research Notes* 25. 15–20.
Philp, Jenefer, Rebecca Adams & Noriko Iwashita. 2014. *Peer interaction and second language learning*. New York: Routledge.
Skehan, Peter. 2001. Tasks and language performance assessment. In Martin Bygate, Peter Skehan & Merrill Swain (Eds.), *Researching pedagogic tasks*, 167–185. London: Longman.
Storch, Neomy. 2002. Patterns of interaction in ESL pair work. *Language Learning* 52(1). 119–158.
Tabachnick, Barbara & Linda Fidell. 2001. *Using multivariate statistics*, 4th edn. Boston: Allyn & Bacon.
Taylor, Lynda & Gillian Wigglesworth. 2009. Are two heads better than one? Pair work in L2 assessment contexts. *Language Testing* 26(3). 325–339.
Thirakunkovit, Ploy, Rodrigo Rodriguez-Fuentes, Kyongson Park & Shelley Staples. 2019. A corpus-based analysis of grammatical complexity as a measure of international teaching assistants' oral English proficiency. *English for Specific Purposes* 53. 74–89.
Winke, Paula. 2013. The effectiveness of interactive group orals for placement testing. In Kim McDonough & Alison Mackey (Eds.), *Second language interaction in diverse educational contexts*, 246–268. Amsterdam: John Benjamins.

Appendix A

Nutrition Information-Exchange Task

You and your partner will pretend to be nutritionists working for a university health center. You have two patients who want to lose weight but need help beyond what a normal diet can provide. After you and your partner describe and make a recommendation about each patient, decide which patient needs more help and should be admitted into the university health center for treatment. You can only admit one student to the health center.

Version A: Melia and Joe

	Melia		Joe
(1)	She is a university freshman	(1)	He is a graduate student
(2)	She has gained 15 pounds	(2)	Since he was a boy, he has always been at least 25 pounds overweight
(3)	Her clothes don't fit	(3)	Obesity runs in his family
(4)	She is in class from 8 a.m. until 7 p.m.	(4)	He's on a diet but just doesn't lost weight
(5)	She studies at the library until midnight	(5)	He's worried about diabetes
(6)	She skips meals and buys snacks at the library	(6)	He sits at his desk for long hours every day

Version B: Cindy and Lou

	Cindy		Lou
(1)	She works at Wells Fargo Bank	(1)	He is a professor
(2)	Obesity runs in her family	(2)	He sleeps only 4 hours a night
(3)	She is depressed because of her job	(3)	He eats at McDonald's three times a week
(4)	She works from 7 a.m. until 5 p.m.	(4)	Cardiovascular disease runs in his family

(continued)

(5)	She has gained 20 pounds	(5)	He's worried about his health
(6)	She eats from the vending machine every day	(6)	He sits at his desk for long hours every day

Version C: Cindy and Jack

Cindy		Jack	
(1)	She has obese parents	(1)	He sleeps 4 hours a night
(2)	She works long hours	(2)	He eats at McDonald's a lot
(3)	She has gained 20 pounds	(3)	He has heart problems in his family
(4)	She eats junk food all day	(4)	He sits at a desk all day

Appendix B

Store Opening Information-Exchange Task

You and your partner will pretend to be business partners. There is a vacant spot at the local mall and you must decide which type of store you want to open in the mall. After you spend some time considering your own idea for the type of store you want to open, discuss your idea with your partner. Then, decide which type of store will be best to open in the mall. You can only open one store. You may use the SWOT Analysis (below) to develop and organize your ideas.

STRENGTHS	WEAKNESSES
OPPORTUNITIES	THREATS

Appendix C

Paired Oral Test Rubric

	Collaboration	Task completion	Style
4	Both learners almost always – Work together on almost all parts of the task – Carefully respond to each other and engage each other's ideas – Offer constructive feedback	– Excellent completion of the task; all required elements of the task are present – Content is rich; ideas developed with elaboration and detail; overall task outcome is outstanding	– Outstanding ability to state an opinion – Show excellent skills in using narrative techniques – Show excellent skills in interrupting politely to ask questions
3	Both learners usually – Work together on most parts of the tasks – Respond to each other and engage each other's ideas – Offer feedback	– Good completion of the task; almost all required elements are present – Responses are appropriate and with some elaboration and detail; overall task outcome is satisfactory	– Good ability to state an opinion – Show good skills in using narrative techniques – Show good skills in interrupting politely to ask questions
2	– There is some engagement in the interaction but only one student generally leads participation during tasks – Sometimes the learners ignore each other's responses – Both learners or one learner sometimes do not offer any feedback	– Acceptable completion of the task; some required elements are missing – Responses are mostly appropriate and adequately developed; overall task outcome is acceptable	– Adequate ability to state an opinion – Show adequate skills in using narrative techniques – Show adequate skills in interrupting politely to ask questions
1	– One learner always takes lead in discussion during tasks or neither of them often try to engage in tasks – Both learners often ignore each other's responses and have high level of disagreements and inability to reach consensus; only claim own opinion – Both learners provide very little feedback to each other	– Partial completion of the task; many required elements are missing – Responses are appropriate yet undeveloped; only basic ideas are expressed without any elaboration or detail; overall task outcome is poor	– Try to state an opinion – Try to use narrative techniques – Try to interrupt politely to ask questions

(continued)

	Collaboration	Task completion	Style
0	- Both learners show no evidence of working with partners - Both learners never pay attention or respond to each other - Both learners demonstrate no evidence of ability to provide feedback to each other	- Unable to complete the task; few or no required elements are present - Responses are inappropriate; overall task outcome is not comprehensible	- Cannot state an opinion - Show no skills in using narrative techniques - Show no skills in interrupting politely to ask questions

Appendix D

Cluster Profiles for Data Set 1

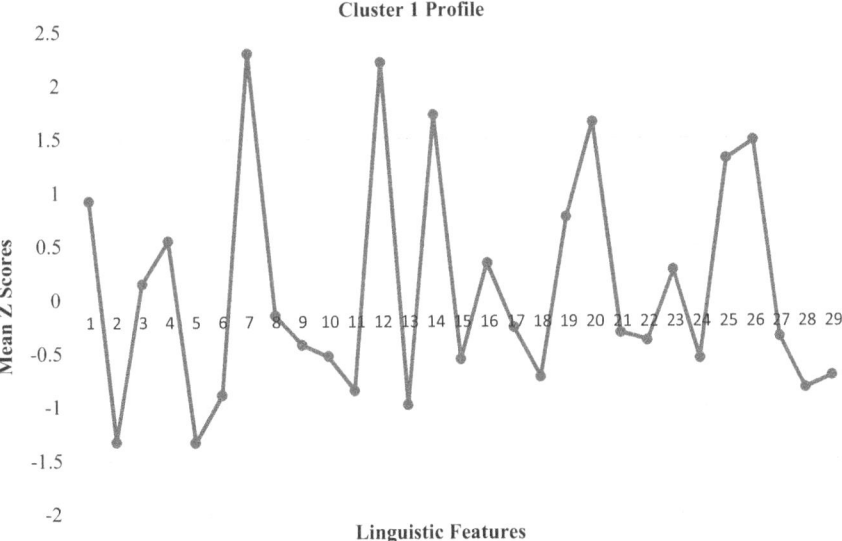

Figure 1: Cluster 1 profile (Data Set 1).

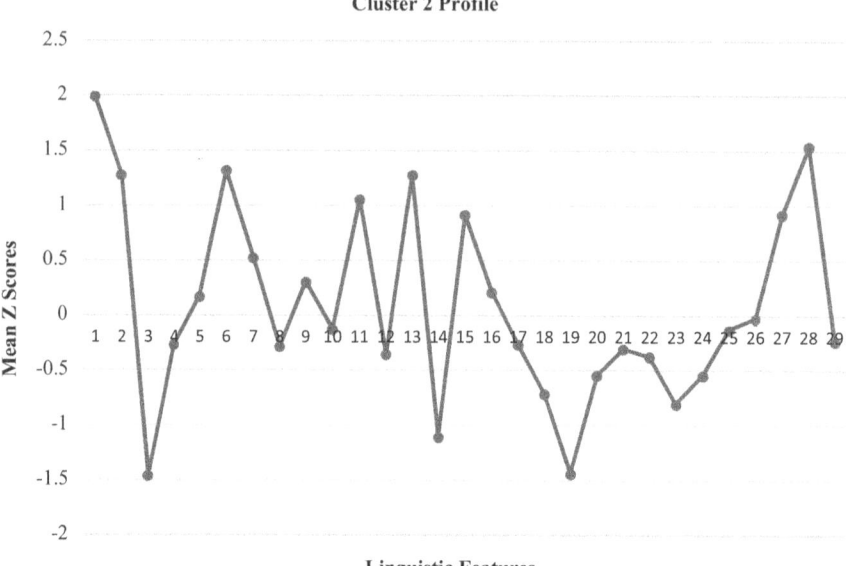

Figure 2: Cluster 2 profile (Data Set 1).

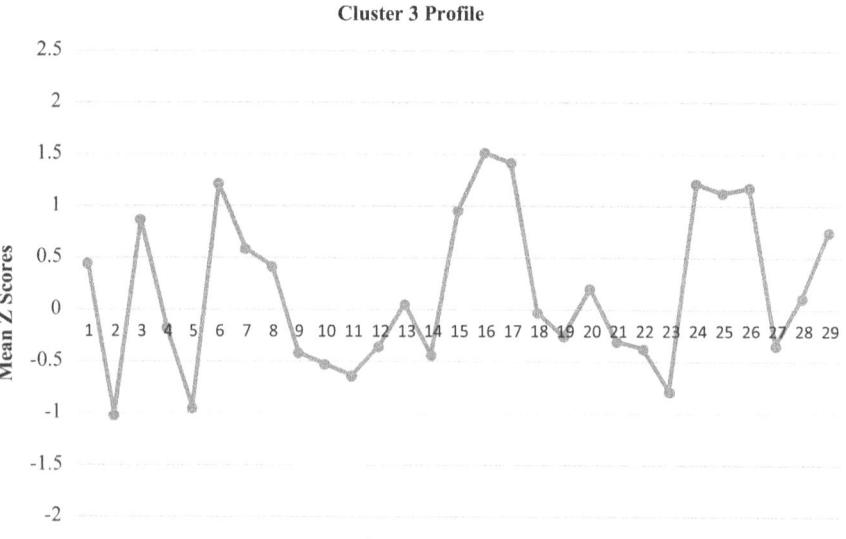

Figure 3: Cluster 3 profile (Data Set 1).

Appendix E

Cluster Profiles for Data Set 2

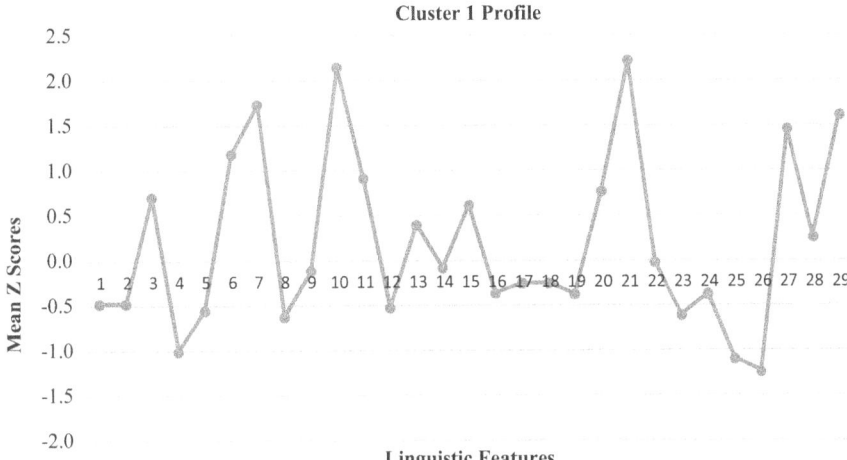

Figure 4: Cluster 1 profile (Data Set 2).

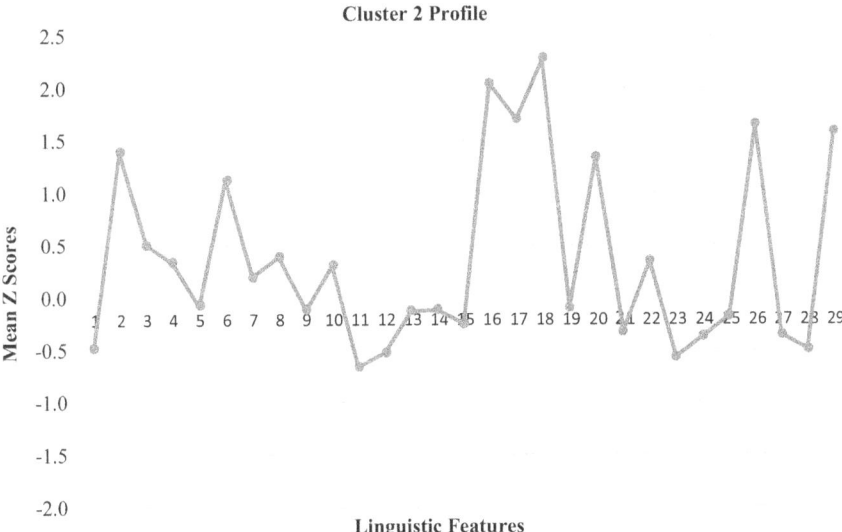

Figure 5: Cluster 2 profile (Data Set 2).

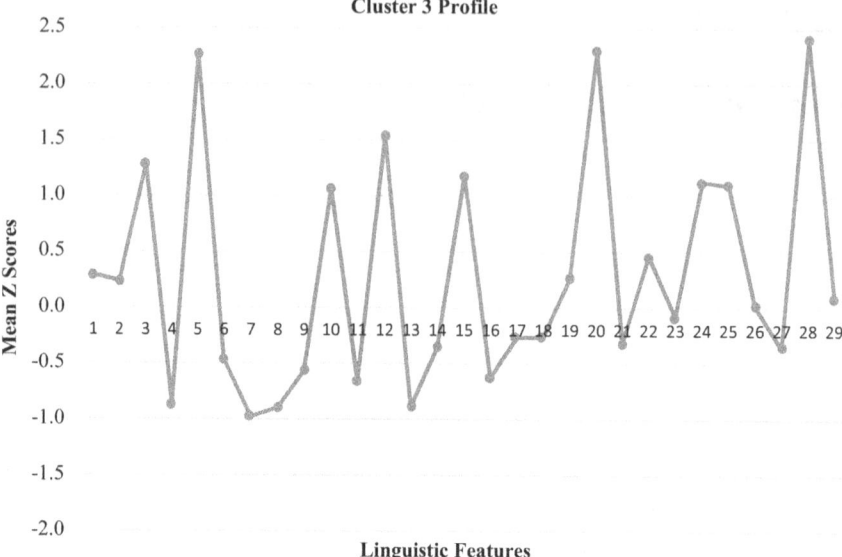

Figure 6: Cluster 3 profile (Data Set 2).

Shelley Staples
Exploring the Impact of Situational Characteristics on the Linguistic Features of Spoken Oral Assessment Tasks

1 Introduction

Research in register analysis (e.g., Biber 1988; Biber 2006) has a long tradition in corpus linguistics of connecting situational characteristics (e.g., purpose, relationship between interlocutors) with linguistic features (e.g., nouns, attributive adjectives, prepositional phrases) through their function in the discourse context (e.g., when the purpose focuses on information sharing, more nouns, attributive adjectives, and prepositional phrases are used). Recently, corpus-based register analysis has been used to explore assessment tasks (Staples, Biber, and Reppen 2018; Staples, LaFlair, and Egbert 2017). In Staples, Biber, and Reppen (2018), for example, the authors show that the frequencies of linguistic features used in the TOEFL integrated writing task are much more similar to those in the disciplinary writing of students at the university when compared with the TOEFL independent writing task. This difference was explained through the variation in situational characteristics between the TOEFL integrated and independent writing tasks (e.g., the integrated task required test takers to integrate informational content, similar to the purposes of many disciplinary writing tasks). This finding clearly has implications for task development in a variety of assessment contexts, both for high stakes and program-specific formative and summative assessment. The findings also show that the method of analysis, which here is called a "register-functional" approach, provides a valuable addition to our understanding of assessment tasks (see Biber, Gray, and Staples 2016; Biber, Gray, Staples, and Egbert in press, for more discussion of the register-functional approach).

To date, few studies using a register-functional approach for the study of assessment tasks have included interactional, pronunciation and fluency features, even though these features have, like lexico-grammatical features, been shown to differ depending on the register in which the interaction takes place (see, e.g., Biber and Staples 2014). This study investigates two assessment tasks that vary in situational characteristics (one has a more informational purpose; one is more argument driven) to determine the impact of these characteristics on a variety of linguistic features, including lexico-grammatical (e.g., involved features such as pronouns and informational features such as nouns), interactional (e.g., discourse markers and backchannels), and pronunciation and fluency fea-

https://doi.org/10.1515/9781501511370-007

tures (e.g., pauses, speech rate, and pitch range). This study adds to the literature on spoken assessment to understand how researchers and test developers may need to take situational characteristics of the task into account when creating and evaluating spoken tasks.

Research questions:
1) How do lexico-grammatical features vary across task types in a spoken dialogic assessment?
2) How do interactional features vary across task types in a spoken dialogic assessment?
3) How do pronunciation and fluency features vary across task types in a spoken dialogic assessment?

2 Linguistic Features in Oral Assessment

2.1 Lexico-grammatical Features in Oral Assessment

Traditionally, in the field of SLA, oral assessments have been analyzed using complexity and accuracy variables such as T-units, C-units, or AS-units as well as fluency variables such as speech rate and pause length. However, more recently researchers have started to look at lexico-grammatical features and how they vary across oral assessments. A subset of these studies have used a register-functional perspective, one in which the situational characteristics of the assessment task are taken into consideration to determine which features are examined. The primary argument for using different discourse features across different contexts is based on the large body of literature that shows dramatic differences in the use of linguistic features across the broad registers of speech and writing (Biber 1988; Biber 2006). Biber, Gray, and Poonpon (2011) replicated this research and showed how register might impact the ways in which development is displayed by L2 speakers and writers. While their focus was on improving measures for the investigation of writing development (as noted in their title: "Should We Use Characteristics of Conversation to Measure Grammatical Complexity in L2 Writing Development?"), their argument also applies to the converse situation: what features are appropriate for investigating L2 speaking development? Previous studies of oral assessments have provided inconclusive results, with some showing increases in lexico-grammatical variables associated with spoken discourse as score level increases and some studies showing increases in variables associated with written discourse as score level increases. To understand these differences, we need to understand the situational characteristics of the tasks, looking beyond mode to other factors such as communicative purpose.

Jamieson and Poonpon (2013), for example, found that relative clauses and passive voice were used most by speakers at the 3.5/4 score level (the highest) in the spoken integrated TOEFL iBT. In addition, prepositional phrases increased between Score Levels 2.5 and 3 (with four being the top score). Biber and Gray (2013) similarly found that passive voice and relative clauses were used to a greater extent by higher scoring test takers on the spoken integrated TOEFL iBT (118, 125). Importantly, this same trend was not found for the independent spoken iBT task (Biber and Gray 2013: 118, 125). Finite adverbial clauses, a feature associated with spoken discourse, decreased as score level increased, in both independent and integrated spoken iBT tasks (Biber and Gray: 123). Different from these studies, Staples, LaFlair and Egbert (2017) found that certainty and likelihood adverbials, two features found more in spoken than in written registers, were used by higher scoring test takers in an oral interview (the MELAB spoken test). On the other hand, nouns and verb + *to* complement clauses were negatively correlated with test score on the same assessment. Thirakunkovit, Rodriguez-Fuentes, Park, and Staples (2019) also explored relationships between lexico-grammatical features and scores on an oral assessment for ITAs (international teaching assistants). They found that while spoken features were more frequent than written features, when proficiency was accounted for, higher scoring speakers actually used more features associated with academic writing (relative clauses and passive voice) and fewer features associated with conversation (adverbial clauses with *because*, stance adverbs, and *that* complement clauses). Finally, Kang (2013) analyzed spoken responses in the Cambridge Exam and found inconsistent results across levels, but general trends for increases in adverbial clauses across score levels, particularly *because* and conditional (*if*) clauses. It is important to note that the tasks for the Cambridge Exam vary across levels, which may have impacted the results. For example, level B2 asks students to describe a photograph while level C2 asks students to give an opinion on a topic.

Many of these studies suggest that even within oral assessments, the use of features traditionally associated with writing may be used at higher rates by higher scoring test takers. To some extent, this is likely a result of the task's communicative purpose. Most of the studies that found relationships between higher speaking scores and written language features included spoken tasks that are more informationally driven. For example, the TOEFL integrated spoken task asks test takers to summarize information from a reading and a lecture. Notably, when other task types were examined (independent TOEFL iBT task, Cambridge CPE task, and oral interview), they seem to rely less on informational features than the integrated iBT task. The results from these studies underscore the importance of considering both mode and task type when examining oral assessments, to determine which features might be of interest.

2.2 Interactional Features in Oral Assessment

Interactional features (e.g., number of turns, length of turns, discourse markers, backchannels, and hesitation markers) have been a focus of oral assessment, particularly for dialogic tasks such as oral proficiency interviews (OPIs; Brown 2003, 2005; Johnson and Taylor 1998; Lazaraton 1992; van Lier 1989). Previous studies have focused on the analysis of OPIs in relation to non-test contexts, such as face to face conversation, finding important differences in the ways that interlocutors manage turns and topics as well as question and answer exchanges within these two registers. In addition, most studies, including those above, have operationalized interactional features through Conversation Analytic approaches to the data (see the 2018 special issue of *Language Testing* on Interactional Competence). Roever and Kasper (2018), for example, discuss the ways in which more advanced speakers use "presequences" in their interactions, while lower-level learners do not. Presequences are "primarily characterized by a delay in the occurrence of the core social action (i.e., the request) by means of explanations and accounts, and it often includes inter-turn and intra-turn hesitations, pauses, and specific prefaces (e.g., 'Well . . . ')" (337). In contrast to this, LaFlair, Staples and Yan (2019) take a corpus linguistic approach to measuring interactional features, investigating length of turn, number of turns, hesitation markers, discourse markers, and backchannels. They show the complementary distribution of two interactional features (number of turns and hesitation markers), with higher scoring test takers using fewer hesitation markers and more turns in the MELAB OPI. Interestingly, LaFlair et al. (2019) also provide evidence for the co-occurrence of interaction, lexico-grammatical, and fluency variables, all of which cluster together to perform the function of "colloquial fluency".

This study follows the methods in LaFlair et al. (2019) and takes a corpus-linguistic approach to measuring interactional features, including number and length of turns, discourse markers, backchannels, and hesitation markers.

2.3 Fluency and Pronunciation Features in Oral Assessment

Fluency features are well documented within oral assessment. The most common features examined are speech rate (operationalized variably as syllables per second, words per minute, mean length of run, or phonation time ratio), number and length of silent pauses, and number and length of filled pauses (e.g., *um*, *uh*, etc.). Many studies have found that speech rate increases with score level (LaFlair, Staples, and Egbert 2015; Kang 2013; Kang, Rubin, and Pickering 2010; Ginther, Dimova, and Yang 2010).

Pronunciation features are less frequently included in analyses of oral assessment (but see Kang 2013; Kang and Yan 2018; Kang et al. 2010). Notably Kang (2013) includes a number of features focusing on intonation, including the number of prominent syllables per run (pace), proportion of prominent words (space), and overall pitch range. Pitch range increased in relation to score level while the proportion of prominent words decreased in relation to score level (Kang 2013).

Very few studies have examined differences in speech rate across task types. However, there are reported differences in speech rate across registers. Rates for read speech have been reported as faster than those for speech in interviews, for example (Derwing and Munro 2001; Götz 2013; Tauroza and Allison 1990). Pitch range has also been shown to differ across read and free speech (Wennerstrom 1994). However, differences in speech rate and pitch range have not been investigated across different types of tasks.

As a first step in examining differences in the use of features that might be predictive of oral development, this study focuses on differences in the use of lexico-grammatical, interactional, fluency and pronunciation features across two task types. As described in more detail in the methods, the primary difference between the two task types is in their communicative purpose: one task type is much more informationally driven while the other has as its primary purpose the defense of a particular argument. The results are interpreted in relation to the ways in which this and other situational characteristics (e.g., interactiveness) vary across tasks.

3 Methods

The subcorpus used in this study consisted of two tasks from the CCOT corpus: "Crime and Economy," which consisted of 13 interactions (26 speakers) and "Workplace Monitoring," which consisted of 15 interactions (30 speakers). Both tasks represent performances by speakers at a scores corresponding to 57–69 on the TOEFL iBT, so the overall proficiency level of the individual speakers is roughly the same (although this total score does not consider differences in test takers across the four sections of the test, speaking, writing, listening, and reading). It should be noted that for each of the two tasks, there was one speaker who contributed to two different interactions. To create the corpus, the interactions were divided by speaker role (A or B) within the files. Thus, the analysis reported on below is of 55 total speakers. Table 1 shows demographic information about the speakers and interactions.

Table 1: Subcorpus for the study.

Task	L1 background	Gender	Mean length of interaction (time)	Mean length of interaction (words)
Crime and Economy	Chinese 12 Arabic 10 Japanese 2 Korean 2	Male 22 Female 4	3 minutes 12 seconds	360
Workplace Monitoring	Chinese 16 Arabic 11 Japanese 3	Male 24 Female 6	3 minutes 1 second	404

Following the register-functional approach, a situational analysis was conducted to understand how the two tasks varied according to characteristics that would impact the linguistic choices of the speakers. This is an essential component of register analysis: the situational analysis is vital for understanding the functional aspects of the linguistic features used in a particular speech situation (in this case, two different oral assessment tasks). Biber and Conrad (2009: 40) provide seven categories of situational characteristics as a framework for understanding variation among registers: participants, relations among participants (including interactiveness), channel, production circumstances, setting, communicative purposes, and topic. This framework is applied here, with a focus on four characteristics: interactiveness, purpose, production circumstances (e.g., degree of planning time), and topic.

Interactiveness in Biber and Conrad's framework refers to the extent to which participants directly interact with one another (42). Here, interactiveness is further operationalized to indicate the degree to which interlocutors are expected to interact. This differs from other conceptualizations of interactiveness and related concepts. For example, in the field of Language Testing, interactiveness refers to "the extent and type of involvement of the test taker's individual characteristics [e.g., language ability, topical knowledge] in accomplishing a test task" (Bachman and Palmer 1996: 25). Interaction in Conversation Analysis represents an entire organizational system, starting with turn construction and turn allocation (Drew and Heritage 2006). While a CA framework is not used here, as discussed above, this study does examine the characteristics of talk-in-interaction through the category of "interactional" features (e.g., number of turns, turn length, backchannels).

To conduct the analysis, an initial top-down evaluation of these characteristics was made using the description of the prompts (see appendix at the end of this book). After the linguistic analysis was conducted, a bottom-up approach was also used to further refine the situational characteristics, based on the actual spoken performances (rather than what the prompt for the task asked the learners to do). For more discussion on how to conduct a situational analysis as part of register analysis, readers are directed to Biber and Conrad (2009: Chapter 2).

For both tasks, the participants were expected to interact to reach a decision within 3 minutes. Both were evaluated according to the same rubric, which included collaboration, task completion, and style. However, the Crime and Economy task provided students with charts that they were asked to summarize to each other (i.e., informational content). Then, the two speakers were asked to reach a decision about which report to present to a class. They were also asked to explain reasons for the crime rates that were reported in their graphs. An examination of the transcribed texts for these tasks shows that all of the interactions contained informational content from the charts. In addition, some of the tasks (but not all) contained arguments about the topic, based on the charts. For this reason, the primary communicative purpose for this task was considered to be informational. This task would also be considered an "integrated task" (see Brown, Iwashita, and McNamara 2005 for a discussion of the characteristics of independent and integrated tasks). One minute of planning time was provided.

The Workplace Monitoring task did not provide any information except what argument/stance each speaker should take. Test takers were explicitly directed to state an argument and interrupt the partner to ask questions about their partners' argument. Thus, the primary purpose of this task was argument, and it does not contain informational content. This would be considered an "independent" task (see Brown, Iwashita, and McNamara 2005). The Workplace Monitoring task included three minutes of planning time.

Table 2 provides a situational analysis of the two tasks, using criteria from Biber and Conrad (2009: 40). As discussed in the introduction, the main situational characteristic that differs across the two tasks is their communicative purpose: the Crime and Economy task is primarily informative while the Workplace Monitoring task is primarily argumentative. Thus, in the results below the two tasks are labelled Informational and Argumentative to reflect this primary difference.

Table 2: Situational analysis of the tasks.

Task	Interactiveness	Communicative Purpose	Production Circumstances	Topic
Crime and Economy	Moderate (participants are directed to communicate information to each other and come to a decision)	Primarily informational, secondary purpose argumentative	Some planning time (1 minute)	Crime rates around the world
Workplace Monitoring	High (participants are directed to ask questions and interrupt)	Primarily argumentative, no informational content	More planning time (3 minutes)	Should workplace monitoring be allowed?

Linguistic variables were selected based on previous research on oral assessments (see Table 3). Lexico-grammatical features fall into three categories: features of involvement (features that are typically used in interactive spoken discourse); informational features (features that are most typically found in informational writing but have also been found in informational spoken discourse); stance features (features used to express opinion/argument). Given the nature of the two tasks, it is hypothesized that the Workplace Monitoring task will contain more features of involvement and stance, due to the argumentative purpose and higher interactiveness promoted by the instructions for this task. On the other hand, it is anticipated that the Crime and Economy task will contain more informational features since the primary purpose of that task is to convey information. It is important to note that a register-functional approach hypothesizes not the presence or absence of a given variable but rather a higher or lower frequency of occurrence. Thus, linguistic variables that rarely occurred in individual texts across the two tasks were excluded from the analysis. For example, passive voice and relative clauses have previously been found to be important distinguishing factors across score levels in oral assessment (Jamieson and Poonpon 2013; Biber and Gray 2013). However, there were many files in which these features did not occur at all so they were not included in the analysis.

The features were identified using different computational programs. For the lexico-grammatical features, the Biber Tagger (Biber 1988; 2006) was used along with post-tagging scripts written by the author to improve the accuracy of the identification of lexico-grammatical features. Verb + *that* complement clauses were checked for accuracy in five randomly selected files, since this feature is known to have lower levels of accuracy based on previous studies of spoken discourse (including both L1 and L2 speakers). The tags were then

Table 3: Linguistic variables included in the analysis.

Feature	Description or examples
Lexico-grammatical features	
Nouns	Country, graph
Attributive adjectives	Poor country, different rates
Pre-modifying nouns	Crime rate, world economy
Causative finite adverbial clauses	I agree with you because …
Conditional finite adverbial clauses	If I use the monitoring it can …
Stance adverbials	Maybe, definitely
Verb + that complement clauses	I think that …
Modal verbs (possibility, prediction, and necessity)	Can, could; will, won't; should, must
Interactional features	
Number of turns	Number of turns (as transcribed)
Turn length	Length of turn in words
Backchannels	Yeah, uh huh
Discourse markers	Now, well
Hesitation markers	Uh, um
Questions	What is your name?
Pronunciation and fluency features	
Speech rate	Words per minute
Mean length of run	Mean length in seconds of a stretch of speech by a speaker between pauses (or turn changes)
Number of silent pauses	Number of silent pauses .25 seconds or greater in length
Mean length of silent pauses	Mean length of silent pauses ≥ .25 seconds
Pitch range	Pitch maxima – pitch minima for a given run (as defined above)

counted and normed to a rate of per 1000 words using the program TagCount (Biber 2006).

The pronunciation and fluency features were analyzed using ELAN (for fluency features) and Praat (for pitch range). The accuracy of the fluency features was established on five interactions with a second coder. The accuracy reached > .90 ICC (intraclass correlation) for all of the variables. Once intercoder reliability was established, the interactions were analyzed by one coder only. Pitch range was calculated using an automated script which measured the maximum and minimum F0 (in Hz) for each run. Frequencies above 350 Hz and below 100 Hz were examined by the coders and modified after removing inaccurate pitch values. Inaccurate pitch can occur due to vocal fry or when a speaker heavily aspirates a consonant.

4 Data Analysis

Data screening revealed that most of the data was distributed normally. However, some of the variables (words per turn, backchannels, 2nd person pronouns, questions, conditionals, and pre-modifying nouns) showed a leptokurtic distribution.

Due to the non-normal distribution of some of the data along with the small sample size (and thus lack of sufficient power), the decision was made to use bootstrapping. Bootstrapping is a statistical procedure that allows for resampling of the data in order to provide a more robust measure of the data, particularly for small sample sizes (see LaFlair, Egbert, and Plonsky 2015). Bootstrapped mean frequencies for each of the dependent variables were examined and are reported below, along with bootstrapped standard deviations and confidence intervals.

5 Results

5.1 Lexico-grammatical Features

As described above, the lexico-grammatical features can be further subdivided into three major categories: features of involvement, stance features, and informational features, as labelled in Table 4 below. The labels "Argumentative" and "Informational" are used below based on the primary communicative purpose of each tasks, from the situational analysis.

First, there was a general trend of greater use of features of involvement in the Argumentative (Workplace Monitoring) task than in the Informational (Crime and Economy) task. In particular, 1st person and 2nd person pronouns/determiners and conditional clauses showed clear differentiation between the two tasks, based on non-overlapping bootstrapped confidence intervals (see Table 4 and Figure 1).

Table 4: Results for lexico-grammatical features across tasks.

Variable	Task	Bootstrapped Mean	Bootstrapped SD	Bootstrapped CIs of the Mean
Features of Involvement				
1st person pronouns	Informational	51.40	20.25	44.10–58.71
	Argumentative	94.10	32.60	82.93–105.27
2nd person pronouns	Informational	16.93	16.57	10.41–23.45
	Argumentative	36.94	34.38	23.94–49.94
Causative subordinate clauses	Informational	4.08	5.62	2.18–5.98
	Argumentative	7.23	4.85	5.55–8.91
Conditional subordinate clauses	Informational	4.94	7.52	1.91–7.97
	Argumentative	13.12	12.31	9.19–17.06
Stance Features				
Possibility modals	Informational	9.57	10.08	6.19–12.96
	Argumentative	14.27	10.90	10.66–17.88
Prediction modals	Informational	12.14	14.90	6.22–18.06
	Argumentative	14.97	14.99	9.91–20.03
Necessity modals	Informational	0.51	1.09	0–1.04
	Argumentative	4.67	5.42	2.83–6.51
Verb + that complement clauses	Informational	11.91	11.25	7.92–15.90
	Argumentative	18.72	10.55	14.96–22.49
Stance adverbials	Informational	4.84	6.32	2.30–7.31
	Argumentative	7.18	7.74	4.39–9.98
Informational Features				
Nouns	Informational	227.34	60.02	205.64–249.04
	Argumentative	151.48	37.94	138.70–164.25
Attributive adjectives	Informational	44.71	26.57	35.87–53.55
	Argumentative	16.51	10.30	13.01–20.02
Nouns as premodifiers	Informational	43.96	28.15	33.22–54.70
	Argumentative	15.90	15.42	10.64–21.15
Word length	Informational	3.94	0.15	3.89–4.00
	Argumentative	3.81	0.25	3.72–3.90

Like features of involvement, stance features were also used more frequently in the Argumentative (Workplace Monitoring) task. Necessity modals in particular were rarely used in the Informational (Crime and Economy) task (see Figure 2).

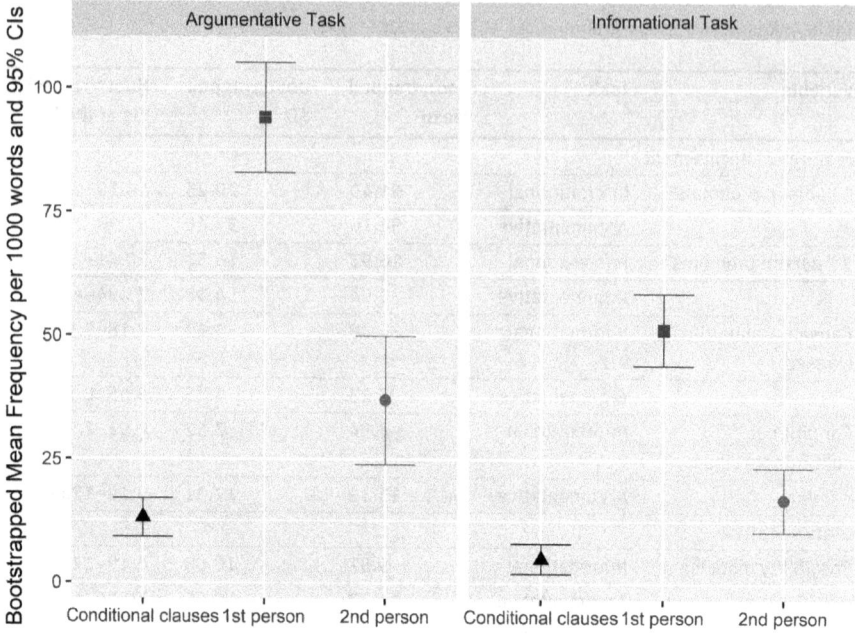

Figure 1: Bootstrapped means and 95% CIs for 1st and 2nd person pronouns/determiners and conditional clauses across Argumentative (Workplace Monitoring) and Informational (Crime and Economy) tasks.

In contrast, informational features (nouns, attributive adjectives, nouns as premodifiers, longer words) were consistently found more in the Informational (Crime and Economy) task (see Table 4). All of these features except word length showed non-overlapping confidence intervals and are displayed in Figure 3.

Examples (1) and (2) illustrate the use of involved and stance features in bold and informational features underlined. The contrast can be seen in the Argumentative (Workplace Monitoring) task (more involved and stance features, Excerpt 1) as compared with the Informational (Crime and Economy) task (more informational features, Excerpt 2).

(1) Interaction 2_2 (Argumentative Task, Workplace Monitoring)
   A: **I think** monitoring **our** <u>employees</u> **would would** be uh they **would** be in <u>pressure</u> and they **might** not work
   B: But the <u>problem</u> is A **that we always** the e <u>employee</u> **always** they have been in <u>pressure</u> by stolen the <u>personal thing</u>
   A: I have another idea **we could we could** uh uh win the trust by raising the <u>salary</u> and **maybe** with good uh

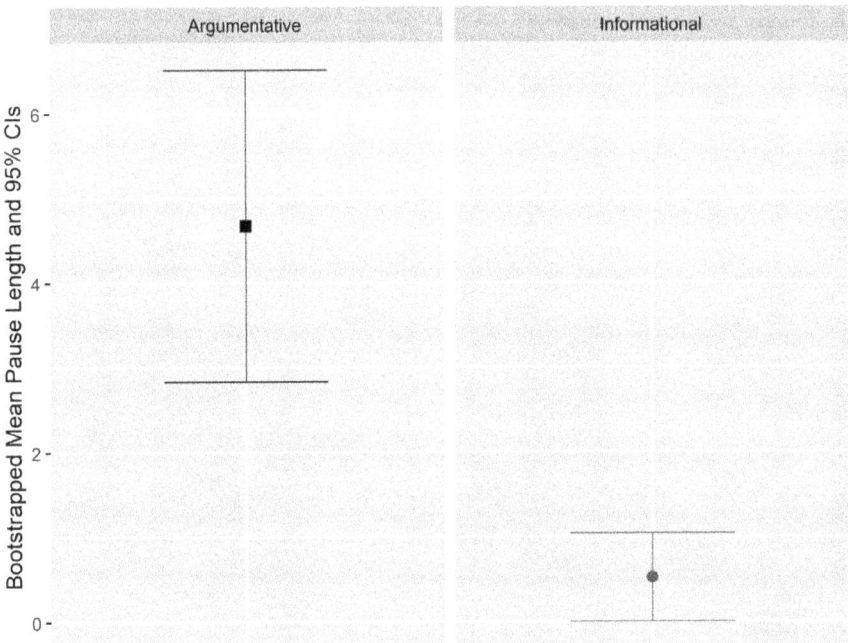

Figure 2: Bootstrapped means and 95% CIs for necessity modals across Argumentative (Workplace Monitoring) and Informational (Crime and Economy) tasks.

    B: Let **me** let let **me** uh convince **you** here uh first of all uh the **that** monitoring **our** <u>company</u> that **we can** protect both <u>side</u> **you can** protect **our** <u>company</u> **our** <u>devices</u> and **our** <u>employees</u>
    A: But **I think** uh the <u>monitoring</u> **would** be expensive for **us**
    B: Yeah but it's get <u>benefits</u> like uh **we** protect **our** <u>devices</u> from being stolen s so **we we** don't need to buy another <u>device</u>
    A: Oh really? Well uh but **I think if we we if we** win their <u>trust</u> **might** be better right?

(2) Interaction 1_6 (Informational Task, Crime and Economy)
    A: Uh **my** <u>graph</u> show the <u>world economy</u>
    B: And **my** <u>graph</u> shows <u>crime rates</u> per capita by uh <u>country</u> and from this <u>graph</u> **I can** see uh like uh many <u>countries</u> uh their uh <u>crime rates</u> are individually uh decline. Uh the order is from uh uh <u>larger amounts</u> uh to the uh <u>less amount</u> and the the most – uh the <u>largest amounts</u> uh <u>crime rate</u> is <u>Dominica</u> uh and the <u>less</u> uh <u>country</u> is <u>Yemen</u> uh what about **you**?

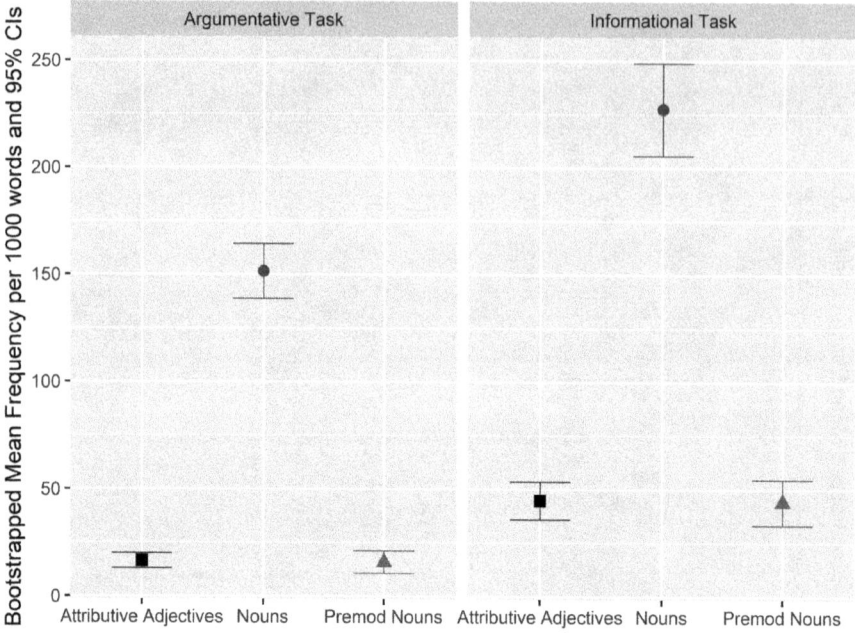

Figure 3: Bootstrapped means and 95% CIs for attributive adjectives, nouns, and premodifying nouns across Argumentative (Workplace Monitoring) and Informational (Crime and Economy) tasks.

A: Uh **my** graph show the relationship between GDP of per person uh and uh less free economy or more free economy uh let **me** think uh the graph shows the more free the economy market is then the GDP of per person will be high uh the highest uh country show in the – show in the graph is United States and the lowest uh the lowest country is uh Burma and also like uh Hong Kong Ireland and Singapore United Kingdom Australia are the uh high uh are the high uh GDP per – of per person and uh their economy market are more free.

5.2 Interactional Features

The results for the interactional features are shown in Table 5. As can be seen, many of the values are quite similar across the two tasks (e.g., turns, words per turn, discourse markers, and even questions). Backchannels were used more in the Informational (Crime and Economy) task, which may reflect greater displays of speaker listenership in this task, and the fact that they are taking in the new information provided by their interlocutor. Hesitation markers, interestingly, were used slightly more in the Argumentative (Workplace Monitoring) task. This contrasts with the speakers' use of silent pauses, as will be seen below, suggesting that hesitation markers are not a measure of fluency here. The bootstrapped confidence intervals show overlaps for all of the interactional features.

Table 5: Results for interactional features across tasks.

Variable	Task	Bootstrapped Mean	Bootstrapped SD	Bootstrapped CIs of the Mean
Turns	Informational	7.11	3.59	5.78–8.43
	Argumentative	7.33	3.29	6.35–8.31
Words per turn	Informational	29.85	14.19	24.53–35.18
	Argumentative	31.79	21.73	24.65–38.94
Backchannels	Informational	0.38	0.58	0.18–0.59
	Argumentative	0.19	0.38	0.02–0.36
Discourse markers	Informational	2.32	2.00	1.60–3.06
	Argumentative	2.58	1.66	1.99–3.18
Hesitation markers	Informational	7.98	5.62	5.92–10.03
	Argumentative	9.18	5.42	7.35–11.00
Questions	Informational	0.96	0.99	0.58–1.34
	Argumentative	1.17	1.01	0.82–1.53

Example (3) below shows the use of backchannels (in bold) to show listenership in an Informational task.

(3) Interaction 1_1 (Informational Task, Crime and Economy)
　　A: Yeah presentation about uh c – c – cri – crime uh and economy
　　B: **Mm hmm**
　　A: Actually I uh I br – I bring one I think it's it's good because it it has like a map and has some statistic numbers and uh it has money some country like very famous country like US and United Kingdom and New Zealand and Singapore. How about yours?
　　B: I think mine it's more obvious than yours it's talk about crime rate per capita by country
　　A: **Mm hmm**
　　B: It's show you many country and many numbers it's good statistic and we will we we we will like show the audience the numbers and the country and it will be obvious for the audience to. . .
　　A: **Mm hmm**

5.3 Fluency and Pronunciation Features

The results for the fluency and pronunciation features are shown in Table 6. As can be seen, speech rate, mean length of run, and pitch range were higher in the Argumentative (Workplace Monitoring) task, while the number and length of silent pauses was higher in the Informational (Crime and Economy) task. Taken together, the fluency variables show that the Argumentative task led to higher speech rates, longer runs, and shorter and fewer pauses. This may be due to the limited informational demands of the task but also could be related to the additional planning time allotted for the Argumentative task. Higher pitch range in the Argumentative task may reflect a need to stress syllables at higher pitch in order to make points more salient and arguments appear stronger. Figure 4 displays the bootstrapped mean and confidence intervals for Mean Length of Pause, for which the confidence intervals did not overlap.

Table 6: Results for fluency and pronunciation features across tasks.

Variable	Task	Bootstrapped Mean	Bootstrapped SD	Bootstrapped CIs of the Mean
Speech Rate	Informational	160.47	24.90	151.31–169.62
	Argumentative	172.88	16.78	166.87–178.88
Mean Length of Run	Informational	1.75	0.48	1.58–1.93
	Argumentative	1.96	0.63	1.75–2.17
Number of Silent Pauses	Informational	31.80	9.95	28.15–35.45
	Argumentative	27.66	10.86	23.94–31.38
Mean length of silent pauses	Informational	0.57	.15	.52–.62
	Argumentative	0.47	.10	.44–.51
Pitch range	Informational	69.01	29.85	58.08–79.94
	Argumentative	81.83	36.28	69.88–93.77

Excerpts 4 and 5 show the use of pauses (in bold) in the Informational task as compared with the Argumentative task.

(4) Interaction 1_9 (Informational task, Crime and Economy)
   A: Yeah in my paragra **<pause .47>** in my graph **<pause .32>** it **<pause .64>** uh **<pause .28>** is uh **<pause .35>** it describes the economy **<pause 1.42>** uh the **<pause .63>** the more – in the **<pause .48>** graph we can see the more free economic are **<pause .62>** uh more GDP.

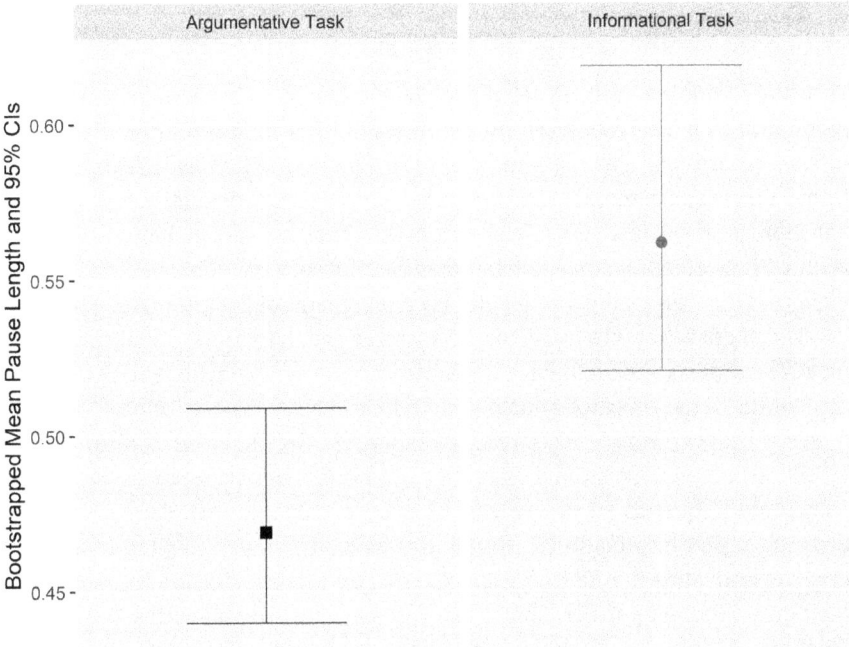

Figure 4: Bootstrapped mean pause length and 95% CIs across Argumentative (Workplace Monitoring) and Informational (Crime and Economy) tasks.

    B: Uh **<pause .52>** my report is **<pause .31>** criminal rates per person by country this is how – it is how many **<pause .41>** how many people crime per **<pause .30>** one thousand **<pause .25>** one thousand person in **<pause .49>** people in eac – in each country.

(5) Interaction 2_6 (Argumentative task, Workplace Monitoring)
    A: Uh huh yeah this is really main problem and uh main issue but however **<pause .33>** I think that if we are going to like moni – uh snoop on employees work **<pause .68>** this is a problem because we need to trust our employee's so you see this point?
    B: But you know I I agree with you in this point but you know A we are losing money our company losing money and we are not selling enough products **<pause .34>** and uh actually the best way **<pause .29>** to protect our – to protect our products is to put the s – to put a surveillance camera you know to **<pause .27>** to monitor the the employees and to monitor our our computer devices.

6 Discussion

This study examined a small set of performances in order to investigate how task types vary in a program-level oral assessment. The findings support previous research that illustrates the impact of task type on the linguistic features used by test takers in other oral assessments but provides data on additional variables and more nuanced task types. In addition, this study investigated interactive peer tasks with whereas most previous studies have focused on monologic oral assessments or OPIs, where the interlocutor is the evaluator of the test taker.

The major difference in the two tasks examined in this study, that of communicative purpose, seems to have impacted the use of linguistic features, in that most of the variation can be attributed to the primary purpose (Informational or Argumentative) of the tasks. Similar to Biber and Gray's (2013) findings for the TOEFL iBT, the informational features (e.g., nouns, attributive adjectives) were used more frequently in the task that provided students with data (Crime and Economy). The Informational (Crime and Economy) task provided a different graph to both student interlocutors and asked them to provide information about their graph to their partner. Conversely, although the Argumentative (Workplace Economy) task promoted the use of evidence to support arguments, the level of informational detail produced by participants was limited. This is reflected linguistically in less use of informational features in the Argumentative task. Features of involvement and stance features, on the other hand, were found more frequently in the Argumentative task, reflecting the participants' use of phrases like *I think* and *we would* as well as conditional phrases (*if* statements). All of these features are used to create arguments and share opinions.

This study also added to the literature on interactional variables within interactive oral assessment, using a corpus-based approach to examine the use of features that are used frequently in interactive spoken discourse. The interactional variables were fairly constant across the two tasks, suggesting that both tasks elicited the same degree of interactiveness. Backchannels were used slightly more in the informational task, likely indicating the uptake of new information from the interlocutor. Of course, a lack of differences in the use of the interactional variables included in this study does not mean that there are not differences in other aspects of interactional competence. Approaching this data set from a conversation analytic perspective would provide additional insights into aspects of speaker exchange in oral assessment (see Plough 2018). However, one way to combine corpus linguistic and conversation analytic analyses would be to investigate linguistic features within interactional phases (e.g., openings and closings). This might provide further insight into how speakers in pair assessment are organizing their interaction through co-constructed discourse level units.

Fluency variables, including speech rate, number of pauses, and pause length, while well represented in previous examinations of oral assessments, have not been widely investigated across task type. This study showed the influence of communicative purpose on fluency variables, showing that the less informational task (Workplace Monitoring) yielded higher fluency rates. The more informationally oriented task (Crime and Economy) presumably required more online processing time, leading to slower speech rate and more and longer pauses. This aligns somewhat with previous findings on speech rates across registers, in that previous studies show that less cognitively demanding tasks (read speech) yield higher fluency rates than those of more cognitively demanding tasks (spontaneous speech in interviews) (Derwing and Munro 2001; Götz 2013; Tauroza and Allison 1990). While test takers showed greater fluency in the Argumentative (Workplace Monitoring) task, they also used more hesitation markers. This provides some evidence that hesitation markers are performing a function beyond fluency (confirming their grouping with interactional rather than fluency variables). Finally, pitch range was higher in the Argumentative (Workplace Monitoring) task, coinciding with the need to emphasize main points of an argument, and perhaps to show enthusiasm for one's opinion as a method of convincing an interlocutor to take up one's position.

Of course, other situational characteristics may have influenced the frequency distributions of the linguistic features analyzed in this study. However, many of them are at least loosely related to the underlying communicative purpose of the task. First, the higher level of interactiveness required for the argumentative task (test takers were directed to ask their interlocutors questions and to interrupt their partners) may have impacted the higher use of features of involvement in that context. This situational characteristic is also somewhat tied to the primary communicative purpose of the task (argumentation): in order to convey one's argument, one might need to directly question one's interlocutor and in order to convince one's interlocutor, interruption might be used. It is not surprising to find more features such as first-person pronouns (and determiners) and *that* complement clauses in the Argumentative (Workplace Economy) task, since these features allow speakers to convey arguments explicitly (*I think that*). By asking the participants to role play as supervisors in a company trying to solve a problem, the task also led the participants to personalize the task more (*our company* instead of *the company*). Fluency may have been affected by the difference in planning time in addition to the informational demands of the task: the Workplace Monitoring task had 3 minutes allotted for planning time, and greater fluency was found in this task (higher speech rate, fewer and shorter pauses). However, it is unclear whether the small difference in planning time (3 minutes vs. 1 minute) would have an impact on the results, since literature exploring such differences in planning time is limited.

7 Implications for Oral Language Assessment

The implications for oral language assessment seem to support the growing call for rethinking the design of oral tasks in general, both in high stakes assessments and program-level assessments. Teachers and assessment specialists can use this information to determine which types of tasks might be more relevant for their test takers, or perhaps to include both types of tasks to address the various discourse functions that learners need for both academic and professional contexts. Future research should investigate similar variables in a larger sample of tasks to determine whether the findings here can be generalized beyond these particular students in this specific context. Tasks could further be controlled by limiting the number of variables that vary (e.g., length of planning time could be held constant across argumentative and informational tasks).

References

Biber, Douglas. 1988. *Dimensions of register variation*. Cambridge: Cambridge University Press.

Biber, Douglas. 2006. *University language: A corpus-based study of spoken and written registers*. Amsterdam: John Benjamins.

Biber, Douglas & Susan Conrad. 2009. *Register, genre, and style*. Cambridge: Cambridge University Press.

Biber, Douglas & Bethany Gray. 2013. *Discourse characteristics of writing and speaking task types on the TOEFL iBT ® Test: A lexico-grammatical analysis*. TOEFL iBT Research Report 19. Princeton, NJ: Educational Testing Service.

Biber, Douglas, Bethany Gray & Kornwipa Poonpon, K. 2011. Should we use the characteristics of conversation to measure grammatical complexity in L2 writing development? *TESOL Quarterly* 45(1). 5–35.

Biber, Douglas, Bethany Gray & Shelley Staples. 2016. Predicting patterns of grammatical complexity across textual task types and proficiency levels. *Applied Linguistics* 37(5). 639–668.

Biber, Douglas, Bethany Gray, Shelley Staples & Jesse Egbert (in press). *The register-functional approach to grammatical complexity: Theoretical foundation, descriptive research findings, applications*. New York: Routledge.

Biber, Douglas & Shelley Staples. 2014. Exploring the prosody of stance: Variation in the realization of stance adverbials. In Tommaso Raso & Heliana Mello (Eds.), *Spoken Corpora and Linguistic Studies*, 271–294. Philadelphia: John Benjamins.

Brown, Annie. 2003. Interviewer variation and the co-construction of speaking proficiency. *Language Testing* 20(1). 1–25.

Brown, Annie. 2005. *Interviewer variability in oral proficiency interviews*. New York: Peter Lang.

Brown, Annie, Noriko Iwashita & Tim McNamara. 2005. *An examination of rater orientations and test-taker performance on English-for-academic-purposes speaking tasks*. TOEFL Monograph. ETS.
Derwing, Tracey M. & Murray J. Munro. 2001. What speaking rates do non-native listeners prefer? *Applied Linguistics* 22. 324–227.
Drew, Paul & John Heritage. 2016. *Conversation analysis*. SAGE.
Ginther, April, Slobodanka Dimova & Rui Yang. 2010. Conceptual and empirical relationships between temporal measures of fluency and oral English proficiency with implications for automated scoring. *Language Testing* 27(3). 379–399.
Götz, Sandra 2013. *Fluency in native and nonnative English speech*. Amsterdam: John Benjamins.
Jamieson, Joan & Kornwipa Poonpon. 2013. *Developing analytic rating guides for TOEFL iBT integrated speaking tasks*. TOEFL iBT Research Report 20. Princeton, NJ: Educational Testing Service.
Johnson, Marysia & Andrea Taylor. 1998. Re-analyzing the OPI: How much does it look like natural conversation? In Agnes Weiyun He & Richard Young (Eds.), *Talking and testing: Discourse approaches to the assessment of oral proficiency*, 27–52. Philadelphia, PA: John Benjamins.
Kang, Okim. 2013. Linguistic analysis of speaking features distinguishing general English exams at CEFR levels. *Cambridge English: Research Notes* 52. 40–48.
Kang, Okim, Don Rubin & Lucy Pickering. 2010. Suprasegmental measures of accentedness and judgments of English language learner proficiency in oral English. *Modern Language Journal* 94. 554–566.
Kang, Okim & Xun Yan. 2018. Linguistic features distinguishing examinees' speaking performances at different proficiency levels. *Journal of Language Testing and Assessment* 1. 24–39, DOI: 10.23977/langta.2018.11003.
LaFlair, Geoffrey, Jesse Egbert & Luke Plonsky. 2015. A practical guide to bootstrapping descriptive statistics, correlations, t Tests, and ANOVAs. In Luke Plonsky (Ed.), *Advancing quantitative methods in second language research*, 46–77. New York: Routledge.
LaFlair, Geoffrey, Shelley Staples & Jesse Egbert. 2015. *Variability in the MELAB speaking task: Investigating linguistic characteristics of test-taker performances in relation to Rater severity and score*. CaMLA Working Papers.
Laflair, Geoffrey, Shelley Staples & Xun Yan. 2019. Connecting corpus linguistics and assessment. In Paul Baker and Jesse Egbert (Eds.), *Using corpus methods to triangulate linguistic analysis*, 109–140. New York: Routledge.
Lazaraton, Anne. 1992. Interlocutor support in oral proficiency interviews: The case of CASE. *Language Testing* 13(2). 151–172.
Plough, India. 2018. Revisiting the speaking construct: The question of interactional competence. *Language Testing* 35(3). 325–329.
Roever, Carsten & Gabriele Kasper. 2018. Speaking in turns and sequences: Interactional competence as a target construct in testing speaking. *Language Testing* 35(3). 331–355.
Staples, Shelley, Douglas Biber & Randi Reppen. 2018. Using corpus-based register analysis to explore authenticity of high-stakes language exams: A register comparison of TOEFL iBT and disciplinary writing tasks. *Modern Language Journal* 102(2). 310–332.
Staples, Shelley, Geoffrey LaFlair, G. & Jesse Egbert. 2017. A multi-dimensional comparison of oral proficiency interviews to conversation, academic and professional spoken registers. *Modern Language Journal* 101(1). 194–213.

Tauroza, Steve & Desmond Allison. 1990. Speech rates in British English. *Applied Linguistics* 11(1). 90–105.

Thirakunkovit, Suthathip, Rodrigo Rodriguez-Fuentes, Kyongson Park & Shelley Staples 2019. A corpus-based analysis of grammatical complexity as a measure of international teaching assistants' oral English proficiency. *English for Specific Purposes Journal* 53. 74–89.

van Lier, Leo. 1989. Reeling, writhing, drawling, stretching, and fainting in coils: Oral proficiency interviews as conversation. *TESOL Quarterly* 23(3). 489–508.

Wennerstrom, Ann. (1994. Intonational meaning in English discourse: A study of nonnative speakers. *Applied Linguistics* 15. 399–421.

SungEun Choi, Mark McAndrews and Okim Kang

Effects of Task and Gender on Interactive Spoken Fluency and the Mediating Role of Alignment

1 Introduction

Fluency has been seen as a crucial component of effective spoken communication (Filmore 1979; Lennon 2000) and as an indicator of overall language proficiency (De Jong, Steinel, Florijn, Schoonen, and Hulstijn 2012; De Jong 2018; Housen, Kuiken, and Vedder 2012; Skehan 2014). Interestingly, studies focusing on fluency in dialogic speech have reported that learners exhibited higher utterance fluency when they were engaged in dialogic discussion, compared to monologic tasks, suggesting that collaborative nature of dialogic tasks is conducive to more fluent speech (Michel 2011; Tavakoli 2016; Witton-Davies 2014). Nevertheless, the factors that contribute to such difference in utterance fluency remain unclear.

Motivated by previous findings on gender effects and the analytic framework of corpus linguistics, the current study examines the effects of interlocutors' gender and speaking tasks on L2 fluency. Previous studies have suggested that a wide range of factors related to task and interlocutors have influence on L2 fluency, including task complexity (De Jong, Steinel, Florijn, Schoonen, and Hulstijn 2012; Kormos and Trebits 2012) and gender of the interlocutor (Gass and Varonis 1986; Kasanga 1996; Ross-Feldman 2005). However, studies on the complex relationship between speaking tasks, interlocutor gender and speech fluency have been underrepresented in L2 studies (Tavakoli and Skehan 2005; Robinson 2005). To explore this issue, this study investigates the effects of task and gender on utterance fluency.

To further investigate potential mechanisms responsible for faster or slower speech, this study adopts an exploratory approach and examines the extent to which the relationship between gender and fluency is mediated by lexical and syntactic alignment. Several studies have shown that the alignment process is influenced by a speaker's perception of interlocutors and can be socially mediated based on the perceived abilities of the interlocutor and their perceived identity (Branigan, Pickering, Pearson, McLean, and Brown 2011; Weatherholtz, Campbell-Kibler, and Jaeger 2014). More fine-grained studies have found that the degree of linguistic alignment between interlocutors is influenced by gender, social intimacy, social membership and the level of priming effects of interlocutors (Balcetis and Dale 2005; Hwang and Chun 2018; Pardo 2006; Schoot,

Menenti, Hagoort, and Segaert 2014; Unger 2010). Working under the assumption that variance in measured fluency might be mediated through alignment, the current study additionally investigates whether pairs of L2 learners of the same gender demonstrate higher degrees of linguistic alignment than different gender pairs and whether gender pairing might contribute to utterance fluency.

2 Literature Review

2.1 Defining and Measuring L2 Fluency

In L2 studies, aspects of fluency have often been regarded as an important indicator of L2 proficiency (De Jong 2018; Housen, Kuiken, and Vedder 2012) and various definitions of fluency have been proposed as L2 studies expanding an understanding of speech. Earlier studies commonly characterize the notion of fluency as performance-based phenomena that are closely related to speakers' ability to produce speech automatically (Filmore 1979) and to translate thoughts into linguistic production with rapidity and accuracy (Lennon 1990; 2000). More recently, the concept of L2 fluency has been divided into three sub-components: cognitive fluency, utterance fluency, and perceived fluency (Segalowitz 2010; 2018). Cognitive fluency refers to fluidity in mobilizing cognitive processes in language production. This type of fluency is manifested, for example, in the efficiency of semantic retrieval or working memory. Utterance fluency refers to objectively measured features of speech, such as speech rate and duration of pauses. Perceived fluency represents the inferences or judgements that listeners make about speech (Segalowitz 2010; 2018).

Moreover, utterance fluency has been operationalized into three distinctive sub-dimensions: breakdown fluency, speed fluency, and repair fluency (Tavakoli and Skehan 2005). Breakdown fluency involves pauses and silences that occur in speech. Repair fluency is related to the frequency of reformulation, false starts and repetition of words and phrases and speed fluency is related to the speed of language production and is commonly measured using speech rate (Kormos and Dénes 2004) and mean length of run. The current study focuses solely on utterance fluency, especially speed fluency, as it can be objective measured using a speech analysis program that can process large amount of data with relatively high accuracy (Kang and Johnson 2018). For this study, speed fluency was operationalized as speech rate and articulation rate.

In L2 research, the majority of fluency-related studies have measured the oral fluency produced during monologic speaking tasks, while comparatively few studies have been conducted on L2 fluency in interaction. To the authors' knowledge, few studies have compared L2 fluency measured both in a monologic and interactive modes; those studies that have looked at this issue have similarly pointed that learners tend to demonstrate higher levels of fluency in dialogic tasks (Michel 2011; Peltonen 2017; Sato 2014; Tavakoli 2016; Witton-Davies 2014). For example, Tavakoli (2016) examined the speech of 35 L2 learners in an EAP course and found that participants produced more fluent speech in dialogic tasks in terms of speed (i.e. faster articulation rate and speech rate), pause (shorter pauses, and more filled pauses), and repair (fewer repairs). Similarly, Witton-Davies (2014) investigated the development of fluency in 17 Taiwanese-L1 English learners and reported that the differences in measured fluency between monologic and dialogic tasks were larger than the gains in fluency that participants made over a four-year period. Although the available data suggests that mode of communication (i.e., monologic versus dialogic speaking) might have a significant impact on fluency, few studies have gone beyond comparing the two modalities and examining the potential impact of interlocutor-related and task-related factors on fluency. In the next section, prior investigation on the effects of these factors on interactions are discussed.

2.2 Relationships between Characteristics of Interaction and L2 Fluency

Task-based research has suggested that the effects of task complexity might not be as strong as that of modality, especially with regard to speaking rate (Kormos and Trebits 2012), repair measures (Iwashita, McNamara, and Elder 2001) and articulation rate (De Jong, Steinel, Florijn, Schoonen, and Hulstijn 2012). De Jong, Steinel, Florijn, Schoonen, and Hulstijn (2012) investigated the effect of task complexity on three types of fluency (breakdown fluency, speed fluency and repair fluency) using data elicited from 208 adult L2 learners of Dutch and 59 adult native Dutch speakers. Task complexity was found to influence repair and breakdown fluency, as both native and non-native speaker participants repaired more and produced more filled pauses during the complex speaking tasks, compared to the simple tasks. However, there was no significant difference in articulation rate, which is one of the main components of speed fluency.

Another line of research indicates modality may have a stronger effect on fluency than task complexity. Michel (2011) investigated the effects of increased task complexity and modality (monologic or dialogic) on the linguistic complexity, accuracy, and fluency of L2 learners' speech. In this study, 64 L2 learners of Dutch performed a decision-making task either individually or in pairs. They were asked to leave a message on an answering machine in the monologic task, whereas they had to discuss the same issue with peers on the phone in the dialogic task. Michel found that modality had a significant main effect on fluency measures, with participants producing more fluent speech in interaction. The results suggest that speakers may find speaking in an interactive mode easier because they might be able to plan of their subsequent speech during the interlocutors' turns; this idea corresponds to earlier research finding that speakers take advantage of the time while their interlocutor speaks (Tavakoli and Foster 2008).

Given the limited impact of task complexity, the current study turns its attention to another task-related feature, communicative purpose. A focus on communicative purpose is theoretically motivated by a corpus-based approach that enables comprehensive description of texts in the light of situational characteristics in which text is produced (Biber and Conrad 2019). Building on this approach, the current study newly attends the situational characteristics of task, specifically, the communicative purpose of tasks. Communicative purpose is one of the major elements in a register framework, encompassing a range of reasons why a specific communication takes place, for instance, to narrative past event, to persuade someone, or to reveal self. It underlies why specific linguistic features occur comparatively more frequently under certain situational characteristics and what functions these features play in relation to a specific communicative purpose (Biber and Conrad 2019: 45). The current analysis focuses on the communicative purposes interlocutors bring into their interaction and the extent to which these communicative purposes have influence on L2 utterance fluency in order to explore the complex relationship among task, gender and fluency.

2.3 Gender of Interlocutors

In addition to task variables, previous studies have investigated relationships between interlocutor characteristics and the fluency of L2 speech produced in interactions with some studies finding that interlocutors' gender might impact conversational development (Coates 2015; Young and Milanovic 1992). In L2 studies, associations between gender, negotiation of meaning, and conversational dominance have received attention. For instance, studies that examining peer-peer interactions showed that male participants tend to use a greater proportion of meaning negotiation strategies (Gass and Varonis 1986; Kasanga 1996; Pica, Holliday, Lewis, Berducci, and Newman 1991; Ross-Feldman 2005) and produce more talk in different-gender dyads, compared to male-male dyads (Gass and Varonis 1986). In the same vein, Kasanga (1996) reported that interlocutor gender was a strong predictor of male participants' use of five types of meaning negotiation (clarification requests, confirmation checks, comprehension checks, elaborations and topicalization). In sum, the reported findings suggest that interlocutor gender influences negotiation of meaning.

In addition to investigating the roles of task and gender in L2 interactive fluency, the current study takes an additional exploratory step. Our assumption was that if gender of interlocutors has effects on speech fluency, it might be reflected not only in speed fluency but also in the lexical or syntactic structures of the speech production. In the current study, we address this assumption by exploring whether linguistic alignment is a mechanism through which gender impacts spoken fluency.

2.4 Linguistic Alignment and Fluency in Interaction

In interaction, interlocutors often reuse some aspects of each other's utterances which reduces the cognitive effort required for speech production and results in greater spoken fluency (Bock 1986; Bock and Loebell 1990; Levelt and Kelter 1982). Alignment has been defined as a phenomenon in which speakers tend to mimic the linguistic and non-linguistic behavior of an interlocutor (Pickering and Garrod 2006).

With available data, it is unknown whether alignment will occur in L2 peer-peer interactions as only few studies investigated alignment in language learning contexts, including alignment in stress patterns (Trofimovich, McDonough, and Foote 2014), *wh-* questions (McDonough and Mackey 2006), and word order (Kootstra, van Hell, and Dijkstra 2010). However, we can reasonably expect alignment might occur considering the previous findings in sociolinguistic studies. Multiple lines of research have investigated interactional characteristics that might influence the degree of alignment between interlocutors. A strand of research in socio-cognitive research on syntactic alignment has tried to understand the phenomenon in terms of one interlocutor's perception of the other. A range of social factors have effects on the degree of alignment, including interlocutor gender (Pardo 2006), social intimacy (Balcetis and Dale 2005; Hwang and Chun 2018), and social group membership (Unger 2010). Pardo (2006) found that pairs of male interlocutors tended to align themselves phonetically to a greater extent than pairs of female interlocutors. Similarly, Unger (2010) reported that participants showed greater lexical alignment with interlocutors they perceived as in-group members compared to those perceived as out-group members. These findings point to the possibility that perceived similarities between interlocutors lead to higher degrees of alignment in their interactive speech. Since the current study is an exploratory approach within the scope of investigation we outlined above, we decided to examine only the relationship between gender, alignment and fluency, leaving group membership to be further explored in future studies.

Taken together, the preceding discussion has highlighted the potential gender effects and task-related effects on L2 speech fluency in peer-peer interactions. Also, it has cautiously assumed that alignment might underscore the variance in speech fluency if any differences are found. The current study addresses the following three research questions:
1. To what extent does L2 utterance fluency differ when participants are involved in speaking tasks that have different communicative purposes?
2. To what extent does L2 utterance fluency differ when participants are paired with an interlocutor of the same gender or different gender?
3. To what extent do lexical and syntactic alignment mediate the relationship between shared gender and fluency?

3 Method

3.1 Participants

The participants in this study were 488 pairs of English learners enrolled in an intensive English program at a university in the southwest U.S. The data analyzed in the current study was a portion of the Corpus of Collaborative Oral Tasks (Crawford and McDonough, this volume), consisting of 775 dyadic interactions with a total of 268,324 words. The data was originally collected from L2 learners of English who participated in achievement tests each semester and as such, some recordings were produced by the same student, but partnered with a different interlocutor and completing a different task. Participants were paired with a partner with various L1 backgrounds: Arabic-Arabic (316 pairs), Arabic-Chinese (77 pairs), Arabic-Korean (9 pairs), Arabic-Japanese (5 pairs), Arabic-Portuguese (2 pairs), Chinese-Chinses (69 pairs), Chinese-Korean (1 pair), Chinese-Japanese (6 pairs), Chinese-Portuguese (1 pair), and Japanese-Japanese (2 pairs). Out of the total number of pairs, 94 pairs were different-gender dyads and 394 pairs were the same-gender dyads, as shown in Table 1 below. Upon enrolling in the intensive English program, participants' English proficiency was assessed based on an in-house English proficiency test, which was modeled on the TOEFL iBT. Their proficiency levels ranged from beginners to low intermediate, with scores falling into the following TOEFL iBT bands: 32–44 (228 pairs), 45–56 (214 pairs), and 57–69 (46 pairs), approximately corresponding to 4.5 to 6 on the IELTS overall band score (Educational Testing Service 2010).

3.2 Paired Speaking Tasks

Data for the current study consisted of 488 audio files that were recorded from participants while carrying out 14 different speaking tasks, and the corresponding written transcripts. The recordings were made as part of regular achievement tests conducted at different times during listening and speaking courses. To investigate potential effects of task characteristics on fluency, the fourteen tasks were grouped by communicative purpose.

The communicative purpose of each of the 14 tasks included in the current study was identified based on the wordings of each task prompt and task requirements, resulting in three different communicative purposes: 1) making a decision (3 tasks); 2) persuasion (4 tasks); and, 3) selecting from multiple alternatives (7 tasks). In the "making a decision" tasks, participants were asked to come up with solutions to problems and decide on the best course of action. In the "persuasion" tasks, each participant was assigned a position for or against a proposition and was asked to make an argument to convince their partner. In the "multiple alternatives" tasks, participants were supplied with multiple pre-existing solutions and had to decide the best alternative through discussion. For "multiple alternatives" tasks, participants were supplied with multiple pre-existing solutions and had to decide the best solution through discussion.

Topics of the speaking tasks included sports, health, politics, and science. With regard to task condition (Pica, Kanagy and Falodun 2009), the tasks required both participants to interact (i.e., two-way) to reach an agreement on a given topic (i.e., convergent) where more than one response was acceptable (i.e., open-ended). Task complexity (Robinson 2005) was similar across the tasks: participants were asked to discuss their thoughts or opinions in present time (+here and now) and to come to a single outcome (+single task) after discussion. The interactions involved formulating opinions (+reasoning demand) and required several steps to complete a given task (+many elements). Participants were given planning time before their task performance (+planning time) (see Appendix A for details of task complexity for each task; Appendix B for a sample task).

In preparation for their task performance, participants were given a written prompt and were allotted time for planning. Participants had between one and five minutes to read the prompt and prepare and two to four minutes to record their joint task performance. They recorded their performance using a hand-held digital voice recorder and were given instructions on its usage beforehand. The mean length of paired speaking task recordings was 2 minutes and 34 seconds (SD = 40 sec).

Table 1: Participants L1 and gender backgrounds.

Communicative Purpose of Task	Making a Decision	Persuasion	Selecting from Multiple Alternatives
First Language			
Arabic-Arabic	123	59	134
Arabic-Chinese	15	16	46
Arabic-Korean	4	4	1
Arabic-Japanese	–	–	5
Arabic-Portuguese	–	–	2
Chinese-Chinese	9	17	43
Chinese-Korean	–	–	1
Chinese-Japanese	–	1	5
Chinese-Portuguese	–	–	1
Japanese-Japanese	–	2	–
Gender			
Male-Male	118	74	157
Female-Female	8	8	29
Male-Female	25	17	52
TOTAL	151	99	238

3.3 Utterance Fluency Analysis

Utterance fluency was operationalized as speaking rate and articulation rate (De Jong 2018; De Jong, Steinel, Florijn, Schoonen, and Hulstijn 2012; Kang 2010). The *Fluency Extractor* (Kang and Johnson 2018) was used to calculate these measures for each audio recording as a whole. As shown in Table 2, speaking rate was calculated as the total number of uttered syllables divided by the total duration of the recording, and articulation rate was calculated as the total number of uttered syllables divided by the duration of continuous speech. Segments of speech that included pauses of less than 100 milliseconds (ms) were considered continuous (cf. Anderson-Hsieh and Venkatagiri 1994; Griffiths 1991; Kang 2010; Kang, Rubin, and Pickering 2010).

Table 2: Measures of utterance fluency.

Measures	Calculation
Speaking rate	Number of syllables / total duration of recording, including pauses
Articulation rate	Number of syllables / total duration of continuous speech

Note: Continuous speech = total duration of recording minus silences of > 100 ms.

3.4 Alignment Analysis

The *Analyzing Linguistic Interactions with Generalizable techNiques Python* library (ALIGN; Duran, Paxton, and Fusaroli 2019) was used to calculate the degree of lexical and syntactic alignment between interlocutors during task performance. Analysis of written transcripts involved several steps. First, punctuation and hesitation markers such as 'uh' and 'um' were removed from each transcript. Next, participants' transcribed turns were transformed into sequences of word tokens, and sequences of part of speech (POS) tags from the Penn Treebank tagset (Marcus, Santorini, and Marcinkiewicz 1993). For example:

Transcribed turn: 'Uh uh your uh . . . idea is a good one also. Uh but uh space travel is dangerous.'

Token sequence: [your, idea, is, a, good, one, also, but, space, travel, is, dangerous]

POS sequence: [PRP$ (possessive personal pronoun), NN (singular noun), VBZ (3rd person singular present tense verb), DT (determiner), JJ (adjective), NN, RB (adverb), CC (coordinating conjunction), NN, NN, VBZ, JJ]

These sequences were then segmented into lists of 2-, 3-, 4-, and 5- grams. Using the above example, the corresponding 5-gram lists were:

Token 5-grams: [your idea is a good], [idea is a good one], [is a good one also], [a good one also but], [good one also but space], [one also but space travel], [also but space travel is], [but space travel is dangerous]

POS 5-grams: [PRP$ NN VBZ DT JJ], [NN VBZ DT JJ NN], [VBZ DT JJ NN RB], [DT JJ NN RB CC], [JJ NN RB CC NN], [NN RB CC NN NN], [RB CC NN NN VBZ], [CC NN NN VBZ JJ]

Next, lexical and syntactic 2-, 3-, 4-, and 5-gram alignment scores were calculated for each pair of consecutive turns by taking the cosine similarity of the relevant n-gram lists, resulting in values between 0 and 1 (cf. Jurafsky and Martin 2009; Tan, Steinbach, and Kumar 2005). Lexical alignment scores were calculated using word token n-gram lists from consecutive turns. Syntactic alignment scores were calculated using POS n-gram lists from consecutive turns. Transcript-level scores for lexical and syntactic 2-, 3-, 4-, and 5-gram alignment were then calculated by taking the mean of all consecutive turn alignment scores. Finally, one overall value for each lexical and syntactic alignment was calculated for each transcript by taking the mean of transcript-level 2-, 3-, 4-, and 5-gram alignment scores.

The following annotated transcript is an example of a task performance that had relatively high syntactic alignment (0.16 cosine degrees). The pair of participants are discussing whether to undertake a manned mission to Mars or to build a powerful telescope. Sequences that align syntactically with those in the following turn are in bold and their correspondence is indicated in subscript.

1. **A:** I think uh with all this money we had what do you think uh **[what do you think of]**$_1$ uh of uh creating a manned mission to Mars?
2. **B:** Uh I think it's uh **[a good idea but]**$_2$ uh maybe you need more uh... uh more uh money and more uh experience for that. Uh **[what do you think about]**$_1$ the uh gigantic space telescope?
3. **A:** I... **[I think]**$_3$ its uh **[a good uh idea and]**$_2$ ...
4. **B:** The telescope can be remotely operated from earth uh twenty-four hours a day. Because uh uh what **[do [you think]**$_3$**]**$_4$?
5. **A:** But **[do you think]**$_4$ its size uh its size maybe cause a problem?
6. **B:** No it's about uh it's about three hundred times more powerful than any space telescope ever made before.
7. **A:** So I think it **[is uh a sensitive uh telescope]**$_5$ ... uh so it maybe it will be damaged.
8. **B:** Uh uh your uh ... idea **[is a good one]**$_5$ also. Uh but uh space travel is dangerous. What do **[you think]**$_6$?
9. **A:** Uh yes **[I think]**$_6$ it's dangerous. Astronauts can ... but **[I think]**$_6$ on the other hand **[I think]**$_6$ the astronauts can monitor how space affect living.
10. **B:** **[I agree]**$_6$ with you. Uh what do **[you think]**$_6$ about uh the ... this telescope help the science to do more experience and study?
11. **A:** Yeah **[I think]**$_6$ uh ... Please can you repeat it again?
12. **B:** **[I think]**$_6$ the ... this uh gigantic space telescope help the scientist to do more experience and study.
13. **A:** Oh yeah **[I agree]**$_6$ with you. I agree with you **[on this point]**$_7$. It's a very useful machine.
14. **B:** **[I'm]**$_8$ satisfied **[for this point]**$_7$ uh what do you think about uh your uh ...

15. **A:** So I think **[I'm]**₈ **[agree with you]**₉ that genetic space telescope is a better uh idea
16. **B:** I **[agree with you]**₉.

In turn 1, Participant A uses the sequence 'what do you think of'. The corresponding POS sequence is the 5-gram [WP (wh-pronoun) VPB (non-3rd person singular present tense verb) PRP (personal pronoun) VB (base-form verb) IN (preposition)]. In the following turn, Participant B uses the same POS 5-gram in the sequence 'what do you think about'. In turn 7, Participant A uses the sequence 'is a sensitive telescope', equivalent to the POS 4-gram [VBZ DT JJ NN]. In the following turn, Participant B uses the same POS 4-gram in the sequence 'is a good one'. In all, there were nine instances in which one participant reused a POS n-gram used by their partner in the previous turn, demonstrating a relatively high degree of syntactic alignment.

3.5 Statistical Analysis

In order to answer the research questions, we performed one-way analysis of variance (ANOVA), independent-samples *t*-test and multiple regression analyses using SPSS (IBM Corp 2016) and the linear model (lm) function in R (R Core Team 2019). First, to examine task effects, utterance fluency measures were compared across the three different communicative purposes of tasks using ANOVAs. Second, to investigate the effect of interlocutors' gender on fluency, utterance fluency measures were compared between same-gender pairs and different-gender pairs using independent samples *t*-tests. To estimate the magnitudes of differences between conditions, effect sizes were calculated as Eta squared (η^2) for ANOVA and Cohen's *d* for *t*-tests.

To address the third research question regarding lexical and syntactic alignment as mediators of the gender-fluency relationship, classic mediation analyses were performed. The purpose of mediation analysis is to investigate whether the influence of a predictor variable on an outcome variable is transmitted through a third, intermediate variable (i.e., a mediator variable). In terms of the current study, mediation analyses were conducted to investigate whether the influence of shared gender on articulation rate was transmitted through lexical or syntactic alignment; in other words, whether shared gender caused greater lexical or syntactic alignment, which in turn caused higher articulation rate. In classic mediation analysis, the influence of a predictor variable on an outcome variable is said to be transmitted by a mediator variable if the following four conditions are met: 1) variation in the predictor predicts variation in the outcome; 2) the predictor predicts the mediator; 3) the mediator predicts the outcome when the predictor is controlled for; and, 4) the regression coefficient for the predictor-outcome association (i.e., condition 1) is reduced in magnitude when the mediator is included in the model (Baron and Kenny 1986; Fairchild and McDaniel 2017; MacKinnon, Fairchild, and Fritz 2007). Figure 1 illustrates conditions 1–3 in terms of relationships between variables in the current study.

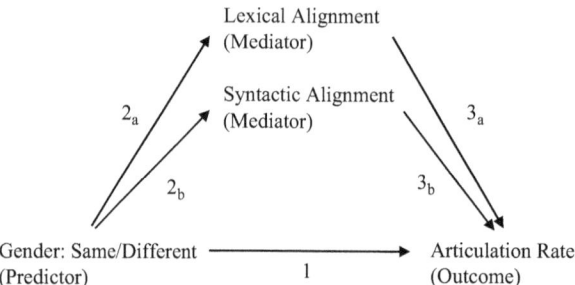

Figure 1: Relationships between variables in mediation analyses.

Separate analyses were performed to investigate lexical and syntactic alignment as potential mediators. In both cases, the same analytical steps were taken with regards to the four necessary conditions for mediation. First, regression was performed to model the relationship between gender and articulation rate, represented as path 1 in Figure 1. To meet the first condition for mediation, the model had to indicate that gender predicted articulation rate. Given that this condition was met, the relationships between gender and lexical alignment (path 2_a) and gender and syntactic alignment (path 2_b) were modeled. To meet the second necessary condition of mediation, these models had to indicate that gender predicted alignment. Given that this condition was met, the final step in the mediation analyses was to create two final models in which the outcome variable was articulation rate, and the predictor variables were (a) gender and lexical alignment; and (b) gender and syntactic alignment. To meet the third necessary condition for mediation, these models had to indicate that alignment predicted articulation rate (i.e., paths 3_a and 3_b). To meet the fourth necessary condition for mediation, the regression coefficient for gender in these final models had to be smaller in magnitude than the coefficient for gender in the model that did not include alignment (i.e., path 1). If all four of these conditions were met, it could be concluded that lexical and/or syntactic alignment was one mechanism through which shared gender influenced articulation rate.

In order to improve the statistical power of the regression models used for the gender-alignment-fluency mediation analysis, task was included as a covariate in each model. The task covariate had 14 levels, one for each of the unique tasks included in the sample. All regression models were checked for linearity, independence of errors, homoscedasticity, and normality; no violations of these assumptions were detected.

4 Results

4.1 Effects of Task on Utterance Fluency

The first research question concerns the effects of the three different communicative purposes of tasks on L2 interactive fluency. To answer this question, ANOVAs were run with communicative purpose (Making a decision, MD; Persuasion, PS; Selecting from multiple alternatives, SA) as an independent variable and the measured speaking rate and articulation rate as dependent variables. As shown in Figure 2 and Table 3, the results revealed a significant effect of communicative purpose on speaking rate ($p < .001$) but no significant effect of communicative purpose on articulation rate ($p = .12$). Since the results of the ANOVA were statistically significant for speaking rate, post-hoc comparisons using Tukey's HSD were additionally conducted. The results of post-hoc comparisons, provided in Table 4, indicated that speaking rate in SA tasks (3.49 syllables/second) was significantly higher than in MD tasks (3.26 syllables/second; $p = .002$) and PS tasks (3.25 syllables/second; $p = .008$). The difference between MD and PS tasks was not significant ($p = .99$).

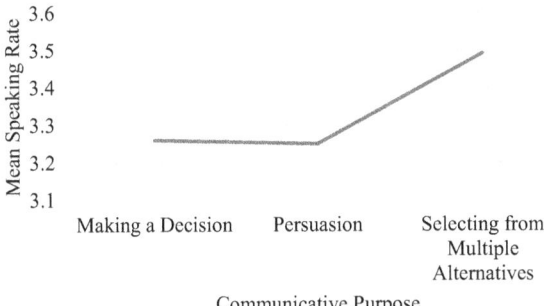

Figure 2: Mean speaking rate across three communicative purposes of speaking tasks.

Table 3: Descriptive and inferential statistics of speaking rate and articulation rate across communicative functions of tasks.

	M (SD)			df	SS	MS	F	Eta Squared	p
	MD (n = 151 pairs)	PS (n = 99 pairs)	SA (n = 238 pairs)						
Speaking rate									
Between	3.26	3.25	3.49	2	6.8	3.4	7.75	.03	< .001*
Within	(0.75)	(0.67)	(0.60)	485	212.93	0.44			
Articulation rate									
Between	3.80	3.88	3.89	2	0.84	0.42	2.13	.009	.12
Within	(0.53)	(0.40)	(0.40)	485	95.373	0.20			

Note. The communicative purposes of tasks were abbreviated as MD (Making a decision), PS (Persuasion), and SA (Selecting from multiple alternatives); * $p < .05$.

Table 4: Post hoc comparisons of speaking rate using Tukey's HSD.

Comparison		Mean Difference (I-J)	p	95% Confidence Interval	
(I) Task	(J) Task			Lower Bound	Upper Bound
SA	MD	0.23	.002*	0.07	0.40
	PS	0.24	.008*	0.05	0.43
MD	PS	0.00	.99	−0.20	0.21

Note. The communicative purposes of task were abbreviated as MD (Making a decision), PS (Persuasion), and SA (Selecting from multiple alternatives); * $p < .05$.

4.2 Effect of Speakers' Gender on Utterance Fluency

The second research question asked whether there was a difference in terms of utterance fluency when L2 learners were paired with a same-gender partner or a different-gender partner. The results showed that participants who interacted with learners of the same gender (i.e., males with males, and females with females) produced higher speaking rates ($M = 3.39$, $SD = 0.68$) compared to those who interacted with learners of the opposite gender (i.e., males with females)

(M = 3.29, SD = 0.64), however, results of an independent samples t-test indicated that this difference was not statistically significant (p = .18), as shown in Table 5. With regard to articulation rate, a similar trend was observed in that same-gender pairs had higher articulation rates (M = 3.89, SD = 0.43) than different-gender dyads (M = 3.74, SD = 0.49). The 0.15 syllables/second advantage for same-gender dyads was statistically significant (p = .003) with a small effect size (d = 0.34) (Oswald and Plonsky 2014).

Table 5: Differences in utterance fluency measures between different- and same-gender Pairs.

	Different gender (n = 96 pairs)		Same gender (n = 393 pairs)		t	df	p	d
	M	SD	M	SD				
Speaking rate	3.29	0.64	3.39	0.68	−1.34	486	.18	0.16
Articulation rate	3.74	0.49	3.89	0.43	−3.03	486	.003*	0.34

Note. * p < .05.

4.3 Lexical and Syntactic Alignment as Mediators of the Gender-Fluency Relationship

The third research question asked whether the relationship between gender and utterance fluency could be explained by higher degrees of linguistic alignment between participants of the same gender. Initial analyses indicated that the mean articulation rate across task performances was 3.86 syllables per second (SD = 0.44). Mean lexical alignment, measured in cosine similarity, was 0.06 degrees (SD = 0.03). Mean syntactic alignment was 0.20 degrees (SD = 0.06).

Mediation analysis consisted of checking four necessary conditions (see section on Statistical Analysis, above). First, the regression model of the relationship between gender and articulation rate revealed that same-gender pairs produced higher utterance fluency than different-gender pairs (B = 0.13, p = 0.01), meaning the first condition was met. Next, the regression model of the relationship between gender and lexical alignment did not indicate that same-gender pairs were more lexically aligned (p = .48). In other words, the second condition for lexical alignment as a mediator was not met. However, the regression model of the relationship between gender and syntactic alignment did indicate that same-gender pairs were more syntactically aligned (B = 0.01, p = 0.049). The second condition was met, therefore, for syntactic alignment as a mediator.

Regarding the third necessary condition for mediation, the regression model of the relationship between gender, syntactic alignment and articulation rate indicated that syntactic alignment predicted articulation rate ($B = 1.28$, $p < .001$). Further, the regression coefficient for same-gender pairs was $B = 0.11$, which was smaller in magnitude than the coefficient for same-gender pairs when syntactic alignment was not included in the model (i.e., the model for condition 1, above, in which $B = 0.13$). In other words, the third and fourth condition were met for syntactic alignment as a mediator of the relationship between gender and utterance fluency. It must be noted, however, that the reduction in the same-gender coefficient when syntactic alignment was included in the model was only 15% (1–0.11/0.13). Therefore, syntactic alignment only *partially* explained the relationship between gender and articulation rate.

To summarize the results of the mediation analysis, we did not find evidence that lexical alignment was part of the mechanism through which same-gender pairs produced higher articulate rates but we did find evidence that syntactic alignment may have done so. Same-gender interlocutors produced speech that was more syntactically aligned, compared to different-gender pairs. Higher degrees of syntactic alignment were associated with higher utterance fluency, even when gender was controlled for. Finally, the magnitude of the association between same-gender pairs and articulation rate was reduced when syntactic alignment was included in the model. In other words, the four necessary conditions for classical mediation were met for syntactic alignment.

5 Discussion

The current study explored the effects of tasks and gender on L2 spoken fluency during paired interactions and examined whether lexical and syntactic alignment might act as a mechanism through which gender influences fluency. Results indicated that L2 learners produced more fluent speech when they performed tasks in which they had to collaborate in order to select one option out of multiple possibilities supplied by the task prompt. Learners produced less fluent speech when they had to persuade their partners about an opposing position or make a joint decision without being given possible solutions in the task prompt. This difference in utterance fluency may be related to the varying cognitive and interpersonal demands of tasks with different communicative purposes. For tasks that require learners to come to a joint decision, task prompts that supply descriptions of possible solutions are less cognitively demanding than those for which no premade solutions are provided to choose from. It is possible that this difference in cognitive demands contributed to observed difference in utterance fluency: less cognitively demanding tasks (i.e., those that supplied multiple alternative solutions) were performed with higher levels of utterance fluency, compared to more cognitively demanding tasks (i.e., those for which learners had to develop their own solutions). In terms of interpersonal demands, learners might have been more forthcoming in their spoken contributions while performing tasks that required collaboration, rather than persuasion. In persuasion tasks, each learner was supplied with a position that was directly opposed to that of their interlocutor, which could have led to negative affective factors such as saving face and avoiding confrontation. These interpersonal factors might have contributed to the observed difference in utterance fluency between collaborative and persuasive tasks involving pre-made solutions. Furthermore, looking into the proficiency level of the participants of the tasks with three different communicative purposes indicate such differences in speaking rate might be due to differing proficiency levels that the participants were in. All of the participants who took the MD task and approximately 70% of the participants who took the PS task were less proficient with their in-house placement test scores ranged between 32 to 44. On the other hand, almost 90% of participants who took the PS task were slightly more proficient learners with test scores ranging between 45 to 56. This suggests that utterance fluency might be shaped under the influence of both task-related factors as well as learners' proficiency level in a target language. The current study assumed that the differences in proficiency levels among the participants were minute and hence largely labeled them as low intermediate learners at study design stage. Interestingly, the findings suggest that such minute differences might influence the utterance fluency of L2 learners, indicating that even slight development in L2 speaking skills might be reflected in their utterance fluency.

The task-related findings support the use of situational analyses of texts to account for patterns of use of linguistic features. In the framework of situational analyses (Biber and Conrad 2019), communicative purpose is one of the major situational characteristics used to describe and compare registers and genres. Previous studies on task effects have mainly focused on the cognitive dimension of tasks (De Jong, Steinel, Florijn, Schoonen, and Hulstijn 2012; Iwashita, McNamara, and Elder 2001; Kormos and Trebits 2012; Michel 2011), or task characteristics such as planning time (Ellis 2009; Tavakoli and Skehan 2005). The findings of the current study suggest that varying communicative purposes might contribute to observed differences in spoken fluency in the performance of L2 paired speaking tasks. In terms of future research on L2 speaking, this suggests communicative purpose as an important variable to help researchers explore and understanding linguistic variation in L2 peer interactions. Also, communicative purpose has pedagogical implications in broadening the range of tasks, allowing practitioners to refer to communicative purpose when design a curriculum focusing on speaking skills.

The current study also found that learners who were paired with a same-gender interlocutor (i.e. male-male pairs, female-female pairs) produced more fluent speech than different-gender (i.e., male-female) dyads. This finding complements results of previous studies that found that interlocutor gender plays a role in shaping interactions (Gass and Varonis 1986; Kasanga 1996; Ross-Feldman 2005). We also examined a potential mechanism through which shared gender could lead to higher utterance fluency in L2 dialogic speaking tasks. Specifically, we investigated the extent to which the gender-fluency relationship could be explained by lexical and syntactic alignment between interlocutors. Previous research has shown that interlocutors tend to exhibit higher levels of linguistic alignment when they interact with those whom they affiliate (Balcetis and Dale 2005; Unger 2010). Further, recycling an interlocutor's lexical items and syntactic constructions in one's own speech reduces cognitive processing burdens and leads to more fluent production (Schoot, Menenti, Hagoort, and Segaert 2014; Smith and Wheeldon 2001). In line with previous research, the current study found that same-gender pairs of speakers exhibited greater syntactic alignment than different-gender pairs, although we did not find evidence of a gender effect on lexical alignment. In other words, L2 English speakers were more likely to re-use syntactic constructions from their interlocutor's previous turn if that interlocutor was of the same gender as themselves. This result is congruent with previous research that found that speakers tend to adjust their linguistic output to make it more similar to that of interlocutors with whom they affiliate.

Further, the current study also found that speech that exhibited greater syntactic alignment also tended to be more fluent. We suggest that the more that interlocutors re-used each other's syntactic constructions, the less they needed to produce cognitively demanding novel language, leading to increased utterance fluency. Given that same-gender pairs exhibited greater syntactic alignment, and that greater syntactic alignment was associated with higher levels of utterance fluency, we performed a classic mediation analysis and concluded that syntactic alignment partially accounted for the observed relationship between shared gender and utterance fluency. In other words, the fact that same-gender pairs had a greater tendency to recycle each other's syntactic constructions on a turn-by-turn basis explained, in part, why they were able to produce more fluent speech than different-gender pairs.

Taken together, results of the current study suggest that variance in spoken fluency during paired L2 interactions is the result of a complex interplay of factors. The findings provide empirical evidence to support the claim that task factors and participant variables influence spoken fluency during interactions.

Previous studies found that L2 learners produced more fluent speech in dialogic tasks than they did in monologic tasks (Michel 2011; Tavakoli 2016; Witton-Davies 2014), showing that speaking modality influences L2 fluency. The reason for increased fluency has been vaguely attributed to the nature of interaction that facilitates the negotiation of meaning (Long 1980). This study took a further step and examined the role of communicative purpose and interlocutors' gender in explaining varying levels of spoken fluency in L2 paired interactions. This approach reflects the triadic componential framework (Robinson 2005) that addresses both task- and learner-related factors with distinctions between task complexity (i.e., cognitive factors), task conditions (i.e., interactional factors such as participant variables) and task difficulty (i.e., learner factors). We suggest that, along with task-related factors, learner variables might account for variation in L2 paired interactions, as demonstrated in the current study through the lens of spoken fluency.

6 Limitations and Directions for Future Research

The current study contributes to our understanding of how L2 spoken fluency is related to the communicative purpose of the task and interlocutor gender. These findings should be considered in light of several limitations. First, L2 fluency has been conceptualized as a multi-faceted phenomenon that encompasses cognitive, utterance and perceived fluency (Segalowitz 2010; 2018). The current study only examined utterance fluency, and particularly its speed measures: speaking rate and articulation rate (Tavakoli and Skehan 2005). Other dimensions of fluency, such as repair fluency and breakdown fluency, should be the focus of future research.

Further, the current study was observational in nature and its results should be interpreted with caution. For example, the analyzed task performances were produced by L2 learners who were classmates for several weeks or months. It is plausible that, over the course of their time spent together, classmates of the same gender developed social relationships to a greater extent with each other, compared to males and females. In other words, shared gender, in the current study, could be confounded with the degree of previous social contact. If this were the case, it would be uncertain how much of the observed effects of shared gender were attributable to previous social contact rather than gender alone. To confirm the observed effects of shared gender on fluency, and the mediating role played by syntactic alignment, future studies should involve L2 speakers who have no previous relationships with each other. Regarding the syntactic alignment analysis conducted in the current study, it is possible that some word sequences uttered by participants represented unanalyzed chunks, rather than syntactic knowledge. For example, in the transcript used above to illustrate a high degree of syntactic alignment, the two participants produced the sequence "I think" in consecutive turns. It is possible that these participants stored "I think" as a single unit of language that could be deployed for a variety of functions (e.g., as a stance marker, or a hesitation marker). If this were the case, the alignment analysis for the current study is not purely indicative of participants' syntactic knowledge, but also of multi-word sequences that participants stored as unanalyzed chunks. Finally, since it was found that the relationship between shared gender and utterance fluency was only partially mediated by syntactic alignment, future studies should be conducted to explore other possible mechanisms through which gender influences fluency in paired speaking tasks.

References

Anderson-Hsieh, Janet & Horabail Venkatagiri. 1994. Syllable duration and pausing in the speech of intermediate and high proficiency Chinese ESL speakers. *TESOL Quarterly* 28(4). 807–812.

Balcetis, Emily & Rick Dale. 2005. An exploration of social modulation of syntactic priming. Paper presented at the *Cognitive Science Society*. Stresa, 21–23 July.

Baron, Reuben M. & David A. Kenny. 1986. The moderator–mediator variable distinction in social psychological research: Conceptual, strategic, and statistical considerations. *Journal of Personality and Social Psychology* 51(6). 1173–1182.

Biber, Douglas & Susan Conrad. 2019 [2009]. *Register, genre, and style,* 2nd edn. Cambridge: Cambridge University Press.

Bock, Kathryn. 1986. Syntactic persistence in language production. *Cognitive Psychology* 18(3). 355–387.

Bock, Kathryn & Helga Loebell. 1990. Framing sentences. *Cognition* 35(1). 1–39.

Branigan, Holly P., Martin J. Pickering, Jamie Pearson, Janet F. McLean & Ash Brown. 2011. The role of beliefs in lexical alignment: Evidence from dialogs with humans and computers. *Cognition* 121(1). 41–57.

Coates, Jennifer. 2015 [1993]. *Women, men and language: A sociolinguistic account of gender differences in language*, 3rd edn. Abingdon-on-Thames, UK: Routledge.

De Jong, Nivja H. 2018. Fluency in second language testing: Insights from different disciplines. *Language Assessment Quarterly* 15(3). 237–254.

De Jong, Nivja H., Margarita P. Steinel, Arjen F. Florijn, Rob Schoonen & Jan H. Hulstijn. 2012. The effect of task complexity on functional adequacy, fluency and lexical diversity in speaking performances of native and non-native speakers. In Alex Housen, Folkert. Kuiken & Ineke Vedder (Eds.), *Dimensions of L2 performance and proficiency: Complexity, accuracy and fluency in SLA*, 121–142. Amsterdam & Philadelphia: John Benjamins.

Duran, Nicholas D., Alexandra Paxton, & Riccardo Fusaroli. 2019. ALIGN: Analyzing Linguistic Interactions with Generalizable techNiques: A Python Library. *Psychological Methods* 24(4). 419–438.

Educational Testing Service. 2010. *Linking TOEFL iBT scores to IELTS.* https://www.ets.org/toefl/score-users/scores-admissions/compare/ (accessed 28 Nov 2020).

Ellis, Rod. 2009. The differential effects of three types of task planning on the fluency, complexity, and accuracy in L2 oral production. *Applied linguistics* 30(4). 474–509.

Fairchild, Amanda J. & Heather L. McDaniel. 2017. Best (but oft-forgotten) practices: Mediation analysis. *The American Journal of Clinical Nutrition* 105(6). 1259–1271.

Filmore, Charles J. 1979. On fluency. In Charles J. Fillmore, Daniel Kempler & William S-Y. Wang (Eds.), *Individual differences in language ability and language behavior*, 85–102. New York: Academic Press.

Gass, Susan M. & Evalgeline Marios Varonis. 1986. Sex differences in NNS/NNS interactions. In Richard R. Day (Ed.), *Talking to learn: Conversation in second language acquisition*, 327–351. Cambridge, MA: Newbury House.

Griffiths, Roger. 1991. Pausological research in an L-2 context: A rationale and review of selected studies. *Applied Linguistics* 12(4). 345–364.

Housen, Alex, Folkert Kuiken & Ineke Vedder (Eds.). 2012. *Dimensions of L2 performance and proficiency: Complexity, accuracy and fluency in SLA.* Amsterdam: John Benjamins.

Hwang, Heeju & Eunjin Chun. 2018. Influence of social perception and social monitoring on structural priming. *Cognitive Science* 42(1). 303–313.

IBM Corp. 2016. *IBM SPSS Statistics for Windows*, Version 24.0. Armonk, NY: IBM Corp.

Iwashita, Noriko, Tim McNamara & Catherine Elder. 2001. Can we predict task difficulty in an oral proficiency test? Exploring the potential of an information-processing approach to task design. *Language learning* 51(3). 401–436.

Jurafsky, Daniel & James H. Martin. 2009 [2000]. *Speech and language processing: An introduction to natural language processing, computational linguistics, and speech recognition*, 2nd edn. Upper Saddle River, NJ: Prentice-Hall.

Kang, Okim. 2010. Relative salience of suprasegmental features on judgments of L2 comprehensibility and accentedness. *System* 38(2). 301–315.

Kang, Okim, Don Rubin & Lucy Pickering. 2010. Suprasegmental measures of accentedness and judgments of language learner proficiency in Oral English. *Modern Language Journal* 94(4). 554–566.

Kang, Okim & David Johnson. 2018. The roles of suprasegmental features in predicting English oral proficiency with an automated system. *Language Assessment Quarterly* 15(2). 150–168.

Kasanga, Luanga A. 1996. Effect of gender on the rate of interaction. Some implications for second language acquisition and classroom practice. *ITL-International Journal of Applied Linguistics* 111(1). 155–192.

Kootstra, Garrit Jan, Janet G. van Hell & Ton Dijkstra. 2010. Syntactic alignment and shared word order in code-switched sentence production: Evidence from bilingual monologue and dialogue. *Journal of Memory and Language* 63(2). 210–231.

Kormos, Judit & Mariann Dénes. 2004. Exploring measures and perceptions of fluency in the speech of second language learners. *System* 32(2). 145–164.

Kormos, Judit & Anna Trebits. 2012. The role of task complexity, modality, and aptitude in narrative task performance. *Language Learning* 62(2). 439–472.

Lennon, Paul. 1990. Investigating fluency in EFL: A quantitative approach. *Language Learning* 40(3). 387–417.

Lennon, Paul. 2000. The lexical element in spoken second language fluency. In Heidi Reiggenbach (Ed.), *Perspectives on fluency*, 25–42. Ann Arbor: University of Michigan.

Levelt, Willem J. M. & Stephanie Kelter. 1982. Surface form and memory in question answering. *Cognitive Psychology* 14(1). 78–106.

Long, Michael H. 1980. *Input, interaction, and second language acquisition*. Los Angeles, CA: University of California dissertation.

MacKinnon, David P., Amanda J. Fairchild & Matthew S. Fritz. 2007. Mediation analysis. *Annual Review Psychology* 58. 593–614.

Marcus, Mitchell, Beatrice Santorini & Mary Ann Marcinkiewicz. 1993. Building a large annotated corpus of English: The Penn Treebank. *University of Pennsylvania Department of Computer and Information Science Technical Report* No. MS-CIS-93-87.

McDonough, Kim & Alison Mackey. 2006. Responses to recasts: Repetitions, primed production, and linguistic development. *Language Learning* 56(4). 693–720.

Michel, Marije C. 2011. Effects of task complexity and interaction in L2 performance. In Peter Robinson (Ed.), *Second language task complexity: Researching the cognition hypothesis of language learning and performance*, 141–174. Amsterdam: John Benjamins.

Pardo, Jennifer S. 2006. On phonetic convergence during conversational interaction. *The Journal of the Acoustical Society of America* 119(4). 2382–2393.

Peltonen, Pauliina. 2017. Temporal fluency and problem-solving in interaction: An exploratory study of fluency resources in L2 dialogue. *System* 70(1). 1–13.

Pica, Teresa, Lloyd Holliday, Nora Lewis, Dom Berducci & Jeanne Newman. 1991. Language learning through interaction: What role does gender play? *Studies in Second Language Acquisition* 13(3). 343–376.

Pica, Teresa, Ruth Kanagy & Joseph Falodun. 2009. Choosing and using communication tasks for second language instruction and research. In Kris van den Branden, Martin Bygate & John M. Norris (Eds.), *Task-based language teaching*, 171–192. Amsterdam: John Benjamins.

Pickering, Martin J. & Simon Garrod. 2006. Alignment as the basis for successful communication. *Research on Language and Computation* 4. 203–228.

Plonsky, Luke & Frederick L. Oswald. 2014. How big is "big"? Interpreting effect sizes in L2 research. *Language Learning* 64(4). 878–912.

R Core Team. 2013. *R: A language and environment for statistical computing*. Vienna: R Foundation for Statistical Computing.

Robinson, Peter. 2005. Cognitive complexity and task sequencing: Studies in a componential framework for second language task design. *International Review of Applied Linguistics in Language Teaching* 43(1). 1–32.

Ross-Feldman, Lauren. 2005. *Task-based interactions between second language learners: Exploring the role of gender*. Washington, D.C.: Georgetown University dissertation.

Sato, Masatoshi. 2014. Exploring the construct of interactional oral fluency: Second Language Acquisition and Language Testing approaches. *System* 45. 79–91.

Schoot, Lotte, Laura Menenti, Peter Hagoort & Katrien Segaert. 2014. A little more conversation-the influence of communicative context on syntactic priming in brain and behavior. *Frontiers in Psychology* 5, Article 208. 1–16.

Segalowitz, Norman. 2010. *The cognitive bases of second language fluency*. New York: Routledge.

Segalowitz, Norman. 2018. Second language fluency and its underlying cognitive and social determinants. *International Review of Applied Linguistics in Language Teaching* 54(2). 79–95.

Skehan, Peter. 2014. Limited attentional capacity, second language performance, and task-based pedagogy. In Peter Skehan (Ed.), *Processing perspectives on task performance*, 211–260. Amsterdam: John Benjamins.

Smith, Mark & Linda Wheeldon. 2001. Syntactic priming in spoken sentence production: An online study. *Cognition* 78(2). 123–164.

Tan, Pang-Ning, Michael Steinbach & Vipin Kumar. 2005. *Introduction to data mining*. Boston: Pearson.

Tavakoli, Parvaneh & Peter Skehan. 2005. Strategic planning, task structure and performance testing. In Rod Ellis (Ed.), *Planning and task performance in a second language*, 239–277. Amsterdam: John Benjamins.

Tavakoli, Parvaneh & Pauline Foster. 2008. Task design and second language performance: The effect of narrative type on learner output. *Language Learning* 58(2). 439–473.

Tavakoli, Parvaneh. 2016. Fluency in monologic and dialogic task performance: Challenges in defining and measuring L2 fluency. *International Review of Applied Linguistics in Language Teaching* 54(2). 133–150.

Trofimovich, Pavel, Kim McDonough & Jennifer A. Foote. 2014. Interactive alignment of multisyllabic stress patterns in a second language classroom. *TESOL Quarterly* 48(4). 815–832.

Unger, Layla. 2010. *The social role of linguistic alignment with in-group and out-group members*. Edinburgh, UK: University of Edinburgh MA thesis.

Weatherholtz, Kodi, Kahryn Campbell-Kibler & T. Florian Jaeger. 2014. Socially-mediated syntactic alignment. Language Variation and Change 26(3). 387–420.

Witton-Davies, Giles. 2014. *The study of fluency and its development in monologue and dialogue*. Lancaster, UK: University of Lancaster dissertation.

Young, Richard, & Michael Milanovic. 1992. Discourse variation in oral proficiency interviews. *Studies in Second Language Acquisition* 14(4). 403–424.

Appendix A

Detailed Description of Speaking Tasks Used

Task	Communicative Purpose	Task Complexity		Planning time	Prior Knowledge	Reasoning demands	Many elements
		Here and now	Single task				
Chen problem	Making a decision	+	+	+ 1–2 min	−	+	+
Spanking		+	+	+ 2 min	+	+	+
Voluntary simplicity		+	+	+ 2 min	−	+	+
Advertisement	Persuasion	+	+	+ 3–5 min	−	+	+
Cancer advice		+	+	+ 1 min	−	+	+
Avoiding extreme sports		+	+	+ 2 min	−	+	+
Workplace monitoring		+	+	+ 3 min	−	+	+
Choosing a patient	Selecting from Multiple Alternatives	+	+	+ 3 min	−	+	+
Crime statistics		−	+	+ 3 min	−	+	+
Election		+	+	+ 3 min	−	+	+
Investing a famous entrepreneur		+	+	+ 3 min	−	+	+
Investing a science funding		+	+	+ 2 min	−	+	+
Opening a barbershop		+	+	+ 2 min	−	+	+
Awarding a scholarship		+	+	+ 1–2 min	+	+	+

Appendix B

Speaking Task Prompt and Rubric

5_ Choosing a Patient

Directions: You and your partner are nutrition advisors at a health center. You have two patients who want to lose weight, but you can only help one of them. Both patients need to eat healthier foods and exercise more. You have 3 minutes to prepare with your partner and 2 minutes and 30 seconds to speak with your partner.
1. Describe Cindy's/Jack's problems. <u>Do not just read the information. Make a story about Cindy/Jack.</u>
2. Talk with Student A/B to make a decision and come to an agreement about who needs more professional help from the health clinic. Make sure to provide reasons to support your ideas.

Cindy	Jack
(1) has obese parents	(1) sleeps 4 hours a night
(2) works long hours	(2) eats McDonalds a lot
(3) gained 20 pounds	(3) has heart problems in his family
(4) eats junk food all day	(4) sits at desk all day

Rubrics

	Collaboration	Task completion	Style
4	Both learners almost always – Work together on almost all parts of the task – Carefully respond to each other and engage each other's ideas – Offer constructive feedback	– Excellent completion of the task; all required elements of the task are present – Content is rich; ideas developed with elaboration and detail; overall task outcome is outstanding	– Outstanding ability to state an opinion – Show excellent skills in using narrative techniques – Show excellent skills in interrupting politely to ask questions

(continued)

	Collaboration	Task completion	Style
3.5	- Both learners usually - Work together on most parts of the tasks - Respond to each other and engage each other's ideas - Offer feedback	- Good completion of the task; almost all required elements are present - Responses appropriate and with some elaboration and detail; overall task outcome is satisfactory	- Good ability to state an opinion - Show good skills in using narrative techniques - Show good skills in interrupting politely to ask questions
3	- Some engagement in the interaction but only one student generally leads participation during tasks - Sometimes the learners ignore each other's responses - Both learners or one learner sometimes do not offer any feedback	- Acceptable completion of the task; some required elements are missing - Responses mostly appropriate and adequately developed; overall task outcome is acceptable	- Adequate ability to state an opinion - Show adequate skills in using narrative techniques - Show adequate skills in interrupting politely to ask questions
2.5	- One learner always takes lead in discussion during tasks or neither of them often try to engage in tasks - Both learners often ignore each other's responses and have high level of disagreements and inability to reach consensus; only claim own opinion - Both learners provide very little feedback to each other	- Partial completion of the task; many required elements are missing - Responses appropriate yet undeveloped; only basic ideas expressed without any elaboration or detail; overall task outcome is poor	- Try to state an opinion - Try to use narrative techniques - Try to interrupt politely to ask questions

(continued)

	Collaboration	Task completion	Style
2	– Bother learners show no evidence of working with partners – Both learners never pay attention or respond to each other – Both learners demonstrate no evidence of ability to provide feedback to each other	– Unable to complete the task; few or no required elements are present – Responses are inappropriate; overall task outcome is not comprehensible	– Cannot state an opinion – Show no skills in using narrative techniques – Show no skills in interrupting politely to ask questions

Romy Ghanem
ESL Students' Use of Suprasegmental Features in Informative and Opinion-Based Tasks

1 Introduction

The evaluation of spoken language has undergone a considerable amount of change and development in the field of second language acquisition. Scores assigned to second language (L2) productions were traditionally provided by expert listeners, who most often underwent some form of norming and/or training for consistency purposes. The reliance on the native speaker as the expert in assessing nonnative productions and their deviancy from the norm has been a longstanding tradition in the subfields of second language production, that is, L2 speaking and writing. However, as with other areas in Second Language Acquisition (SLA), recent research has called for a move towards a more ecologically realistic model for second language learners (Murphy 2014; Munro and Derwing 2001). In other words, a highly intelligible second language speaker has become the more achievable goal for L2 speakers, even with the retention of some L1 influence (also referred to as accentedness). This has led to a push for a less biased form of assessment by including two types of evaluative data: a) quantifiable and measurable data in the form of pronunciation features and b) scores provided by listeners. Researchers (e.g., Kang and Pickering 2013) thus advocate for an alternative method by combining objective and systematic measurements of speaking features with rater evaluations, which allows for a more comprehensive depiction of pronunciation constructs and a learner's proficiency.

A number of speaking features have been shown to predict second language (L2) speakers' proficiency level. Earlier studies in pronunciation research highlighted the importance of segmental features (i.e., consonant and vowel production) with a focus on the deviation from a native speaker norm (Flege and Port 1981; Macken and Ferguson 1983). More recent studies have maintained the importance of suprasegmental features (i.e., features that go beyond consonants and vowels, such as prosody – intonation, stress, and rhythm) particularly regarding the extent to which prosodic features may contribute to a listener's perception of a speaker's intelligibility or comprehensibility (Hahn 2004; Kang 2010; Kang, Rubin, and Pickering 2010). However, consensus is yet to be reached with regard to the most prominent linguistic components that contribute to NNSs' production of intelligible speech. In addition, the connection between pronunciation features and various components of speech assessment is yet to be solidified, especially when it comes to comparing pronunciation measures across different task types.

2 Literature Review

2.1 Relationship between Scores and Pronunciation Features

The call for the use of more objective methods for evaluating second language speech was primarily promoted by the need for an unbiased form of rating that assesses a learner's speech production and is not swayed by the learner's L1, cultural background, or any other factor that may influence a rater's score. In fact, some studies have demonstrated that 18–23% of the variance in scores could be attributed to a listener's bias or some other background factors (Kang and Rubin 2009). This does not indicate, however, that a rater solely relies on external factors to assess an individual's speech. A human ear may be unable to detect and record segmental and suprasegmental features as a computer program would, yet raters do rely on such components when evaluating speech production. A tester cannot perhaps measure the deviation of learner's voice onset timing (VOT) or the length of their pauses, but a long pause and a VOT that does not correspond to the correct voiced or voiceless consonant will certainly affect the rater's perception of the test taker's speech.

Additionally, pronunciation scores have been shown to correlate with values for certain pronunciation features produced by the speaker, particularly suprasegmental variables (Ginther, Dimova, and Yang 2010; Kang et al. 2010). Ginther et al. (2010) maintain that raters' judgments of speech segments correlate with certain fluency measures such as speech rate and pauses. This could be due to the raters' attention to these features when evaluating a speech production or to other factors that correlate highly with fluency measures. Whether negatively or positively affecting a learner's scores, pronunciation features have assumed a vital role for both second/foreign language pronunciation classrooms and automatic speech recognizing (ASR) algorithms (Kang and Johnson 2018). Cucchiarini, Strik, and Boves (2002) demonstrated through ASR technology that six fluency measures are able to account for a high percentage of the variance (>80%) of the fluency scores provided by human raters. For most of the research that examines the relationship between fluency measures and scores, two main types of studies emerge: the first type of study includes holistic scores as their outcome variables (Jin and Mak 2012) and the second type incorporates intelligibility or comprehensibility ratings from trained pronunciation raters (Trofimovich and Isaacs 2012). Fewer studies explore the relationship between pronunciation features and analytic scores (or score bands).

2.2 Features Affecting Pronunciation Scores

In recent research, the identification of the most relevant pronunciation features to the assessment or recognition of speech has come into focus due to the heightened interest in ASRs. The ability to include a large number of variables in an algorithm has allowed for a much more comprehensive view of the gamut of pronunciation features that affect the perception and/or evaluation of first or second language speech. Segmental features, for instance, have recently reclaimed their role in speech assessment, especially in research on automated speech assessment which examines segmental deviations such as phone duration, vowel quality, syllable production, voice onset time (VOT), and stop closure duration (Kazemzadeh et al. 2006; Jin and Mak 2012). However, suprasegmental features, particularly fluency and prosodic features retain their primary role in the evaluation of speech production, particularly since they are easier to be identified and evaluated by human raters.

2.3 Fluency Features

The term fluency has been used to refer to different concepts; some studies consider this notion as synonymous to proficiency. That is, a speaker is evaluated based on his/her fluency level (Peters and Guitar 1991). Others treat this construct as an umbrella term that houses several other pronunciation features. Combined, the ways speakers use these sub-features distinguish among proficiency levels (Trofimovich and Baker 2006). For the purposes of this study, fluency is used as a term that includes several suprasegmental pronunciation features that affect listeners' perceptions of how fluid a speaker's speech seems. The most widely used fluency features as identified by Blake (2006) are the following: speech time or speech units (e.g. words, syllables) produced, speech rate (whether in second or minutes), and speech interruptions (including various characteristics of silent and filled pauses).

2.3.1 Speaking Time Difference

As a construct, speaking time frequently refers to the total time spent by a speaker to produce speech. This number could either include (phonation time ratio) or exclude (articulation rate) pauses. Such a calculation is effective for monologic tasks. When two speakers interact, however, the manner in which time is distributed between them is equally important. Conversational Analysis (CA) research has compared the lengths or the complexity of the runs (stretches of uninterrupted speech) between monologic and dialogic tasks (Nitta and Nakatsuhara 2014). Yet the actual distribution of the task time between two participants is rarely (if ever) included in the analyses.

2.3.2 Speech Rate

The speech rate of a speaker is usually calculated by dividing the total number of words by the total amount of time of the speech or per one minute of speaking time. Some researchers also consider hesitations and false starts when counting the number of words (Riggenbach 1991). The total speaking time in this case also includes the pauses between individual stretches of speech. Studies have shown that speech rate is a suprasegmental feature that correlates with accentedness, especially when, most often than not, nonnative speakers are slower than native speakers (Munro and Derwing 1998; Kang et al. 2010). Speech rate has been likewise employed as a variable in L2 pronunciation for two main reasons: to differentiate between L1 and L2 speech and to evaluate oral proficiency. This fluency measure, in particular, has been said to strongly correlate with accentedness (Munro and Derwing 1998).

2.3.3 Pauses

A pause is identified as the silent or filled time between two stretches of speech or a run. Two types of pauses are frequently examined in L2 pronunciation research: filled and silent pauses. Filled pauses (e.g., *um* and *uh*) have been described by some research as having a function, e.g., as discourse markers used to prevent lull time or gain some time for thought. Studies have revealed that filled pauses are least associated with disfluency and often introduce rather complex grammatical structures (Lennon 1990; Swerts 1998).

Silent pauses are identified as the absence of speech between runs. L2 speaking research has focused on the correlation between the number of silent pauses and accentedness ratings. Some studies have demonstrated that a pause as short as 0.1 seconds is effective enough to cue accentedness (Kang 2010). Research has consistently demonstrated that pauses are longer and more frequent in a learner's second language than their first (Cucchiarini, Strik, and Boves 2001;

Riazantseva 2001; Riggenbach 1991). Interest has also emerged in assessing the location of these pauses (particularly silent ones). Studies have revealed that the location of a pause (at a phrasal boundary or within a phrase) and its duration (Freed 2000; Kang and Wang 2014) vary among proficiency levels. Silent pauses can also affect another measure: average run duration. Since pauses of various lengths interrupt runs, then the mean length of a run would be negatively correlated with the number and length of pauses. This fluency feature has also been shown to correlate with fluency measures and ratings (Towell et al. 1996).

2.4 Prosodic Features

Prosodic features are suprasegmental measures that relate to connected speech. Several constructs are often included within this category, such as tone choice, prominent syllables, among others. The current study only focuses on one prosodic feature: pitch range. A speaker's overall pitch variation is used to determine the extent to which a speaker fluctuates his/her pitch. Studies in L2 pronunciation have revealed that L2 speakers often exhibit a more restricted pitch range than L1 speakers (Kang 2013; Staples 2015). L2 learners particularly struggle with falling intonation to indicate the finality of a statement. That is most often the case because their pitch does not fall far enough to indicate a change (Binghadeer 2008). The potential lack in pitch variation might create a monotonous speech pattern and possibly even hinder comprehension. This has been shown to be particularly true with nonnative speakers who have been shown to use a more restricted pitch range than native speakers (Wennerstrom 1997; Pickering 2004; Busa and Urbani 2011).

2.5 Collaboration

Numerous studies have investigated the construct of collaboration or "communicative competence" in oral communication (Arter 1989; Celce-Murcia et al. 1995). The measure is most often defined as the speaker's ability to interact with his/her interlocutor in such a way that s/he responds to the interlocutor's ideas and builds upon them (Ron 2011). In other words, it is the speaker's ability to truly make a conversation dialogic in nature.

For collaboration to occur, a speaker should maintain communicative competence. This characteristic has been defined as the speaker's use of linguistic competence in a specific social context (Arter 1989). For this reason, the measure is most often defined as the speaker's ability to interact with their interlocutor in such a way that s/he builds upon the interlocutor's ideas in order to achieve some purpose or complete a task (Ron 2011). Research has demonstrated that many language learners exhibit proficient linguistic competence when in monologic or isolated environments (Okada 2015). Natural conversation, however, involves more than simply understanding the interlocutor's meaning. It is the speaker's ability to respond to that utterance or extend it in such a way that makes the conversation essentially dialogic. Research has shown that collaboration in dialogic tasks has a significant effect on the overall communication success of a particular interaction. Okada (2015) determined that Oral Proficiency Interviews (OPIs) cannot be successful unless the interviewer and interviewee play a certain role and they both produce utterances that are consistent with the roles they have. Ohta (2001) demonstrated that collaboration during a peer-to-peer interaction enhanced performance and was itself a form of learning while performing a speaking task. Collaboration while performing a speaking task influenced both high and low proficiency speakers, particularly in the grammatical and lexical complexity of their productions.

Second language speakers' suprasegmental features have frequently been investigated in relation to their effect on intelligibility, accentedness, and comprehension. Research into second language pronunciation has revealed that speakers employ a much more restricted pitch range while producing speech in English (Binghadeer 2008; Busa and Urbani 2011; Taniguchi 2001). Other studies have demonstrated that L2 speakers are more likely to produce longer silent pauses than native speakers (Riggenbach 1991; Riazantseva 2001) which could cause loss of a message or idea. Few studies, however, specifically investigate the effect of a speakers' use of pronunciation features (mainly suprasegmental features) on the collaboration scores of a given task.

2.6 Pronunciation Scores and Task Type Differences

The effect of task manipulation on L2 speaker production has been a topic of interest to many SLA researchers in the last few decades (Long 2016; Skehan 2014). Task Based Language Teaching (TBLT) has gained traction as its own sub-field in SLA and second language teaching. Studies have been able to prove that linguistic resources, task complexity, and task type play a major role in a learner's ability to complete a task successfully (Kormos 2011; Robinson 2011). The data that are typically analyzed, however, are most often related to writing features such as lexico-grammatical factors (Plonksy and Kim 2016). The relationship between task complexity and pronunciation features have rarely been investigated and even when they are, not as the primary focus of the study. In fact, even when speech production and task types are investigated, pronunciation is only one of several factors being explored, most often including grammar and lexis (Gurzynski-Weiss, Long, and Solon 2017). Some research has focused on the production of segmentals based on the formality of the task whereas other studies examined the effects of task type on both the accuracy and complexity of the production (Rau, Chang, and Tarone 2009; Robinson 2011). Accuracy and complexity, however, were measured from a lexico-grammatical standpoint.

Similarly, studies in L2 speaking, particularly those investigating the relationship between pronunciation features and rater perceptions frequently include one type of task in the analysis. More recent pronunciation research has attempted to fill the gap between TBLT research and the evaluation of L2 spoken discourse (Crowther, Isaacs, and Saito 2015; Derwing et al. 2004). However, as these studies mention, research is still not quite robust and the range of variables as they relate to pronunciation output are still limited (Crowther et al. 2015).

As can be seen from the above review, a large number of studies have demonstrated the relationship between pronunciation features, particularly, suprasegmental features and various measures of evaluation. However, few studies have examined analytic scores or those related to collaboration. Additionally, task type difference is still an under-researched area in the field of second language pronunciation. The following study examines the relationship between rater-assigned scores as they relate to communication success and pronunciation features, namely suprasegmental features as produced by ESL students. The variation between two types of tasks (informative and opinion-based) is also investigated in order to determine the effect of task type on the production of suprasegmental features as well as collaboration scores. In order to address these matters, the following research questions were explored:

1. To what extent do certain prosodic and fluency features predict scores in dialogic tasks?
   a. To what extent do certain prosodic and fluency features predict overall scores in dialogic tasks?
   b. To what extent do certain prosodic and fluency features predict collaboration scores in dialogic tasks?
2. To what extent do certain prosodic and fluency features predict scores in informative tasks?
   a. To what extent do certain prosodic and fluency features predict overall scores in informative tasks?
   b. To what extent do certain prosodic and fluency features predict collaboration scores in informative tasks?

3. To what extent do certain prosodic and fluency features predict scores in opinion-based tasks?
   a. To what extent do certain prosodic and fluency features predict overall scores in opinion-based tasks?
   b. To what extent do certain prosodic and fluency features predict collaboration scores in opinion-based tasks?
4. How does task type (informative vs. opinion-based) affect the values of pronunciation features?

3 Methods

3.1 The Corpus

The data used in this study were extracted from the Corpus of Collaborative Oral Tasks (CCOT) (Crawford and McDonough this volume), which includes 775 tasks and is a little over 250,000 words in total. The corpus is a collection of evaluative tasks produced by second language learners in an Intensive English Program and covers a range of various proficiency levels as well as first languages. The student proficiency levels include Level 1(TOEFL iBT score range: 32–44), Level 2 (TOEFL iBT score range: 45–56) and Level 3 (TOEFL iBT score range: 57–69). The speech files had already been transcribed and reviewed by the corpus creators. Each file was deidentified and the speakers were referred to as A or B throughout the interaction.

3.2 Rubric

Every speech file included in this study was graded by two trained raters whose scores were averaged for each participant. The two speakers received the same scores which included the following: 1) collaboration (out of 4); 2) task completion (out of 4); 3) style (out of 4); 4) overall score (out of 12). The focus of the study is collaboration between the two speakers. For this reason, the style and task completion components were excluded from the analyses. The two main outcome variables explored were thus the overall scores and the collaboration component allocated for each interaction.

For three of the interactions, the rubric included 5 bands instead of 4 and therefore the scores were recalculated in order to align with the rest of the participant scores. For all the tasks examined in this paper, two raters provided each pair of speakers a single score for collaboration, task completion, and style. The participant overall score was calculated by first averaging the two raters' scores for each construct and then adding all three sub-scores for an overall score.

3.3 Data

A total of 28 speech files were analyzed in this study, with two task types included: informative and opinion-based/argumentative tasks. Both tasks were dialogic in nature and each participant's pronunciation features were analyzed individually, therefore a total number of 56 data points were included in the statistical analyses. The informative task (N=13 files) provided both speakers with pieces of information in relation to crime and economy. The students were asked to share this information with each other and come up with the most pertinent cause to crime statistics in a particular country. Students compared graphs as well as numbers and were asked to discuss reasons as well as solutions for the crime statistics they share. Both speakers were each given 3 minutes to plan their ideas individually before starting the activity.

The second task (N=15 files) gave the two students opposing views with regard to workplace monitoring. One student was asked to push for the surveillance of employees especially due to issues in productivity and thefts. The other student would oppose monitoring and was asked to counter the arguments that support such a practice. For this task, students were provided with specific guidelines in relation to polite interruptions as well as respecting their partner's opinions while disagreeing with them. Both students had three minutes to plan their arguments and/or rebuttals.

3.4 Speakers

The speakers whose speech data was analyzed consisted of 34 individuals in total: 28 male and 6 female speakers. Several L1s were represented: Arabic (12), Japanese (3), Korean (2), and Chinese (17). The speaker description identified the proficiency level as Level 3, which corresponds to a score range of 57–69 on the TOEFL iBT.

Several students contributed more than one file to the analysis; however, no student performed the same task twice with the same interlocutor. Therefore, for each speaker, every interaction was a new one with a different partner. For this reason, the analyses conducted in this study focused on the speech files and the contributions by the speakers in that interaction. Thus, even though there were only 34 individuals whose speech was examined, 56 separate contributions (or individual data points) were in fact analyzed.

3.5 Data Coding

The speech files were coded by two phonologically trained researchers. Ten percent of the total number of files were coded by both, with a high inter-rater reliability (α >.90). The rest of the files were distributed equally and analyzed by each individual separately.

The variables were extracted using two computer programs: ELAN and PRAAT (Boersma and Weenink 2019). PRAAT was first used to automatically identify pause location and ELAN was used to manually edit the PRAAT Textgrid for inconsistencies. ELAN was also used to distribute transcriptions, speaking time, and silent pauses for each of the two speakers. This was done through the creation of separate tiers for each speaker and their silent pauses. The program then automatically calculated the following: average turn length, silent pause count and average length, total speaking time for each participant (time difference was calculated by subtracting the two speakers' speech values). A computer program was then utilized to calculate total number of words for each speaker. PRAAT was used to identify the average pitch range for each participant, by extracting the pitch range for each run. Since the tasks were conducted in a room with other students participating, background noise was common in the various recordings, and values were sometimes affected by this factor. Extreme values, such as pitches that were too high or too low for the speaker, were manually checked and modified by the researchers when needed.

3.6 Data Analysis

Seven pronunciation features were analyzed in this study: six fluency features (speech rate, average run duration, number and length of silent pauses, number of filled pauses, and speaking time difference), and one prosodic feature (mean pitch range). Table 1 provides a summary of the description and operationalization of each variable. The pronunciation features from each speaker were considered as a single data point even though raters provided a common score for the two speakers. The primary reason to adopt this type of analysis is to evaluate each speaker's individual phonological contribution to the scores attained as a pair, particularly features that relate to communicative success and collaboration.

Speech rate is often calculated by one of two methods: 1) dividing the number of syllables by the total speaking time, or 2) calculating the number of words per minute. The latter calculation was adopted for this study. Pauses that were less than 0.25 seconds were disregarded in the analysis of the data. The primary reason for this decision is the research that has shown that shorter pauses can usually be regarded as hesitations or may occur due to other segmental phenomena such as voicing (De Jong and Bosker 2013; Towell et al. 1996). Runs, therefore, were calculated as any speaking time between two pauses equal or greater than .25 seconds. Mean pitch range values were obtained by calculating the average pitch variation (F_0 maxima – F_0 minima) for total runs produced by individual speakers. Pronunciation studies might focus on pitch values assigned to prominent syllables in a tone unit rather than the overall pitch variation (Brazil 1997). The calculations in this case are performed by examining the pitch values on the key (first) and termination (last) prominent syllable in a given tone unit. A large body of research, however, has demonstrated that L2 speakers tend to produce an inaccurate number of prominent syllables, usually more than what is required (Wennerstrom 1997; Kang 2010). Thus, pitch range was calculated by subtracting the highest F_0 value from the lowest value in each run. This allowed for a better description of the student's variation in pitch which may or may not have been used on the termination or key syllables as would be expected from a native speaker. The collaboration and overall scores were obtained by averaging the two raters' scores for both speakers of that task.

Table 1: Description of suprasegmental measures.

Variable	Description	Measurement
Speech Rate	mean number of words produced per minute for each speaker	number of words/minute
Speaking Time Difference	distribution of speaking time between the two speakers	Speaker A total time-Speaker B total time
Average Run Duration	average uninterrupted speaking time between two pauses	Mean speaking time between two pauses = or >.25 seconds
Silent Pauses	total number of silent pauses per speaker	silence = or >.25 seconds
Mean Pause Length	average length of silent pauses for each speaker	Mean (silence = or >.25 seconds)
Filled Pauses	total number of filled pauses per speaker	words including uh, um
Mean Pitch Range	range of pitch variation for the entire speech of each speaker	Mean (F_0 maxima – F_0 minima) per run

4 Results

The first three research questions investigated the correlation between seven pronunciation features and outcome scores on individual (informative and opinion-based) or combined dialogic tasks. Multiple Regression models were examined as well as various correlation values between the scores and values of pronunciation features. The fourth research question explored the differences in the production of pronunciation features between the informative and opinion-based task. The results for RQ4 were thus descriptive in nature and sought to simply explore pronunciation trends as they relate to various task types.

4.1 Combined Tasks

The first research question examined the extent to which certain prosodic and fluency features predict scores for the combined tasks (informative and argumentative). Two Multiple Regression analyses were conducted with all seven pronunciation features acting as the predictor variables. The two outcome variables were: 1) the overall student score (first general model), and 2) the collaboration component of the student score (second general model).

4.1.1 First General Model (Total Score for Combined Tasks)

Results of the regression show that the model was a good fit $F(7,48)=18.56$, p=.000). The pronunciation features accounted for 69% of the variance in the total score for both task types. Four features were significant predictors: average run duration (p=.000) with a moderate positive correlation coefficient (r=.4), speech rate (p=.000) with a low negative correlation coefficient (r= −.22), number of pauses (p=.035) with a moderate negative correlation coefficient (r= −.42), and pause mean length (p=.013) with a moderate negative correlation coefficient (r= −.49).

Table 2: Coefficient and correlation results for total score.

Model		Unstandardized Coefficients		Standardized Coefficients	t	Sig.	Correlations		
		B	Std. Error	Beta			Zero-order	Partial	Part
1	(Constant)	12.381	1.182		10.471	.000			
	Av Run Duration	2.331	.390	.824	5.969	.000	.395	.653	.447
	Speech Rate (WPM)	−.115	.015	−.903	−7.686	.000	−.217	−.743	−.576
	Number of Pauses	−.032	.015	−.221	−2.174	.035	−.415	−.299	−.163
	Pause Mean Length	−3.049	1.179	−.245	−2.586	.013	−.486	−.350	−.194
	Average Pitch Range	−.006	.004	−.117	−1.342	.186	.168	−.190	−.101
	Speaking Time Difference	−.010	.006	−.133	−1.646	.106	−.067	−.231	−.123
	Filled Pauses	.009	.014	.055	.618	.540	.162	.089	.046

4.1.2 Second General Model (Collaboration Score for the Combined Tasks)

Results of the regression show that the model was a good fit $F(7,48)=4.748$, p=.000). The pronunciation features accounted for 32% of the variance in the collaboration component for both task types. Three features were significant predictors: average run duration (p=.000) with a low positive correlation coefficient (r=.38), speech rate (p=.000) with a low positive correlation coefficient (r= .01) and pause mean length (p=0.31) with a moderate negative correlation coefficient (r=−.46).

Table 3: Coefficient and correlation results for collaboration component.

Model		Unstandardized Coefficients		Standardized Coefficients	t	Sig.	Correlations		
		B	Std. Error	Beta			Zero-order	Partial	Part
1	(Constant)	8.487	.352		24.088	.000			
	Av Run Duration	.608	.543	.488	1.119	.278	.319	.255	.214
	Speech Rate (WPM)	−.578	.436	−.540	−1.326	.202	.151	−.298	−.253
	Number of Pauses	−.259	.351	−.221	−.737	.471	−.414	−.171	−.141
	Pause Mean Length	−.330	.255	−.325	−1.295	.212	−.426	−.292	−.248
	Average Pitch Range	−.074	.265	−.064	−.280	.782	.122	−.066	−.054
	Speaking Time Difference	−.202	.241	−.181	−.839	.413	−.012	−.194	−.160
	Filled Pauses	−.205	.317	−.167	−.646	.527	−.260	−.150	−.123

4.2 Informative Task

The second research question investigated the extent to which certain prosodic and fluency features predict scores for the informative task. Two Multiple Regression analyses were conducted with the seven pronunciation features acting as the predictor variables. The two outcome variables were: 1) the total score for the informative task (first general model), and 2) the collaboration component of the informative task score (second general model).

4.2.1 First General Model (Total Score for Informative Task)

Results of the regression show that the model was not a good fit $F(7,18)=1.336$, $p=.290$). No pronunciation features were significant predictors of the total score for the informative task. The following pronunciation features had high correlation values: average run duration ($r=.32$), number of pauses ($r=-.41$), and pause mean length ($r=-.43$).

Table 4: Coefficient and correlation results for informative task total score.

Model		Unstandardized Coefficients		Standardized Coefficients	t	Sig.	Correlations		
		B	Std. Error	Beta			Zero-order	Partial	Part
1	(Constant)	8.487	.352		24.088	.000			
	Av Run Duration	.608	.543	.488	1.119	.278	.319	.255	.214
	Speech Rate (WPM)	−.578	.436	−.540	−1.326	.202	.151	−.298	−.253
	Number of Pauses	−.259	.351	−.221	−.737	.471	−.414	−.171	−.141
	Pause Mean Length	−.330	.255	−.325	−1.295	.212	−.426	−.292	−.248
	Average Pitch Range	−.074	.265	−.064	−.280	.782	.122	−.066	−.054
	Speaking Time Difference	−.202	.241	−.181	−.839	.413	−.012	−.194	−.160
	Filled Pauses	−.205	.317	−.167	−.646	.527	−.260	−.150	−.123

4.2.2 Second General Model (Collaboration Score for the Informative Task)

Results of the regression show that the model was not a good fit $F(7,18)=.893$, $p=.532$). No pronunciation features were significant predictors of the collaboration score for the informative task. The following pronunciation features had correlation values worth mentioning: average run duration (r=.35), speech rate (r=.38), number of pauses (r= −.41), and pause mean length (r=−.36).

Table 5: Coefficient and correlation results for collaboration score of informative task.

Model		Unstandardized Coefficients		Standardized Coefficients	t	Sig.	Correlations		
		B	Std. Error	Beta			Zero-order	Partial	Part
1	(Constant)	2.909	.225		12.930	.000			
	Av Run Duration	-.097	.347	-.130	-.280	.783	.346	-.066	-.057
	Speech Rate (WPM)	.167	.278	.260	.601	.555	.375	.140	.122
	Number of Pauses	-.145	.224	-.205	-.644	.528	-.408	-.150	-.131
	Pause Mean Length	-.160	.163	-.262	-.982	.339	-.364	-.225	-.199
	Average Pitch Range	-.003	.169	-.005	-.020	.984	.120	-.005	-.004
	Speaking Time Difference	-.058	.154	-.086	-.375	.712	-.099	-.088	-.076
	Filled Pauses	-.067	.203	-.091	-.332	.744	-.202	-.078	-.067

4.3 Opinion Based Task

The third research question examined the extent to which the selected pronunciation features predict scores for the opinion-based task. Two Multiple Regression analyses were conducted with the seven pronunciation features acting as the predictor variables. The two outcome variables were: 1) the total score for the opinion-based task (first general model), and 2) the collaboration component of the opinion-based task score (second general model).

4.3.1 First General Model (Total Score for the Opinion-Based Task)

Results of the regression show that the model was a good fit $F(7,22)=16.996$, p=.000). The pronunciation features accounted for 79% of the variance in the opinion-based task total score. Three pronunciation features were significant predictors of the score: average run duration (p=.000) with a moderate positive correlation coefficient (r= .46), speech rate (p=.000) with a low positive correlation coefficient (r=.13), and speaking time difference (p=.018) with a moderate negative correlation coefficient (r=−.40). Average pitch range was also near significant (p=.090). Other features with significant correlation values include number of pauses (r= −.36) and number of filled pauses (r= .23).

Table 6: Coefficient and correlation results for opinion-based task total score.

Model		Unstandardized Coefficients		Standardized Coefficients	t	Sig.	Correlations		
		B	Std. Error	Beta			Zero-order	Partial	Part
1	(Constant)	9.202	.151		61.136	.000			
	Av Run Duration	1.611	.196	1.873	8.223	.000	.457	.869	.693
	Speech Rate (WPM)	−1.895	.245	−1.691	−7.747	.000	.132	−.855	−.652
	Number of Pauses	−.103	.105	−.114	−.980	.338	−.358	−.204	−.083
	Pause Mean Length	−.177	.136	−.150	−1.299	.207	−.187	−.267	−.109
	Average Pitch Range	−.170	.096	−.189	−1.774	.090	−.045	−.354	−.149
	Speaking Time Difference	−.240	.094	−.266	−2.566	.018	−.398	−.480	−.216
	Filled Pauses	.105	.085	.120	1.224	.234	.231	.252	.103

4.3.2 Second General Model (Collaboration Score for the Opinion-Based Task)

Results of the regression show that the model was a good fit $F(7,22)=2.853$, p=.028). The pronunciation features accounted for 31% of the variance in the collaboration component of the opinion-based task score. Two pronunciation features were significant predictors of the score: average run duration (p=.010) with a moderate positive correlation coefficient (r= .37) and speech rate (p=.021) with a low positive correlation coefficient (r=.19). Speaking time difference was also near significant (p=.065). Other features with significant correlation values include number of pauses (r= −.28), pause mean length (r= −.26) and speaking time difference (r= −.48).

Table 7: Coefficient and correlation results for collaboration score of opinion-based task.

Model		Unstandardized Coefficients		Standardized Coefficients	t	Sig.	Correlations		
		B	Std. Error	Beta			Zero-order	Partial	Part
1	(Constant)	3.348	.118		28.380	.000			
	Av Run Duration	.433	.154	1.177	2.820	.010	.368	.515	.435
	Speech Rate (WPM)	−.477	.192	−.995	−2.488	.021	.189	−.469	−.384
	Number of Pauses	−.002	.082	−.005	−.026	.980	−.281	−.005	−.004
	Pause Mean Length	−.096	.107	−.189	−.898	.379	−.256	−.188	−.139
	Average Pitch Range	−.055	.075	−.142	−.729	.474	−.054	−.154	−.113
	Speaking Time Difference	−.142	.073	−.369	−1.940	.065	−.477	−.382	−.299
	Filled Pauses	−.025	.067	−.067	−.375	.711	.043	−.080	−.058

4.4 Task-Based Pronunciation Differences

The fourth research question examined whether the selected fluency and prosodic features were produced differently in the two tasks. Since the two tasks were not completed by the same students, this part of the study adopted a descriptive approach by simply exploring the mean differences in the pronunciation values between the two tasks. As can be seen Table 8 below, the opinion-based task registered higher means for the following suprasegmental features: average run duration, average pitch range, speaking time difference, and number of filled pauses. Students who completed the informative task, on the other hand, produced a higher speech rate and a higher number of pauses and pause length.

Table 8: Descriptive statistics for differences in pronunciation features between both tasks.

	TT	N	Mean	Std. Deviation	Std. Error Mean
Av Run Duration	Inf	26	1.7475	.46944	.09206
	Op	30	1.9497	.57409	.10481
Speech Rate (WPM)	Inf	26	44.0193	12.08049	2.36918
	Op	30	34.5244	9.75894	1.78173
Number of Pauses	Inf	26	31.788	9.6728	1.8970
	Op	30	27.167	10.6028	1.9358
Pause Mean Length	Inf	26	.5610	.13085	.02566
	Op	30	.4689	.09497	.01734
Average Pitch Range	Inf	26	67.7372	29.49070	5.78360
	Op	30	79.7215	32.01201	5.84457
Speaking Time Difference	Inf	26	18.5300	18.74897	3.67698
	Op	30	22.0552	19.69104	3.59508
Filled Pauses	Inf	26	12.9231	8.63446	1.69336
	Op	30	17.0000	10.23853	1.86929

Note: Op=Opinion-based task; Inf=informative task.

5 Discussion

The first three research questions investigated the degree to which seven pronunciation features: speech rate, speaking time difference, average run duration, length and number of silent pauses, number of filled pauses, and mean pitch range successfully predicted various scores on two types of dialogic tasks. Table 9 summarizes the significant correlations between pronunciation features and various scores. As the results below demonstrate, general patterns emerge for general speaking tasks whereas others are more task-specific. A fluency feature that is consistently positively correlated with all types of scores is average run duration. Additionally, the two features that are frequently shown to yield a negative correlation with scores are silent pause length and number. All three features point towards the same outcome: a learner's ability to form long stretches of speech without any long hesitations and interruptions. These fluency markers have been consistently shown to discriminate among various proficiency levels and affect raters' perception of the speech production (Cucchiarini, Strik, and Boves 2001; Riazantseva 2001; Riggenbach 1991; Towell et al. 1996).

Table 9: Summary of the correlations between pronunciation features and various scores.

	Both Tasks		Informative		Opinion-Based	
	Overall	Collab	Overall	Collab	Overall	Collab
Speech Rate	−	+		+	+	+
Speaking Time Difference					−	−
Average Run Duration	+	+	+	+	+	+
Silent Pauses	−		−	−	−	−
Mean Pause Length	−	−	−	−		−
Filled Pauses					+	
Mean Pitch Range						

Note: Collab=collaboration score.

The first research question examined the extent to which values for certain pronunciation features predict second language learners' collaboration and overall scores on both dialogic tasks. Multiple regression results demonstrated that the model was a good fit and that the features accounted for 69% of the variance of the total score and 32% of the collaboration component. The findings corroborate those from previous studies which show that pronunciation features, particularly suprasegmental ones, frequently account for a high variance in scores and speaker proficiency (Kang et al. 2010). The features that correlated the highest with the scores were speech rate, average run duration, as well as number and mean length of pauses. This finding is also consistent with research which demonstrated that fluency features tend to correlate highly with rater scores even when raters are not consciously listening for or paying attention to such constructs (Ginther et al. 2010). Certain pronunciation features additionally showed some correlation with specific components of the score or with a particular task.

The second research question explored the relationship between pronunciation features and informative task scores. Results demonstrated that the model was not a good fit for the overall score and the collaboration component. This finding reveals that when it comes to exchanging information, the selected pronunciation features for this study may not be as important as they are for opinion-based tasks. Previous studies have shown that the spontaneous relaying of information is usually less accurate but more complex than scripted texts (Rau, Chang, and Tarone 2009). It is possible, therefore, that the features that strongly predicted the scores for this particular task type are more closely related to grammatical and lexical factors. It is also possible that more task-specific pronunciation features, such as narrative tone choice, could be more accurate predictors of this particular model. These features, however, are beyond the purview of this study.

The third research question investigated the correlation between pronunciation features and the various speaking scores for the opinion-based task. Findings showed that the models were a good fit for both outcome variables: total score and collaboration score. In fact, the selected pronunciation features accounted for 79% of the variance in the total score of the opinion-based task. The results confirm that certain pronunciation features are good predictors of a student's communication success, especially when it comes to opinion-based activities. The ability to collaborate with an interlocutor and complete the task at hand require a learner to not only use the correct lexico-grammatical tools but also be able to communicate effectively through phonological processes (Arter 1989). In this study, these processes included having a wide enough pitch range, utilizing pauses effectively, speaking with a high enough speech rate and yielding (or taking) the floor when necessary.

The results also suggest that when it comes to the opinion-based task, certain fluency and prosodic features do influence the rater's overall and various component scores. Unlike the informative task, some of the pronunciation features are quite critical to the completion and success of an opinion-based task. One particular feature that is of interest is speaking time difference. This feature proved to be significantly correlated with the total task score and the collaboration component of the rubric. While reviewing the speech files, it became clear that a disproportionate time distribution frequently indicated one of two things: a) consistent interruptions from one of the speakers without giving the other speaker a chance to respond or b) a constant relinquishing of the floor by one of the speakers and agreeing with what their partner says almost instantly instead of providing valid arguments.

The fourth research question compared the use of the seven pronunciation features between the informative and opinion-based task. Even though some of the same students did undertake both tasks at different points in time, the two groups of participants were not identical and so the results analyzed for this question simply show a possible trend in the use of pronunciation features by intermediate nonnative speakers. Descriptive statistics showed that the speech rate was much higher for the informative task than for the opinion-based task. This finding is consistent with research that has examined task effects on L2 speech production. Tasks that are discursive in nature allow for speech outputs to be less accurate but more complex, hence the higher number of filled pauses and slower speech rate (Skehan and Foster 1997). However, for all other suprasegmental features that frequently discriminate among proficiency levels, the values were consistently better for the opinion-based task. Students produced a wider pitch range, fewer and shorter silent pauses, and longer runs with the opinion-based task. In contrast, they produced a higher number of and longer silent pauses while participating in the informative task. This finding could indicate that opinion-based tasks were better designed for this level of students or that argumentation encourages learners to produce more intelligible speech. In addition, scores on both tasks proved to counter the literature that suggests that more complex tasks lead to lower scores and lower accuracy. This was verified by comparing the overall scores between the two tasks and it was shown that opinion-based task scores ($M=10.25$) were in fact higher than informative task scores ($M=8.00$). However, since the two groups compared were not identical, the results may not be accurately comparing the task effects on students' performance.

6 Conclusion

This study examined the relationship between seven pronunciation features and various score components of two types of speaking tasks: opinion-based and informative. While pronunciation research has explored a vast number of segmental and suprasegmental variables that best predict pronunciation scores, very few studies have compared these variables across different task types and score components. Results demonstrated that certain pronunciation features are better predictors for specific speaking tasks. When combined, the seven pronunciation features accounted for a high percentage in the score variation for both tasks. However, when analyzed individually, findings revealed that the fluency and prosodic features selected were better suited predictors for the opinion-based task. The results have implications that extend to pronunciation research in general and second language pronunciation classrooms.

This study has explored an area that has not been thoroughly investigated when it comes to the evaluation of spoken discourse. Most studies rely on specific types of tasks, including monologic or a single type of dialogic task. Very few studies have explored the variation in suprasegmental features across various task types. The results demonstrate that this is an important area to investigate as some features have proven to be more crucial to overall speaking scores or collaboration for some tasks than others. Future studies could compare speech production for multiple tasks produced by the same second language learners. Such studies may also include a larger number of segmental and suprasegmental features in the analysis with the use of ASRs. A more systematic examination of these speech files could provide a better understanding of what specific pronunciation features cue raters to provide a particular score on a given task type.

Another area that is important to mention is the pronunciation classroom. Although textbooks have recently included an array of suprasegmental features as part of the curriculum, the features are rarely associated with a particular task type. Findings in this study suggest that certain fluency features are much more important for opinion-based tasks than they are for informative tasks. This type of information is important to relay to students when explaining the characteristics of communication success and how it is measured in the classroom. It would also be of value to the learner to know that certain fluency features are of interest to native speakers during specific types of interactions. Thus, when a learner is expressing an opinion, or disagreeing with an interlocutor, they should be aware that politeness is not only exhibited through word choice and grammatical construction. The use of a wide pitch range, relinquishing the floor, and using pauses appropriately can also play a role in promoting interlocutor understanding and avoiding communication breakdown.

References

Arter, Judith. 1989. *Assessing communication competence in speaking and listening: A consumer's guide*. Portland, OR: Northwest Regional Educational Laboratory.
Binghadeer, Nora. 2008. An acoustic analysis of pitch range in the production of native and nonnative speakers of English. *Asian EFL Journal* 10(4). 96–113.
Blake, Christopher. 2006. *The potential of text-based internet chats for improving ESL oral fluency*. West Lafayette, IN: Purdue University dissertation.
Boersma, Paul & David Weenink 2019. Praat: doing phonetics by computer [Computer program]. Version 6.1.01, retrieved 14 August 2019 from http://www.praat.org/
Brazil, David. 1997. *The communicative value of intonation in English*. Cambridge, UK: Cambridge University Press.
Busà, Grazia & Martine Urbani. 2011. A cross linguistic analysis of pitch range in English L1 and L2. In *Proceedings of the 17th International Congress of Phonetic Sciences (ICPhS XVII)*, 380–383. Hong Kong: City University of Hong Kong.

Celce-Murcia, Marianne, Zoltan Dörnyei & Sarah Thurrell. 1995. Communicative competence: A pedagogically motivated model with content specifications. *Issues in Applied Linguistics* 6(2). 5–35.

Crowther, Dustin, Pavel Trofimovich, Talia Isaacs & Kazuya Saito. 2015. Does a speaking task affect second language comprehensibility? *The Modern Language Journal* 99(1). 80–95.

Cucchiarini Catia, Helmer Strik & Lou Boves L. 2002. Quantitative assessment of second language learners' fluency: Comparisons between read and spontaneous speech. *Journal of the Acoustical Society of America* 111(6). 2862–2873.

De Jong, Nivja & Hans Bosker. 2013. Choosing a threshold for silent pauses to measure second language fluency. Paper presented at the 6th Workshop on Disfluency in Spontaneous Speech.

Derwing, Tracey, Marian Rossiter, Murray Munro & Ron Thomson. 2004. Second language fluency: Judgments on different tasks. *Language Learning* 54(4). 655–679.

Flege, James & Robert Port. 1981. Cross-language phonetic interference: Arabic to English. *Language and Speech* 24(2). 125–146.

Freed, Barbara. 2000. Is fluency, like beauty, in the eyes (and ears) of the beholder? In Heidi Riggenbach (Ed.), *Perspectives on fluency*, 243–265. Michigan: The University of Michigan Press.

Ginther, April, Slobodanka Dimova & Rui Yang. 2010. Conceptual and empirical relationships between fluency measures of fluency and oral English proficiency with implications for automated scoring. *Language Testing* 27(3). 379–399.

Gurzynski-Weiss, Laura, Avizia Long & Megan Solon. 2017. TBLT and L2 pronunciation: Do the benefits of tasks extend beyond grammar and lexis? *Studies in Second Language Acquisition* 39(2). 213–224.

Hahn, Laura. 2004. Primary stress and intelligibility: Research to motivate the teaching of suprasegmentals. *TESOL Quarterly* 38(2). 201–223.

Jin, Tan & Barely Mak. 2012. Distinguishing features in scoring L2 Chinese speaking performance: How do they work? *Language Testing* 30(1). 23–47.

Kang, Okim. 2010. Salient prosodic features on judgments of second language accent. *System* 38. 301–315

Kang, Okim. 2013. Linguistic analysis of speaking features distinguishing general English exams at CEFR levels B1 to C2 and examinee L1 backgrounds. *Research Notes* 52. 40–48.

Kang, Okim & David Johnson. 2018. The roles of suprasegmental features in predicting English oral proficiency with an automated system. *Language Assessment Quarterly* 15(2). 150–168.

Kang, Okim & Lucy Pickering. 2013. Using acoustic and fluency analysis for assessing speaking. In Antony Kunnan (Ed.) *Companion to Language Assessment*, 1047–1062. West Sussex, UK: Wiley-Blackwell.

Kang, Okim & Donald Rubin. 2009. Reverse linguistic stereotyping: Measuring the effect of listener expectations on speech evaluation. *Journal of Language & Social Psychology* 28. 441–456.

Kang, Okim & Linxiao Wang. 2014. Impact of different task types on candidates' speaking performances. *Research Notes* 57. 40–49.

Kang, Okim, Donald Rubin & Lucy Pickering. 2010. Suprasegmental measures of accentedness and judgments of language learner proficiency in oral English. *The Modern Language Journal* 94(4). 554–566.

Kazemzadeh, Abe, Jospeh Tepperman, Jorge Silva, Hong You, Sungbok Lee, Abeer Alwan, & Shrikanth Narayanan. 2006. Automatic detection of voice onset time contrasts for use in pronunciation assessment. Paper presented at the *Ninth International Conference on Spoken Language Processing*.

Kormos, Judit. 2011. Speech production and the Cognition Hypothesis. In Peter Robinson (Ed.), *Second language task complexity: Researching the Cognition Hypothesis of language learning and performance*, 39–59. Philadelphia, PA: John Benjamins Publishing Company.

Lennon, Paul. 1990. Investigating fluency in EFL: A quantitative approach. *Language Learning* 40(3). 387–417.

Long, Michael. 2016. In defense of tasks and TBLT: Nonissues and real issues. *Annual Review of Applied Linguistics 36*. 5–33.

Macken, Marlys & Charles Ferguson. 1983. Cognitive aspects of phonological development: Model, evidence, and issues. In: Keith Nelson (Ed.), *Children's Language*, Vol. 4, 255–282. Hillsdale, NY: Erlbaum.

Munro, Murray & Tracey Derwing. 1998. The Effects of Speaking Rate on Listener Evaluations of Native and Foreign-Accented Speech. *Language Learning*. 48(2). 159–182.

Munro, Murray & Tracey Derwing. 2001. Modeling perceptions of the accentedness and comprehensibility of L2 speech the role of speaking rate. *Studies in Second Language Acquisition*. 23(4). 451–468.

Murphy, John. 2014. Teacher training programs provide adequate preparation in how to teach pronunciation. In Linda Grant (Ed.), *Pronunciation myths: Applying second language research to classroom teaching*, 188–224. Ann Arbor, MI: The University of Michigan Press.

Nitta, Ryo & Fumiyo Nakatsuhara. 2014. A multifaceted approach to investigating pre-task planning effects on paired oral test performance. *Language Testing* 31(2). 147–175.

Okada, Yusuke. 2015. Building rapport through sequentially linked joke-serious responses in second language job interviews. *Pragmatics and Society* 6(4). 593–614.

Ohta, Amy. 2001. Peer interactive tasks and assisted performance in classroom language learning. In Amy Ohta (Ed.), *Second language acquisition processes in the classroom: Learning Japanese*, 73–128. Mahwah, NJ: Lawrence Erlbaum.

Peters, Theodore & Barry Guitar. 1991. *Stuttering: An integrated approach to its nature and treatment*. Baltimore, MD: William & Wilkins.

Pickering, Lucy. 2004. The structure and function of intonational paragraphs in native and nonnative speaker instructional discourse. *English for Specific Purposes* 23(1). 19–43.

Plonsky, Luke & Youjin Kim. 2016. Task-based learner production: A substantive and methodological review. *Annual Review of Applied Linguistics 36*. 73–97.

Rau, Victoria, Hui-Huan Chang, Ann & Elaine Tarone. 2009. Think or sink: Chinese learners' acquisition of the English voiceless interdental fricative. *Language Learning* 59(3). 581–621.

Riazantseva, Anastasia. 2001. Second language proficiency and pausing a study of Russian speakers of English. *Studies in Second Language Acquisition* 23(4). 497–526.

Riggenbach, Heidi. 1991. Toward an understanding of fluency: A microanalysis of nonnative speaker conversations. *Discourse Processes* 14(4). 423–441.

Robinson, Peter. 2011. Task-based language learning: A review of issues. *Language learning* 61. 1–36.

Ron, Martin. 2011. A pilot EFL oral communication test for Japanese elementary school students. *Language, Culture, and Communication* 3. 153–173.

Skehan, Peter. 2014. *Processing perspectives on task performance*. Amsterdam, The Netherlands: Benjamins.

Staples, Shelley. 2015. *The Discourse of Nurse-Patient Interactions: Contrasting the communicative styles of U.S. and international nurses*. Philadelphia: John Benjamins.

Swerts, Marc. 1998. Filled pauses as markers of discourse structure. *Journal of Pragmatics* 30. 485–496.

Taniguchi, Masaki. 2001. *Japanese EFL learners' weak points in English intonation*. Paper presented at the 2001 Phonetics Teaching and Learning Conference, London.

Towell, Richard, Roger Hawkins & Nives Bazergui. 1996. The development of fluency in advanced learners of French *Applied Linguistics* 17(1). 84–119.

Trofimovich, Pavel & Wendy Baker. 2006. Learning second language suprasegmentals: Effect of L2 experience on prosody and fluency characteristics of L2 speech. *Studies in Second Language Acquisition* 28 (1). 1–30.

Trofimovich, Pavel & Talia Isaacs. 2012. Disentangling accent from comprehensibility. *Bilingualism: Language and Cognition* 15(4). 905–916.

Wennerstrom, Ann. 1997. Discourse intonation and second language acquisition: Three genre based studies. Seattle, WA: University of Washington dissertation, Seattle.

Appendix
A Detailed Description of Tasks in the Corpus of Collaborative Oral Tasks (CCOT)

Because the tasks in the CCOT were a part of the formative assessment purposes, some tasks or rubrics were modified for curricular or administrative reasons. Most of the differences within and across tasks are related to 1) when the task was done in relation to the other part of the exam; 2) planning time differences; 3) whether the planning was done individually, collaboratively, or both individually and collaboratively; 4) time to complete task; 5) whether grading requirements were shared with the students prior to doing the task; and 6) rubric differences concerning format, descriptors and point spreads (e.g., some rubrics contain aspects scored from 0–4; others are scored from 2.5–4). In cases where there are differences in tasks and/or rubrics, all versions of the tasks and rubrics are provided. Below are descriptions of each task, including any differences across tasks. For each task, the following information is provided:

1. Task name (and number)
2. Proficiency level of students
3. The number of different task versions
4. Administration time for each task: By semester (F=Fall; SP=Spring; SU=Summer); Year (09=2009; 10=2010; 11=2011; 12=2012) and week of the semester (e.g., 5, 7, 10)
5. Planning time allotted for each task
6. Planning type (collaborative, individual)
7. Version(s) of each task
8. Rubric(s) used to score the tasks

Advertisement (Task #2)

Proficiency level: 1
Task versions: 1
Administration time: 3: A: F10wk5, SP11wk5; B: F11wk5; C: F12wk7
Planning time: A 5 minutes; B, C 3 minutes
Planning type: Collaborative
Task completion time: A: 3–4 minutes; B, C: 2 minutes
Rubric types: 2

Task

Look at the following products or ads. With you partner, choose one of the ads or products to create a radio advertisement. You will have X minutes to discuss and plan your advertisement with your partner. Your commercial must be X minutes. Use the blank space on the next page to plan your radio advertisement.

Your radio commercial must include the following elements:
1) clear identification of your product
2) the effective use of a positive or negative appeal
3) the effective use of one of the "Attention Grabbers" discussed in Unit 1
4) equal speaking parts for you and your partner

Picture of a sports drink	Picture of a person smoking
Picture of a razor	Picture of a camera

Rubrics

Version A, B

	Collaboration	Task completion	Style
4	Both learners: – Work together on almost all parts of the task – Carefully respond to each other and engage each other's ideas – Offer constructive feedback	– Excellent completion of the task; all required elements of the task are present – Content is rich; ideas developed with elaboration and detail; overall task outcome is outstanding	– Excellent use of attention grabbers – Have excellent skills in providing reasons and elaborating ideas – Have excellent skills in utilizing positive and/or negative appeals
3	Both learners: – Work together on most parts of the tasks – Respond to each other and engage each other's ideas – Offer some feedback	– Good completion of the task; almost all required elements are present – Responses appropriate and with some elaboration and detail; overall task outcome is satisfactory	– Good use of attention grabbers – Have good skills in providing reasons and elaborating ideas – Have good skills in utilizing positive and/or negative appeals

(continued)

	Both learners:	Task completion	Skills
2	– Both learners: – Engage in interaction, but only one student generally leads participation during task – Sometimes ignore each other's responses – Sometimes do not offer any feedback	– Acceptable completion of the task; some required elements are missing – Responses mostly appropriate and adequately developed; overall task outcome is acceptable	– Adequate use of attention grabbers – Have adequate skills in providing reasons and elaborating ideas – Have adequate skills in utilizing positive and/or negative appeals
1	– Both learners: – Engage each other very little in the task – Often ignore each other's responses and have high level of disagreements and inability to reach consensus – Provide very little feedback to each other	– Partial completion of the task; many required elements are missing – Responses appropriate yet undeveloped; only basic ideas expressed without any elaboration or detail; overall task outcome is poor	– Have some difficulties in using attention grabbers – Have difficulties in providing reasons and elaborating ideas – Have difficulties in utilizing positive and/or negative appeals
0	– Both learners: – Show no evidence of working with their partner – Never pay attention or respond to each other – Demonstrate no evidence of ability to provide feedback to each other	– Unable to complete the task; few or no required elements are present – Responses are inappropriate; overall task outcome is not comprehensible	– Cannot use attention grabbers – Have no skills in providing reasons and elaborating ideas – Have no skills in utilizing positive and/or negative appealsa

Version C

Collaboration Check List	Number of Features Checked	Score
☐ Maintains a balance of talk between speakers ☐ Introduces topics or opens/closes conversation ☐ Listens and responds to create cohesion/flow in conversation ☐ Uses comprehension checks (e.g., *You mean there is no bargain tour?*), confirmation checks (e.g., *You see what I said?*), clarification requests (e.g., *What does it mean?*)	3	4
	Strong 2 or weak 3	3.5
	2	3
	Strong 1 or weak 2	2.5
	1	2
	0	0

(continued)

Task Completion Check List	Number of Features Checked	Score
☐ Introduces opinions and ideas	3	4
☐ Introduces reasons for opinions/ideas	Strong 2 or weak 3	3.5
☐ Develops ideas with details; gives creative reasons/examples	2	3
☐ Agrees on a choice	Strong 1 or weak 2	2.5
	1	2
	0	0

Style Check List	Number of Features Checked	Score
☐ States an opinion effectively	3	4
☐ States strong (e.g., *We definitely should/shouldn't, I think we should*) and weak suggestions (e.g., *We might/could; Why don't we, how about*) effectively	Strong 2 or weak 3	3.5
	2	3
☐ Uses a variety of strategies and a range of language to express opinions and ideas	Strong 1 or weak 2	2.5
	1	2
☐ Uses intonation and stress to help communicate meaning	0	0

Cancer Advice (Task #3)

Level: 3
Task versions: 1
Administration time: SP10, wk 5
Planning time: 1 minute
Planning type: Individual
Task completion time: 4 minutes
Rubric types: 1

Task

Provided to both students
- A 65-year-old man comes to his physician (doctor) with complaints of persistent, but not extreme pains in his stomach.
- Tests reveal that he has cancer of the stomach.
- The man has just retired from a busy professional career, and he and his wife are about to leave on a round-the-world cruise that they've been planning for over a year.

- The wife knows her husband has cancer but she doesn't want him to know that he's dying.
- His wife asks his physician to keep the cancer a secret.

Student A	Student B
You believe that the physician should tell the patient the **truth** about the cancer.	You believe that the physician should lie to the patient about the cancer.
Consider using the following expressions:	Consider using the following expressions:
– One way to look at ___ is… – And another way could be…	– One way to look at ___ is… – And another way could be…
– Of course, it depends on… – It could also depend on…	– Of course, it depends on… – It could also depend on…
– On the one hand, you could say… – On the other hand…	– On the one hand, you could say… – On the other hand…
– One way to think about ___ is… – But the flip side would be…	– One way to think about ___ is… – But the flip side would be…
– If you look at it from the angle of… – But seen from another angle…	– If you look at it from the angle of… – But seen from another angle…
You have one minute to prepare your ideas.	You have one minute to prepare your ideas.

- Step 1: Exchange your ideas with your partner. Ask questions to make sure you understand your partner's ideas.
- Step 2: Try to convince your partner that your opinion is more justified. Together, decide what the physician should do.

You have four minutes to exchange ideas and agree on what the physician should do.

Rubric

	4	3	2	1	0
Collaboration	Both consistently and actively work toward group goals. Value the knowledge, opinion and skills of group members and encourage contribution. The amount of contribution is fairly equal.	Both work toward group goals without prompting. Value the knowledge, opinion and skills of group members. The amount of contribution is fairly equal but turn is clearly controlled by one member.	One works toward group goal but the other contributes occasionally. Opinion and knowledge of group members do not receive equal attention. There is a clear difference in the amount of contribution.	One works toward group goal but the other contributes only when prompted. Only the dominant member's opinion is valued; or the other member is disinterested. One member largely dominates the conversation.	Both learners show no evidence of working with partners. Both learners never pay attention or respond to each other. Both learners demonstrate no evidence of ability to provide feedback to each other.
Task completion	Both complete task with excellent ideas relevant to topic. Good use of examples to illustrate idea. Ideas are exceptionally well developed and coherent; relationship between ideas is clear.	Both complete the task with valid ideas relevant to topic. Sufficient number of ideas, but may lack elaboration or specificity. Relationships between ideas may not be immediately clear.	One or both complete part of the task with ideas relevant to topic, but with an insufficient number. Some ideas lack elaboration or specificity. Connections of ideas may not always be clear.	Both complete part of the task with only a few ideas relevant to topic. Ideas are limited and lack elaboration or specificity. Unclear connection between ideas.	Unable to complete the task; few or no required elements are present Responses are inappropriate; overall task outcome is not comprehensible

(continued)

| Style | Both demonstrate use of a variety of expressions for giving opinions, agreeing, disagreeing, and building on other member's idea. Shows appropriate use of the expressions and vocabulary. Exhibits a fairly high degree of automaticity. Some errors are noticeable but do not obscure meaning. | Both demonstrate use of a few expressions for giving opinions, agreeing, and disagreeing, and building on other member's idea. Show fairly automatic and effective use of the expression and vocabulary. | One or both demonstrates limited range and control of expressions for giving opinions, agreeing, and disagreeing, and building on other member's idea. May rely on one or two general expressions. Show difficulty using the more complex expression and can be inappropriate at times. | Both demonstrate a very limited range of expressions for giving opinions, agreeing, and disagreeing, and building on other member's ideas. Rely heavily on one or two general expressions. Show limited use of the more complex and specific expressions. | No use of more complex and specific expressions for giving opinions, agreeing, disagreeing, and building on other member's ideas. |

A score of "0" is also given when learners make no attempt to fulfill the task.

Chen Problem (Task #4)

Level: 1
Task versions: 3:
Administration times: A: F12wk14, SU12 wk5; B: F11wk10; C: SU11wk5
Planning time: A, C 1–2 minutes; B 2 minutes
Planning type: A, B individual and then collaborative planning; C: individual planning only
Task completion time: 2 minutes for all tasks
Rubric types: 2

Tasks

Version A

Directions: Read the situation below. You and your partner need to describe, discuss and agree on a solution to this person's problem.

> Chen's test score at the PIE is high enough to go to the university next semester. Chen is happy, but he is also worried. He is feeling self-conscious because he thinks his teachers and classmates won't understand him because of his accent. How could you help Chen? You and your partner need to introduce your solutions, discuss the reasons for your choices, and agree on one solution.

- You will have 2 minutes by yourself to prepare your opinion.
- Then you will have 1 minute to prepare with your partner.
- Finally, you will have 2 minutes to record your conversation and agree on a solution.
- Remember that you need to take turns, discuss, and agree on a solution in the end.

Version B, C

Directions: Read the situation below. You and your partner need to discuss and decide on a solution to this person's problem.
- Version B: You will have 2 minutes by yourself to prepare your opinion of what the person should do. Then you will have 1 minute to prepare with your partner.

Finally, you will have 2 minutes to record your conversation and agree on a solution. Version C: You will have 2 minutes to prepare your opinion of what the person should do and 2 minutes to speak with your partner to decide on a solution.

> Chen has just been informed that his test score was high enough at PIE to move on to the university next semester. Chen is excited, but he is also worried. He is feeling self-conscious because he thinks that his accent might be too heavy and that his teachers and classmates might not understand him very well.

Imagine that you and your partner are sitting at the Union and talking about Chen's problem.
  You need to **describe, discuss** and **offer a solution** to Chen's problem.

Remember that you need **to take turns, collaborate and agree on a solution** in the end.

Try to use the vocabulary and grammar presented in Unit 4.

Rubrics

Version A

Collaboration Check List	Number of Features Checked	Score
☐ Maintains a balance of talk between speakers	3	4
☐ Introduces topics or opens/closes conversation	Strong 2 or weak 3	3.5
☐ Listens and responds to create cohesion/flow in conversation	2	3
☐ Uses comprehension checks (e.g., you mean there is no bargain tour?), confirmation checks (e.g., you see what I said?), clarification requests (e.g., what does it mean?)	Strong 1 or weak 2	2.5
	1	2
	0	0

Task Completion Check List	Number of Features Checked	Score
☐ Introduces opinions and ideas	3	4
☐ Introduces reasons for opinions/ideas	Strong 2 or weak 3	3.5
☐ Develops ideas with details	2	3
☐ Agrees on a choice	Strong 1 or weak 2	2.5
	1	2
	0	0

Style Check List	Number of Features Checked	Score
☐ States an opinion effectively	3	4
☐ States strong (e.g., we definitely should/shouldn't, I think we should) and weak suggestions (e.g., we might/could, why don't we, how about) effectively	Strong 2 or weak 3	3.5
	2	3
☐ Uses a variety of strategies and a range of language to express opinions and ideas	Strong 1 or weak 2	2.5
	1	2
☐ Uses intonation and stress to help communicate meaning	0	0

*Students are scored individually in all domains above.

Version B, C

	Collaboration	Task completion	Style
4	Both learners: – Work together on almost all parts of the task – Carefully respond to each other and engage each other's ideas – Offer constructive feedback	– Excellent completion of the task; all required elements of the task are present – Content is rich; ideas developed with elaboration and detail; overall task outcome is outstanding	– Excellent use of attention grabbers – Have excellent skills in providing reasons and elaborating ideas – Have excellent skills in utilizing positive and/or negative appeals
3	Both learners: – Work together on most parts of the tasks – Respond to each other and engage each other's ideas – Offer some feedback	– Good completion of the task; almost all required elements are present – Responses appropriate and with some elaboration and detail; overall task outcome is satisfactory	– Good use of attention grabbers – Have good skills in providing reasons and elaborating ideas – Have good skills in utilizing positive and/or negative appeals
2	– Both learners: – Engage in interaction, but only one student generally leads participation during task – Sometimes ignore each other's responses – Sometimes do not offer any feedback	– Acceptable completion of the task; some required elements are missing – Responses mostly appropriate and adequately developed; overall task outcome is acceptable	– Adequate use of attention grabbers – Have adequate skills in providing reasons and elaborating ideas – Have adequate skills in utilizing positive and/or negative appeals
1	– Both learners: – Engage each other very little in the task – Often ignore each other's responses and have high level of disagreements and inability to reach consensus – Provide very little feedback to each other	– Partial completion of the task; many required elements are missing – Responses appropriate yet undeveloped; only basic ideas expressed without any elaboration or detail; overall task outcome is poor	– Have some difficulties in using attention grabbers – Have difficulties in providing reasons and elaborating ideas – Have difficulties in utilizing positive and/or negative appeals

(continued)

0	– Both learners: – Show no evidence of working with their partner – Never pay attention or respond to each other – Demonstrate no evidence of ability to provide feedback to each other	– Unable to complete the task; few or no required elements are present – Responses are inappropriate; overall task outcome is not comprehensible	– Cannot use attention grabbers – Have no skills in providing reasons and elaborating ideas – Have no skills in utilizing positive and/or negative appeals

Choosing a Patient (Task #5)

Level: 2
Task versions: 4
Administration time: A: F10wk5, SP11wk5; B: F11wk10; C: SU11wk8; D: SP12wk7
Planning time: 3 minutes for all tasks
Planning type: Collaborative
Task completion time: A, C = 3 minutes; B, D = 2.5 minutes
Rubric types: 2

Directions: You and your partner will pretend to be nutritionists working for a university health center. You have two patients who want to lose weight but need help beyond what a normal diet can provide. After you and your partner describe and make a recommendation about each patient, decide which patient needs more help and should be admitted into the university health center for treatment. You can only admit one student to the health center.

(1) You are in charge of X's health plan. Describe X's problem, and then make a recommendation about how she can best lose weight.
Do not just read the information. Make a story about X/Y.

(2) While listening to your partner, fill out the following table about X/Y.

Your partner's recommended treatment

(3) Talk with Student A and make a decision about who needs more professional help from the health clinic. Make sure to provide reasons to support your ideas.

Version A

Melia	Joe
(1) Is a university freshman	(1) Is a graduate student
(2) She has gained 15 pounds	(2) Since he was a boy, he has always been at least 25 pounds overweight
(3) Her clothes don't fit	(3) Obesity runs in his family
(4) She is in class from 8am until 7pm	(4) He's on a diet but just doesn't lose weight
(5) She studies at the library until 12am	(5) He's worried about diabetes
(6) She buys snacks at the library	(6) He sits at his desk for long hours every day

Version B, C

Cindy	Lou
(1) She works at Wells Fargo Bank.	(1) He is a professor.
(2) Obesity runs in her family.	(2) He sleeps only 4 hours a night.
(3) She is depressed because of her job.	(3) He eats at McDonalds three times a week.
(4) She works from 7am until 5pm.	(4) Cardiovascular disease runs in his family.
(5) She has gained 20 pounds.	(5) He's worried about his health.
(6) She eats from the vending machine every day.	(6) He sits at his desk for long hours every day.

You and your partner are nutritionists at a health center. You have two patients who want to lose weight. Both patients need to eat healthier foods and exercise more. You have **3** minutes to prepare (don't show your instructions to your partner) and **2.5** minutes to speak with your partner.

(2) While listening to your partner, take notes in the following table about X/Y.

Version D

Directions: You and your partner are nutrition advisors at a health center. You have two patients who want to lose weight, but you can only help one of them. Both patients need to eat healthier foods and exercise more. You have 3 minutes to prepare with your partner and 2 minutes and 30 seconds to speak with your partner.

(1) Describe Cindy's/Jack's problems. Do not just read the information. Make a story about Cindy/Jack.
(2) Talk with Student A/B to make a decision and come to an agreement about who needs more professional help from the health clinic. Make sure to provide reasons to support your ideas.

Cindy	Jack
– Has obese parents	– Sleeps 4 hours a night
– Works long hours	– Eats McDonalds a lot
– Gained 20 pounds	– Has heart problems in his family
– Eats junk food all day	– Sits at desk all day

Rubrics

Versions A, C

	Collaboration	Task completion	Style
4	Both learners almost always – Work together on almost all parts of the task – Carefully respond to each other and engage each other's ideas – Offer constructive feedback	– Excellent completion of the task; all required elements of the task are present – Content is rich; ideas developed with elaboration and detail; overall task outcome is outstanding	– Outstanding ability to state an opinion – Show excellent skills in using narrative techniques – Show excellent skills in interrupting politely to ask questions
3	Both learners usually – Work together on most parts of the tasks – Respond to each other and engage each other's ideas – Offer feedback	– Good completion of the task; almost all required elements are present – Responses appropriate and with some elaboration and detail; overall task outcome is satisfactory	– Good ability to state an opinion – Show good skills in using narrative techniques – Show good skills in interrupting politely to ask questions

(continued)

2	– Some engagement in the interaction but only one student generally leads participation during tasks – Sometimes the learners ignore each other's responses – Both learners or one learner sometimes do not offer any feedback	– Acceptable completion of the task; some required elements are missing – Responses mostly appropriate and adequately developed; overall task outcome is acceptable	– Adequate ability to state an opinion – Show adequate skills in using narrative techniques – Show adequate skills in interrupting politely to ask questions
1	– One learner always takes lead in discussion during tasks or neither of them often try to engage in tasks – Both learners often ignore each other's responses and have high level of disagreements and inability to reach consensus; only claim own opinion – Both learners provide very little feedback to each other	– Partial completion of the task; many required elements are missing – Responses appropriate yet undeveloped; only basic ideas expressed without any elaboration or detail; overall task outcome is poor	– Try to state an opinion – Try to use narrative techniques – Try to interrupt politely to ask questions
0	– Bother learners show no evidence of working with partners – Both learners never pay attention or respond to each other – Both learners demonstrate no evidence of ability to provide feedback to each other	– Unable to complete the task; few or no required elements are present – Responses are inappropriate; overall task outcome is not comprehensible	– Cannot state an opinion – Show no skills in using narrative techniques – Show no skills in interrupting politely to ask questions

Versions B, D

	Collaboration	Task completion	Style
4	Both learners almost always – Work together on almost all parts of the task – Carefully respond to each other and engage each other's ideas – Offer constructive feedback	– Excellent completion of the task; all required elements of the task are present – Content is rich; ideas developed with elaboration and detail; overall task outcome is outstanding	– Outstanding ability to state an opinion – Show excellent skills in using narrative techniques – Show excellent skills in interrupting politely to ask questions
3.5	Both learners usually Work together on most parts of the tasks – Respond to each other and engage each other's ideas – Offer feedback	– Good completion of the task; almost all required elements are present – Responses appropriate and with some elaboration and detail; overall task outcome is satisfactory	– Good ability to state an opinion – Show good skills in using narrative techniques – Show good skills in interrupting politely to ask questions
3	– Some engagement in the interaction but only one student generally leads participation during tasks – Sometimes the learners ignore each other's responses – Both learners or one learner sometimes do not offer any feedback	– Acceptable completion of the task; some required elements are missing – Responses mostly appropriate and adequately developed; overall task outcome is acceptable	– Adequate ability to state an opinion – Show adequate skills in using narrative techniques – Show adequate skills in interrupting politely to ask questions
2.5	– One learner always takes lead in discussion during tasks or neither of them often try to engage in tasks – Both learners often ignore each other's responses and have high level of disagreements and inability to reach consensus; only claim own opinion – Both learners provide very little feedback to each other	– Partial completion of the task; many required elements are missing – Responses appropriate yet undeveloped; only basic ideas expressed without any elaboration or detail; overall task outcome is poor	– Try to state an opinion – Try to use narrative techniques – Try to interrupt politely to ask questions

(continued)

2	- Bother learners show no evidence of working with partners - Both learners never pay attention or respond to each other - Both learners demonstrate no evidence of ability to provide feedback to each other	- Unable to complete the task; few or no required elements are present - Responses are inappropriate; overall task outcome is not comprehensible	- Cannot state an opinion - Show no skills in using narrative techniques - Show no skills in interrupting politely to ask questions

Crime Statistics (Task #6)

Level: 3
Task versions: 2
Administration time: A: F09wk10; C: SU10wk5
Planning time: 3 minutes
Planning type: Individual
Task completion time: A: 2 minutes; B: 3 minutes
Rubric types: 1

Task

Scenario: You and your partner are taking Sociology at NAU. Your assignment was to find two different statistical reports on crime rates in the USA. You and your partner have chosen two different reports.

You have three minutes to individually prepare your own ideas before discussing it with your partner. You have two minutes to complete this task with your partner.

Directions
Step 1: In pairs, explain what each of your statistical reports present.
Step 2: Based on the amount of information that each report includes, discuss two possible reasons for types of crimes and crime rates and two solutions to decrease crime rates.
Step 3: Agree on the biggest factor contributing to crime rates in large cities.

Types of crimes in 2004
   Student A

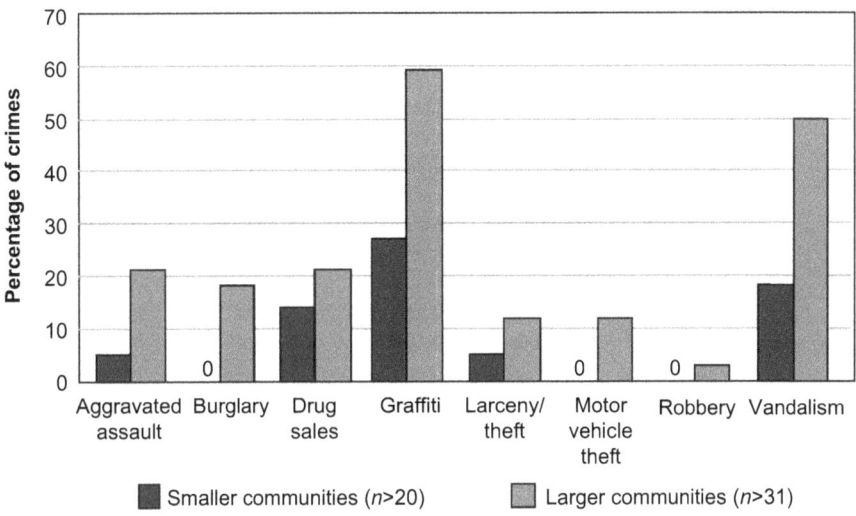

   Student B

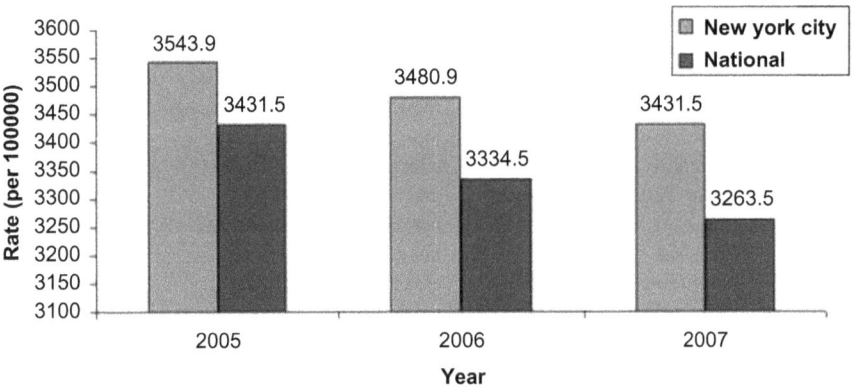

Rubric

	4	3	2	1	0
Collaboration	Both consistently and actively work toward group goals. Value the knowledge, opinion and skills of group members and encourage contribution. The amount of contribution is fairly equal.	Both work toward group goals without prompting. Value the knowledge, opinion and skills of group members. The amount of contribution is fairly equal but turn is clearly controlled by one member.	One works toward group goal but the other contributes occasionally. Opinion and knowledge of group members do not receive equal attention. There is a clear difference in the amount of contribution.	One works toward group goal but the other contributes only when prompted. Only the dominant member's opinion is valued; or the other member is disinterested. One member largely dominates the conversation.	Both learners show no evidence of working with partners. Both learners never pay attention or respond to each other. Both learners demonstrate no evidence of ability to provide feedback to each other.
Task completion	Both complete task with excellent ideas relevant to topic. Good use of examples to illustrate idea. Ideas are exceptionally well developed and coherent; relationship between ideas is clear.	Both complete the task with valid ideas relevant to topic. Sufficient number of ideas but may lack elaboration or specificity. Relationships between ideas may not be immediately clear.	One or both complete part of the task with ideas relevant to topic, but with an insufficient number. Some ideas lack elaboration or specificity. Connections of ideas may not always be clear.	Both complete part of the task with only a few ideas relevant to topic. Ideas are limited and lack elaboration or specificity. Unclear connection between ideas.	Unable to complete the task; few or no required elements are present. Responses are inappropriate; overall task outcome is not comprehensible

(continued)

Style	Both demonstrate use of a variety of expressions for giving opinions, agreeing, disagreeing, and building on another member's idea. Shows appropriate use of the expressions and vocabulary. Exhibits a fairly high degree of automaticity. Some errors are noticeable but do not obscure meaning.	Both demonstrate use of a few expressions for giving opinions, agreeing, and disagreeing, and building on other member's idea. Show fairly automatic and effective use of the expression and vocabulary.	One or both demonstrates limited range and control of expressions for giving opinions, agreeing, and disagreeing, and building on another member's idea. May rely on one or two general expressions. Show difficulty using the more complex expression and can be inappropriate at times.	Both demonstrate a very limited range of expressions for giving opinions, agreeing, and disagreeing, and building on other member's ideas. Rely heavily on one or two general expressions. Show limited use of the more complex and specific expressions.	No use of more complex and specific expressions for giving opinions, agreeing, disagreeing, and building on other member's ideas.

Election (Task #7)

Level: 2
Task versions: 2
Administration time: A: F11wk5; B: SU11wk5
Planning time: 3 minutes
Planning type: Individual
Task completion time: A: 2 minutes; B: 3 minutes
Rubric types: A: half points, no score below 2; B: no half points

Task

Version A

Imagine that you and your partner will be voting for the candidates for the student government president at the PIE. There are two candidates who are leading in the polls. After you and your partner discuss the strengths and weaknesses of each candidate, decide which one you will both vote for.

You will have three minutes to prepare your answer and two minutes to complete the task with your partner.

(1) You are Student A/B and you support Bill in the election
Do not just read the information. Make a story about Bill – be sure to talk about his qualifications to try to convince your partner to pick him.

Student A
Bill
1) Has many classes;
2) Talkative, hard-working;
3) Promises: Fun activities at the PIE, free course books;
4) Plans: Start an international soccer team;
5) Languages: German, English, Arabic.

Student B
Maria
1) Has no classes on Fridays
2) Intelligent, organized
3) Promises: New chairs, student break room
4) Plans: Open an international restaurant at NAU
5) Languages: Spanish, English, Chinese

(2) While listening to your partner, take notes about Maria.
(3) Talk with Student B and agree about who deserves to be elected. Make sure to provide reasons to support your ideas. Negotiate to make a decision.

Version B

Imagine that you and your partner will be voting for the candidates for the student government president in PIE. There are two candidates who are leading in the

polls. After you and your partner discuss about the strength and weaknesses of each candidate, decide which one you will vote for.
(1) You are Student A/B and you support Majed in the election
Do not just read the information. Make a story about Majed – be sure to talk about his qualifications to try to convince your partner to pick him.

Student A
Majed
(1) Is from Kuwait.
(2) Is a level 4 student.
(3) Has to be in class for 25 hours in a week.
(4) Is very talkative, hardworking and intelligent.
(5) Has a good relationship with the administration and teachers.
(6) Promises to bring more fun activities to the PIE.
(7) Wants to give out free course-books each semester.
(8) Dresses very professionally.
(9) Likes to tell people what to do.

Student B
Felah
(1) Is from Saudi Arabia.
(2) Is a level 5 student.
(3) Has to be in class only 15 hours in a week.
(4) Is a good negotiator.
(5) Knows how to manage his time.
(6) Has a lot of friends from other NAU departments.
(7) Promises to get the PIE involved in different university organizations.
(8) Wants to open a Saudi restaurant on Campus.
(9) Is a little lazy.

Rubrics

Version A

	Collaboration	Task completion	Style
4	Both learners almost always - Work together on almost all parts of the task - Carefully respond to each other and engage each other's ideas - Offer constructive feedback	- Excellent completion of the task; all required elements of the task are present - Content is rich; ideas developed with elaboration and detail; overall task outcome is outstanding	- Outstanding ability to state an opinion - Show excellent skills in using narrative techniques - Show excellent skills in interrupting politely to ask questions
3.5	Both learners usually - Work together on most parts of the tasks - Respond to each other and engage each other's ideas - Offer feedback	- Good completion of the task; almost all required elements are present - Responses appropriate and with some elaboration and detail; overall task outcome is satisfactory	- Good ability to state an opinion - Show good skills in using narrative techniques - Show good skills in interrupting politely to ask questions
3	- Some engagement in the interaction but only one student generally leads participation during tasks - Sometimes the learners ignore each other's responses - Both learners or one learner sometimes do not offer any feedback	- Acceptable completion of the task; some required elements are missing - Responses mostly appropriate and adequately developed; overall task outcome is acceptable	- Adequate ability to state an opinion - Show adequate skills in using narrative techniques - Show adequate skills in interrupting politely to ask questions
2.5	- One learner always takes lead in discussion during tasks or neither of them often try to engage in tasks - Both learners often ignore each other's responses and have high level of disagreements and inability to reach consensus; only claim own opinion. - Both learners provide very little feedback to each other	- Partial completion of the task; many required elements are missing - Responses appropriate yet undeveloped; only basic ideas expressed without any elaboration or detail; overall task outcome is poor	- Try to state an opinion - Try to use narrative techniques - Try to interrupt politely to ask questions

(continued)

2	– Bother learners show no evidence of working with partners – Both learners never pay attention or respond to each other – Both learners demonstrate no evidence of ability to provide feedback to each other	– Unable to complete the task; few or no required elements are present – Responses are inappropriate; overall task outcome is not comprehensible	– Cannot state an opinion – Show no skills in using narrative techniques – Show no skills in interrupting politely to ask questions

Version B

	Collaboration	Task completion	Style
4	Both learners almost always – Work together on almost all parts of the task. – Respond to each other at least twice – Sometimes offer constructive feedback	– Excellent completion of the task; all required elements of the task are present – Content is rich; ideas developed with elaboration and detail; overall task outcome is outstanding	– Outstanding ability to state an opinion – Show excellent skills in using narrative techniques – Show excellent skills in interrupting politely to ask questions
3	Both learners usually – Work together on most parts of the tasks – Respond to each other and engage each other's ideas – Sometimes offer feedback or back channel.	– Good completion of the task; almost all required elements are present – Responses appropriate and with some elaboration and detail; overall task outcome is satisfactory	– Good ability to state an opinion – Show good skills in using narrative techniques – Show good skills in interrupting politely to ask questions

(continued)

2	− Some engagement in the interaction but only one student generally leads participation during tasks − Sometimes the learners ignore each other's responses − Both learners or one learner sometimes do not offer any feedback	− Acceptable completion of the task; some required elements are missing − Responses mostly appropriate and adequately developed; overall task outcome is acceptable	− Adequate ability to state an opinion − Show adequate skills in using narrative techniques − Show adequate skills in interrupting politely to ask questions
1	− One learner always takes lead in discussion during tasks or neither of them often try to engage in tasks − Both learners often ignore each other's responses and have high level of disagreements and inability to reach consensus; only claim own opinion. − Both learners never back channel or one does not provide feedback	− Partial completion of the task; many required elements are missing − Responses appropriate yet undeveloped; only basic ideas expressed without any elaboration or detail; overall task outcome is poor	− Try to state an opinion − Try to use narrative techniques − Try to interrupt politely to ask questions
0	− Bother learners show no evidence of working with partners − Both learners never pay attention or respond to each other − Both learners demonstrate no evidence of ability to provide feedback to each other	− Unable to complete the task; few or no required elements are present − Responses are inappropriate; overall task outcome is not comprehensible	− Cannot state an opinion − Show no skills in using narrative techniques − Show no skills in interrupting politely to ask questions

Avoid an Extreme Sport (Task #8)

Level: 1
Task versions: 1
Administration time: F09wk5, SP10wk5
Planning time: 2 minutes
Planning type: Individual
Task completion time: 3 minutes
Rubric types: 1

Task

Student A
Directions: Your partner really likes extreme sports. You think they are too dangerous. You want your partner to stop doing extreme sports. Your partner does not want to stop. You and your partner must make a decision.
(1) These are pictures of some extreme sports. Describe what could happen to someone playing these sports and tell your partner why you think he or she should stop participating in extreme sports.

Picture of a skateboarder	Picture of rock climbing	Picture of a slackline jumper	Picture of people skydiving
Picture of a snowboarder	Picture of motorcycle jumping	Picture of speedboat racing	

Listen to your partner's reasons for doing extreme sports. Use the table below to take notes. Ask questions to get enough information.

Reasons you like extreme sports	Reasons why your partner thinks extreme sports are too dangerous

(2) Make a decision. While sharing your opinions, make sure to provide reasons to support your ideas.

Student B

Directions: You really like extreme sports. Your partner thinks they are too dangerous. Your partner wants you to stop doing extreme sports. You do not want to stop. You and your partner must make a decision.

(1) These are pictures of some extreme sports. Describe what you like about extreme sports and explain to your partner why you do not want to stop participating in them.

Picture of a skateboarder	Picture of rock climbing	Picture of a slackline jumper
Picture of a snowboarder	Picture of motorcycle jumping	Picture of speedboat racing

(2) Listen to your partner's reasons for why extreme sports are too dangerous. Use the table below to take notes. Ask questions to get enough information.

Reasons you like extreme sports	Reasons why your partner thinks extreme sports are too dangerous

(3) Make a decision. While sharing your opinions, make sure to provide reasons to support your ideas.

Rubric

	Collaboration	Task completion	Style
4	Both learners often – Work together on almost all parts of the task – Carefully respond to each other and engage each other's ideas. – Offer constructive feedback	– Excellent completion of the task; all required elements of the task are present – Content is rich; ideas developed with elaboration and detail; overall task outcome is outstanding	– Excellent use of attention grabbers – Have excellent skills in providing reasons and elaborating ideas – Have excellent skills in asking for partner's opinion

(continued)

3	Both learners usually – Work together on most parts of the tasks – Respond to each other and engage each other's ideas – Offer feedback	– Good completion of the task; almost all required elements are present – Responses appropriate and with some elaboration and detail; overall task outcome is satisfactory	– Good use of attention grabbers – Have good skills in providing reasons and elaborating ideas – Have good skills in asking for partner's opinion
2	– Some engagement in the interaction but only one student generally leads participation during tasks – Sometimes the learners ignore each other's responses. – Both learners or one learner sometimes do/does not offer any feedback	– Acceptable completion of the task; some required elements are missing – Responses mostly appropriate and adequately developed; overall task outcome is acceptable	– Adequate use of attention grabbers – Have adequate skills in providing reasons and elaborating ideas – Have adequate skills in asking for partner's opinion
1	– One learner always takes the lead in discussion during tasks or neither of them often try to engage in tasks – Both learners often ignore each other's responses and have high level of disagreements and inability to reach consensus; only claim own opinion. – Both learners provide very little feedback to each other	– Partial completion of the task; many required elements are missing – Responses appropriate yet undeveloped; only basic ideas expressed without any elaboration or detail; overall task outcome is poor	– Have some difficulties in using attention grabbers – Have difficulties in providing reasons and elaborating ideas – Have difficulties in asking for partner's opinion
0	– Bother learners show no evidence of working with partners – Both learners never pay attention or respond to each other – Both learners demonstrate no evidence of ability to provide feedback to each other	– Unable to complete the task; few or no required elements are present – Responses are inappropriate; overall task outcome is not comprehensible	– Cannot use attention grabbers – Have no skills in providing reasons and elaborating ideas – Have no skills in asking for partner's opinion

Hiring (Task #9)

Level: 2
Task versions: 1
Administration time: F09wk10, SP10wk9
Planning time: 2 minutes
Planning type: Individual
Task completion time: 2 minutes
Rubric types: 1

Task

Student A

Scenario: You work at a marine conservation center (e.g., protecting the ocean and its wildlife) in Miami. There is an opening for a new employee.

(1) You have Sam's profile and believe he is a good fit for the job. Try to convince your partner that Sam should get the job by using the information below. You must reach a decision about who to hire by the end of 2 minutes.

Do not just read the list but provide explanations or examples to support your idea. You have 2 minutes to prepare and 2 minutes to talk.

Sam
- Ability to finish task
- Good communication skills
- Attention to detail
- Sense of humor

(2) While listening to your partner, you may take notes about Greg.
(3) Make a decision. Make sure to provide enough reasons for supporting your ideas.

Student B

Scenario: You work at a marine conservation center (e.g., protecting the ocean and its wildlife) in Miami. There is an opening for a new employee.

(1) You have Greg's profile and believe he is a good fit for the job. Try to convince your partner that Greg should get the job by using the information below. You must reach a decision about who to hire by the end of 2 minutes.

Do not just read the list but provide explanations or examples to support your idea. You have 2 minutes to prepare and 2 minutes to talk.

Greg
- Compassionate
- Assertive
- Public speaking experience
- Ability to work with many kinds of people

(2) While listening to your partner, you may take notes about Sam.
(3) Make a decision. Make sure to provide enough reasons for supporting your ideas

Rubric

	Collaboration	Task completion	Style
4	Both learners almost always - Work together on almost all parts of the task. - Carefully respond to each other and engage each other's ideas. - Offer constructive feedback	- Excellent completion of the task; all required elements of the task are present - Content is rich; ideas developed with elaboration and detail; overall task outcome is outstanding	- Outstanding ability to state an opinion - Show excellent skills in using narrative techniques - Show excellent skills in interrupting politely to ask questions
3	Both learners usually - Work together on most parts of the tasks - Respond to each other and engage each other's ideas - Offer feedback	- Good completion of the task; almost all required elements are present - Responses appropriate and with some elaboration and detail; overall task outcome is satisfactory	- Good ability to state an opinion - Show good skills in using narrative techniques - Show good skills in interrupting politely to ask questions
2	- Some engagement in the interaction but only one student generally leads participation during tasks - Sometimes the learners ignore each other's responses - Both learners or one learner sometimes do not offer any feedback	- Acceptable completion of the task; some required elements are missing - Responses mostly appropriate and adequately developed; overall task outcome is acceptable	- Adequate ability to state an opinion - Show adequate skills in using narrative techniques - Show adequate skills in interrupting politely to ask questions

(continued)

1	One learner always takes lead in discussion during tasks or neither of them often try to engage in tasks Both learners often ignore each other's responses and have high level of disagreements and inability to reach consensus; only claim own opinion. Both learners provide very little feedback to each other	Partial completion of the task; many required elements are missing Responses appropriate yet undeveloped; only basic ideas expressed without any elaboration or detail; overall task outcome is poor	Try to state an opinion Try to use narrative techniques Try to interrupt politely to ask questions
0	Bother learners show no evidence of working with partners Both learners never pay attention or respond to each other Both learners demonstrate no evidence of ability to provide feedback to each other	Unable to complete the task; few or no required elements are present Responses are inappropriate; overall task outcome is not comprehensible	Cannot state an opinion Show no skills in using narrative techniques Show no skills in interrupting politely to ask questions

Choosing an Extreme Sport (Task #10)

Level: 1
Task versions: 1
Administration time: SP12wk14
Planning time: 1minute individual; 2 minutes collaborative
Planning type: Individual then collaborative
Task completion time: 2 minutes
Rubric types: 1; Score of 2 is the minimum

Student A
Step 1: Choose one extreme sport you want to do this summer

skydiving   ice climbing   cave diving   river rafting   ultramarathon

Step 2: You have one minute to prepare the reasons for your choice.

Step 3: Then you have two minutes to discuss and plan with your partner who has a different list.

Step 4: You and your partner have two minutes to record the following:
- Introduce your own choice.
- Discuss reasons for your choice.
- Agree on one extreme sport.

Student B

Step 1: Choose one extreme sport you want to do this summer

skydiving   ice climbing   cave diving   river rafting   ultramarathon

Step 2: You have one minute to prepare the reasons for your choice.
Step 3: Then you have two minutes to discuss and plan with your partner who has a different list.
Step 4: You and your partner have two minutes to record the following:
- Introduce your own choice.
- Discuss reasons for your choice.
- Agree on one extreme sport.

Rubric

	Collaboration	Task completion	Style
4	Both learners almost always - Work together on almost all parts of the task - Carefully respond to each other and engage each other's ideas - Offer constructive feedback	- Excellent completion of the task; all required elements of the task are present - Content is rich; ideas developed with elaboration and detail; overall task outcome is outstanding	- Outstanding ability to state an opinion - Show excellent skills in using narrative techniques - Show excellent skills in interrupting politely to ask questions
3.5	Both learners usually - Work together on most parts of the tasks - Respond to each other and engage each other's ideas - Offer feedback	- Good completion of the task; almost all required elements are present - Responses appropriate and with some elaboration and detail; overall task outcome is satisfactory	- Good ability to state an opinion - Show good skills in using narrative techniques - Show good skills in interrupting politely to ask questions

(continued)

3	– Some engagement in the interaction but only one student generally leads participation during tasks – Sometimes the learners ignore each other's responses. – Both learners or one learner sometimes do not offer any feedback	– Acceptable completion of the task; some required elements are missing – Responses mostly appropriate and adequately developed; overall task outcome is acceptable	– Adequate ability to state an opinion – Show adequate skills in using narrative techniques – Show adequate skills in interrupting politely to ask questions
2.5	– One learner always takes lead in discussion during tasks or neither of them often try to engage in tasks – Both learners often ignore each other's responses and have high level of disagreements and inability to reach consensus; only claim own opinion. – Both learners provide very little feedback to each other	– Partial completion of the task; many required elements are missing – Responses appropriate yet undeveloped; only basic ideas expressed without any elaboration or detail; overall task outcome is poor	– Try to state an opinion – Try to use narrative techniques – Try to interrupt politely to ask questions
2	– Both learners show no evidence of working with partners – Both learners never pay attention or respond to each other – Both learners demonstrate no evidence of ability to provide feedback to each other	– Unable to complete the task; few or no required elements are present – Responses are inappropriate; overall task outcome is not comprehensible	– Cannot state an opinion – Show no skills in using narrative techniques – Show no skills in interrupting politely to ask questions

Investing in a Famous Entrepreneur (Task #11)

Level: 2
Task versions: 1
Administration time: F11wk15
Planning time: 3 minutes
Planning type: Individual
Task completion time: 2.5 minutes
Rubric types: 1 Minimum score of 2

Task

Student A
Situation: You and your partner have been given 2 million dollars to invest in a company developed by a famous entrepreneur.

Based on SWOT analyses of both companies, you and your partner will:
1. debate the pros and cons of each company
2. decide which company in which you want to invest together

Do NOT just read the list but provide details or examples to support your ideas.

The Unique and Amazing Computer Store
Strength: unique help for each customer
Weakness: expensive; takes more time
Opportunity: no competing businesses nearby
Threat: the online shopping trend

Student B
Situation: You and your partner have been given 2 million dollars to invest in a company developed by a famous entrepreneur.

Based on SWOT analyses of both companies, you and your partner will:
1. debate the pros and cons of each company
2. decide which company in which you want to invest together

Do NOT just read the list but provide details or examples to support your ideas.

The Super Awesome International Drive-thru Restaurant
Strength: delicious, and inexpensive international food
Weakness: difficult to find a location with enough space
Opportunity: large international population
Threat: high taxes for this kind of business

Rubric

	Collaboration	Task completion	Style
4	Both learners almost always – Work together on almost all parts of the task – Carefully respond to each other and engage each other's ideas – Offer constructive feedback	– Excellent completion of the task; all required elements of the task are present – Content is rich; ideas developed with elaboration and detail; overall task outcome is outstanding	– Outstanding ability to state an opinion – Show excellent skills in using narrative techniques – Show excellent skills in interrupting politely to ask questions
3.5	Both learners usually – Work together on most parts of the tasks – Respond to each other and engage each other's ideas – Offer feedback	– Good completion of the task; almost all required elements are present – Responses appropriate and with some elaboration and detail; overall task outcome is satisfactory	– Good ability to state an opinion – Show good skills in using narrative techniques – Show good skills in interrupting politely to ask questions
3	– Some engagement in the interaction but only one student generally leads participation during tasks – Sometimes the learners ignore each other's responses – Both learners or one learner sometimes do not offer any feedback	– Acceptable completion of the task; some required elements are missing – Responses mostly appropriate and adequately developed; overall task outcome is acceptable	– Adequate ability to state an opinion – Show adequate skills in using narrative techniques – Show adequate skills in interrupting politely to ask questions
2.5	– One learner always takes lead in discussion during tasks or neither of them often try to engage in tasks – Both learners often ignore each other's responses and have high level of disagreements and inability to reach consensus; only claim own opinion – Both learners provide very little feedback to each other	– Partial completion of the task; many required elements are missing – Responses appropriate yet undeveloped; only basic ideas expressed without any elaboration or detail; overall task outcome is poor	– Try to state an opinion – Try to use narrative techniques – Try to interrupt politely to ask questions

(continued)

| 2 | – Bother learners show no evidence of working with partners
– Both learners never pay attention or respond to each other
– Both learners demonstrate no evidence of ability to provide feedback to each other | – Unable to complete the task; few or no required elements are present
– Responses are inappropriate; overall task outcome is not comprehensible | – Cannot state an opinion
– Show no skills in using narrative techniques
– Show no skills in interrupting politely to ask questions |

Investing in Science Funding (Task #12)

Level: 2
Task versions: 1
Administration time: A F10wk15; B: SP11wk15
Planning time: 2 minutes
Planning type: Individual
Task completion time: 3 minutes
Rubric types: 1

Task A

Student A

Scenario: You and your partner are scientists, and you are discussing the possibilities of different scientific projects. The government has given your team $5 Billion dollars to explore space. You must discuss with your partner your different ideas and reach an agreement about how to best use the money.
(1) You think the money would best be spent by creating a manned mission to Mars. You want to convince your partner that the most knowledge can be gained by sending people to another planet, but it is also your duty to inform your partner of all the positive and negative factors.

Do NOT just read the list but provide explanations or further examples to support your idea.

Manned Mission to Mars	
Positive	**Negative**
1. People will be able to conduct new experiments (not previously planned for) based on what they discover on Mars. 2. The astronauts can monitor how space affects living organisms. 3. (Think of a new, original positive reason)_____	1. Space travel is dangerous 2. It's hard to plan for everything that the astronauts might need on their mission 3. (Think of a new, original negative reason)_____

(2) While listening to your partner, you may take notes about positive and negative factors of building a gigantic space telescope.

(3) Make a decision about which project should be completed. Make sure to provide enough reasons for supporting your ideas.

Student B

Scenario: You and your partner are scientists, and you are discussing the possibilities of different scientific projects. The government has given your team $5 Billion dollars to explore space. You must discuss with your partner your different ideas and reach an agreement about how to best use the money.

(1) You think the money would best be spent by creating a gigantic space telescope. You want to convince your partner that the most knowledge can be gained by using a powerful telescope to look into the farthest corners of the universe, but it is also your duty to inform your partner of all the positive and negative factors.

Do NOT just read the list but provide explanations or further examples to support your idea.

Gigantic Space Telescope	
Positive	**Negative**
– The telescope can be remotely operated from Earth 24 hours a day. – It is 300 times more powerful than any space telescope ever made before. – Think of a new, original positive reason)_____	– Because of its size, the telescope must be fully assembled in space, which requires several trips by astronauts. – The telescope could easily be damaged by comets, meteorites, or space junk. – Think of a new, original negative reason)_____

(2) While listening to your partner, you may take notes about positive and negative factors of a manned mission to Mars.
(3) Make a decision about which project should be completed. Make sure to provide enough reasons for supporting your ideas.

Rubric

	Collaboration	Task completion	Style
4	Both learners almost always - Work together on almost all parts of the task - Carefully respond to each other and engage each other's ideas. - Offer constructive feedback	- Excellent completion of the task; all required elements of the task are present - Content is rich; ideas developed with elaboration and detail; overall task outcome is outstanding	- Outstanding ability to state an opinion - Show excellent skills in using narrative techniques - Show excellent skills in interrupting politely to ask questions
3	- Both learners usually - Work together on most parts of the tasks - Respond to each other and engage each other's ideas - Offer feedback	- Good completion of the task; almost all required elements are present - Responses appropriate and with some elaboration and detail; overall task outcome is satisfactory	- Good ability to state an opinion - Show good skills in using narrative techniques - Show good skills in interrupting politely to ask questions
2	- Some engagement in the interaction but only one student generally leads participation during tasks - Sometimes the learners ignore each other's responses. - Both learners or one learner sometimes do not offer any feedback	- Acceptable completion of the task; some required elements are missing - Responses mostly appropriate and adequately developed; overall task outcome is acceptable	- Adequate ability to state an opinion - Show adequate skills in using narrative techniques - Show adequate skills in interrupting politely to ask questions

(continued)

1	– One learner always takes lead in discussion during tasks or neither of them often try to engage in tasks – Both learners often ignore each other's responses and have high level of disagreements and inability to reach consensus; only claim own opinion – Both learners provide very little feedback to each other	– Partial completion of the task; many required elements are missing – Responses appropriate yet undeveloped; only basic ideas expressed without any elaboration or detail; overall task outcome is poor	– Try to state an opinion – Try to use narrative techniques – Try to interrupt politely to ask questions
0	– Bother learners show no evidence of working with partners – Both learners never pay attention or respond to each other – Both learners demonstrate no evidence of ability to provide feedback to each other	– Unable to complete the task; few or no required elements are present – Responses are inappropriate; overall task outcome is not comprehensible	– Cannot state an opinion – Show no skills in using narrative techniques – Show no skills in interrupting politely to ask questions

Matt Test Score (Task #13)

Level: 1
Task versions: 1
Administration time: SP12wk7
Planning time: 3 minutes
Planning type: Individual
Task completion time: 2
Rubric types: 1

Task (Given to Both Participants)

Matt's test score at the PIE is high enough to go to the university next semester. Matt is happy, but he is also worried. He is feeling self-conscious because he thinks his teachers and classmates might not understand him because of his accent.

First, think about your opinion of what Matt should do. Then, with your partner, you need to describe, discuss and agree on a solution to Matt's problem.

Remember that you need to take turns, discuss, and agree on a solution in the end.

Rubric

	Collaboration	Task completion	Style
4	Both learners almost always – Work together on almost all parts of the task – Carefully respond to each other and engage each other's ideas. – Offer constructive feedback	– Excellent completion of the task; all required elements of the task are present – Content is rich; ideas developed with elaboration and detail; overall task outcome is outstanding	– Outstanding ability to state an opinion – Show excellent skills in using narrative techniques – Show excellent skills in interrupting politely to ask questions
3	Both learners usually – Work together on most parts of the tasks – Respond to each other and engage each other's ideas – Offer feedback	– Good completion of the task; almost all required elements are present – Responses appropriate and with some elaboration and detail; overall task outcome is satisfactory	– Good ability to state an opinion – Show good skills in using narrative techniques – Show good skills in interrupting politely to ask questions
2	– Some engagement in the interaction but only one student generally leads participation during tasks – Sometimes the learners ignore each other's responses – Both learners or one learner sometimes do not offer any feedback	– Acceptable completion of the task; some required elements are missing – Responses mostly appropriate and adequately developed; overall task outcome is acceptable	– Adequate ability to state an opinion – Show adequate skills in using narrative techniques – Show adequate skills in interrupting politely to ask questions
1	– One learner always takes lead in discussion during tasks or neither of them often try to engage in tasks – Both learners often ignore each other's responses and have high level of disagreements and inability to reach consensus; only claim own opinion – Both learners provide very little feedback to each other	– Partial completion of the task; many required elements are missing – Responses appropriate yet undeveloped; only basic ideas expressed without any elaboration or detail; overall task outcome is poor	– Try to state an opinion – Try to use narrative techniques – Try to interrupt politely to ask questions

Music and Vocabulary (Task #14)

Level: 3
Task versions: 1
Administration time: F09wk15
Planning time: 3 minutes
Planning type: Individual
Task completion time: 3 minutes
Rubric types: 1

Task (Given to Both A and B)

Scenario: You and your partner are taking Psychology at NAU. Your assignment is to design a research experiment to find out the relationship between vocabulary learning and classical music. You and your partner have to write a report on how you would carry out the study.

You have three minutes to individually prepare your own ideas before discussing it with your partner. You have three minutes to complete this task with your partner.
Step 1: In pairs, decide a research question which you would like to examine. For instance, in Unit 9, several experiments related to music and reasoning were introduced.
Step 2: Based on your decision for Step 1, discuss how you would like to design your study.

You should consider the following:
(1) Who are your participants (e.g., age, nationality, educational background)?
(2) What groups are you going to include?
(3) What is each group going to do?
(4) What are your predictions regarding the results of the study?

Rubric

	4	3.5	3	2.5	0
Collaboration	Both consistently and actively work toward group goals. Value the knowledge, opinion and skills of group members and encourage contribution. The amount of contribution is fairly equal.	Both work toward group goals without prompting. Value the knowledge, opinion and skills of group members. The amount of contribution is fairly equal but interaction is clearly controlled by one member.	One works toward group goal but the other contributes only occasionally. Opinion and knowledge of group members do not receive equal attention. There is a clear difference in the amount of contribution.	One works toward group goal but the other contributes only when prompted. Only the dominant member's opinion is valued; or the other member is disinterested. One member largely dominates the conversation.	Both learners show no evidence of working with partners. Both learners never pay attention or respond to each other. Both learners demonstrate no evidence of ability to provide feedback to each other.
Task completion	Both complete task with excellent ideas relevant to topic. (see "task completion requirements" below) Good use of examples to illustrate idea. Ideas are exceptionally well developed and coherent; relationship between ideas is clear.	Both complete the task with valid ideas relevant to topic. Sufficient number of ideas, but may lack elaboration or specificity. Relationships between ideas may not be immediately clear.	Both complete part of the task with ideas relevant to topic, but with an insufficient number. Some ideas lack elaboration or specificity. Connections of ideas may not always be clear.	Both complete part of the task with only a few ideas relevant to topic. Ideas are limited and lack elaboration or specificity. Unclear connection between ideas.	Unable to complete the task; few or no required elements are present. Responses are inappropriate; overall task outcome is not comprehensible

(continued)

Style	Variety of expressions for emphasizing points, giving opinions, agreeing, disagreeing, and building on other member's idea. Shows appropriate use of the expressions and vocabulary. Exhibits a fairly high degree of automaticity. Some errors are noticeable but do not obscure meaning.	A few expressions for emphasizing points, giving opinions, agreeing, and disagreeing, and building on other member's idea. Show fairly automatic and effective use of the expression and vocabulary.	Demonstrate limited range and control of expressions for emphasizing points, giving opinions, agreeing, and disagreeing, and building on other member's idea. May rely on one or two general expressions. Show difficulty using the more complex expression and can be inappropriate at times.	Demonstrate a very limited range of expressions for emphasizing points, giving opinions, agreeing, and disagreeing, and building on other member's ideas. Rely heavily on one or two general expressions. Show limited use of the more complex and specific expressions.	No use of more complex and specific expressions for emphasizing points, giving opinions, agreeing, disagreeing, and building on other member's ideas.

Nonverbal Communication (Task #15)

Level: 3
Task versions: 1
Administration time: F10wk15
Planning time: 2 minutes
Planning type: Individual
Task completion time: 3 minutes plus time to make a decision (no time limit given for this part)
Rubric types: 1

Task (Given to Both A and B)

Background information: You and your partner are talking about non-verbal communication. You have 2 minutes to plan and 3 minutes total to discuss with your partner.

Step 1 (2 minutes): Your friend is coming from your home country and is new to America. He does not know any non-verbal communication (e.g., hand gestures) that Americans often use. With your partner, discuss useful non-verbal communication that your friend can use in various situations. Then, develop a helpful list that you could give to your friend. Both student A and B should provide at least 1–2 suggestions.

Step 2 (3 minutes): Explain your points to your partner. Listen to your partner's main points for useful non-verbal communication that your friend can use. You and your partner only have 3 minutes to discuss this information.

Step 3: Decide together which types of non-verbal communication would be most helpful to put on the list for your friend.

Rubric

	Collaboration	Task completion	Style
5	Students always: – Work together – Carefully respond to each other – Engage each other's ideas – Offer constructive feedback	– Excellent completion of the task; all required elements are present – Content is rich; ideas developed with elaboration and detail	– Outstanding ability to state an opinion – Excellent skills in using narrative techniques – Excellent skills in interrupting politely to ask questions
4	Students almost always: – Work together – Carefully respond to each other – Engage each other's ideas – Offer constructive feedback	– Good completion of the task; almost all required elements are present – Responses appropriate and with some elaboration and detail	– Good ability to state an opinion – Good skills in using narrative techniques – Good skills in interrupting politely to ask questions

(continued)

3	- Some engagement but one student generally leads - Sometimes ignore each other's responses - One or both learner(s) usually do(es) not offer feedback	- Acceptable completion of the task; some required elements are missing - Responses mostly appropriate and adequately developed	- Adequate ability to state an opinion - Adequate skills in using narrative techniques - Adequate skills in interrupting politely to ask questions
2	- One learner always takes lead or neither engages the other in task - Often ignore each other's responses - High level of disagreement or are unable to reach agreement - Neither provides feedback to other	- Partial completion of the task; many required elements are missing - Responses appropriate yet undeveloped; only basic ideas expressed without any elaboration or detail	- Try to state an opinion - Try to use narrative techniques - Try to interrupt politely to ask questions
1	- Neither works with partner - Neither pays attention or responds to other - Neither demonstrates ability to provide feedback	- Unable to complete the task; few or no required elements are present - Responses are inappropriate or not comprehensible	- Cannot state an opinion - No skills in using narrative techniques - No skills in interrupting politely to ask questions

Presentation on Healthy Food (Task #16)

Level: 2
Task versions: 1
Administration time: F12wk7; SU12wk5
Planning time: 2 minutes
Planning type: Individual
Task completion time: 2.5 minutes
Rubric types: 1

Task (Given to Both A and B)

You and your partner are going to discuss the topic of a new presentation called: Our Favorite Healthy Food
  In your discussion with your partner you should:
- State what food you think should be in the presentation and why
- Listen and respond to your partner's healthy food ideas
- Make a decision together about what food you will talk about in your presentation

You have 2 minutes to think on your own and, then, 2 minutes and 30 seconds to speak with your partner.

```
Think on your own (Plan for 2 minutes):
```

Rubric

	Collaboration	Task completion	Style checklist
4	Both learners almost always – Work together on almost all parts of the task – Carefully respond to each other and engage each other's ideas	– Excellent completion of the task; all required elements of the task are present – Content is rich; ideas developed with elaboration and detail; overall task outcome is outstanding	☐ Declare/reject ideas (e.g., in my opinion, I'm not sure that's…) ☐ Asking for information (e.g., like what, what does x mean) ☐ Giving information (e.g., for example, I mean) ☐ Persuading (e.g., don't you agree/think) ☐ Countering (e.g., but, even though) ☐ Conceding (e.g., I see what you mean, that makes sense) ☐ Transition words (e.g., first, second, next, in addition, also)
3.5	Both learners usually – Work together on most parts of the tasks – Respond to each other and engage each other's ideas	– Good completion of the task; almost all required elements are present – Responses appropriate and with some elaboration and detail; overall task outcome is satisfactory	

(continued)

Score	Interaction	Task completion	No. of Features	Score
3	– Some engagement in the interaction but only one student generally leads participation during tasks – Sometimes the learners ignore each other's responses	– Acceptable completion of the task; some required elements are missing – Responses mostly appropriate and adequately developed; overall task outcome is acceptable	4	4
			Strong 3 or Weak 4	3.5
			3	3
			Strong 2 or Weak 3	2.5
2.5	– One learner always takes lead in discussion during tasks or neither of them often try to engage in tasks – Both learners often ignore each other's responses and have high level of disagreements and inability to reach consensus; only claim own opinion	– Partial completion of the task; many required elements are missing – Responses appropriate yet undeveloped; only basic ideas expressed without any elaboration or detail; overall task outcome is poor	2	2
			Strong 1 or Weak 2	1.5
			1	1
			0	0

Presentation on Immigration (Task #17)

Level: 2
Task versions: 1
Administration time: F09wk15; SP10wk15
Planning time: 2 minutes
Planning type: Individual
Task completion time: 2 minutes
Rubric types: 1

Task

Scenario: You are taking ENG 105 (an introductory writing class) at NAU. You have an assignment to do a 10-minute presentation with a partner. Student B is your partner. Your presentation should be about immigration. Today, you are meeting with your partner. You must decide – together – what topics to include and how to organize your presentation.

You have 2 minutes to prepare and 2 minutes to talk.
You must prepare separately but speak together.
(1) Discuss the presentation plan.

You must share your ideas for topics with your partner. You would like to suggest the following ideas to your partner.

Ideas for the presentation for Student A
(1) Concerns related to teenage immigrants
(2) Ways to help immigrants improve their English
(3) Types of jobs that immigrants have or might have in the USA
Ideas for the presentation for student B
(1) Common reasons for immigration by different countries
(2) Educational policy for immigrants in the USA
(3) Child-immigrants' difficulties

(2) Decide with your partner how to structure (i.e., how you will organize it) the topics for your presentation. Your plan should meet the following criteria:
   a. Include at least three topics related to immigration from you and your partner's lists and *why* those topics are important.
   b. Provide a visual aid
   c. State the order of your topics and *why* you chose that order

(3) You must agree on a plan that includes contributions by both partners.

Rubric

	Collaboration	Task completion	Style
4	Both learners almost always – Work together on almost all parts of the task – Carefully respond to each other and engage each other's ideas – Offer constructive feedback	– Excellent completion of the task; all required elements of the task are present – Content is rich; ideas developed with elaboration and detail; overall task outcome is outstanding	– Outstanding ability to state an opinion – Show excellent skills in using narrative techniques – Show excellent skills in interrupting politely to ask questions

(continued)

3	Both learners usually – Work together on most parts of the tasks – Respond to each other and engage each other's ideas – Offer feedback	– Good completion of the task; almost all required elements are present – Responses appropriate and with some elaboration and detail; overall task outcome is satisfactory	– Good ability to state an opinion – Show good skills in using narrative techniques – Show good skills in interrupting politely to ask questions
2	– Some engagement in the interaction but only one student generally leads participation during tasks – Sometimes the learners ignore each other's responses – Both learners or one learner sometimes do not offer any feedback	– Acceptable completion of the task; some required elements are missing – Responses mostly appropriate and adequately developed; overall task outcome is acceptable	– Adequate ability to state an opinion – Show adequate skills in using narrative techniques – Show adequate skills in interrupting politely to ask questions
1	– One learner always takes lead in discussion during tasks or neither of them often try to engage in tasks – Both learners often ignore each other's responses and have high level of disagreements and inability to reach consensus; only claim own opinion – Both learners provide very little feedback to each other	– Partial completion of the task; many required elements are missing – Responses appropriate yet undeveloped; only basic ideas expressed without any elaboration or detail; overall task outcome is poor	– Try to state an opinion – Try to use narrative techniques – Try to interrupt politely to ask questions
0	– Bother learners show no evidence of working with partners – Both learners never pay attention or respond to each other – Both learners demonstrate no evidence of ability to provide feedback to each other	– Unable to complete the task; few or no required elements are present – Responses are inappropriate; overall task outcome is not comprehensible	– Cannot state an opinion – Show no skills in using narrative techniques – Show no skills in interrupting politely to ask questions

Opening up a Barbershop (Task #18)

Level: 2
Task versions: 1
Administration time: A: F10wk10; B: SP10wk10
Planning time: 2 minutes
Planning type: Individual
Task completion time: 3 minutes
Rubric types: 2

Task

Student A

Scenario: You and your friend are investors. A business plan has just arrived at your office, and you need to complete a SWOT analysis to determine if this is a good business to invest in.

(1) You have the positive aspects of the new business idea. You must try to convince your partner that this is a good business to invest in. You must reach a decision about whether to invest in this business or not within 3 minutes.

Do NOT just read the list but provide explanations or examples to support your idea.

Student A

Cutting Edge Barber Shop and Hair Design	
Strengths	Opportunities
1. Highly trained stylists and barbers with good reputations	1. They are entering into a new location for businesses
2. Discounts are offered to repeat customers	2. There is no competition (no competing barber shops or hair salons) within a 10 mile area
3. They have a large advertising budget	

Student B

Cutting Edge Barber Shop and Hair Design

Weaknesses	Threats
1. Location- the barber shop and salon is located in an office park (a large group of office buildings) away from where people shop 2. The salon charges more money than customers are used to paying	1. The office park is often under construction and is difficult to find the location of the barber shop/salon 2. The state raised taxes on businesses

(2) While listening to your partner, you may take notes about the Weaknesses and Threats that the new business faces.
(3) Make a decision. Make sure to provide enough reasons for supporting your ideas.

Rubrics

Version A

	Collaboration	Task completion	Style
4	Both learners almost always − Work together on almost all parts of the task − Carefully respond to each other and engage each other's ideas − Offer constructive feedback.	− Excellent completion of the task; all required elements of the task are present − Content is rich; ideas developed with elaboration and detail; overall task outcome is outstanding	− Outstanding ability to state an opinion − Show excellent skills in using narrative techniques − Show excellent skills in interrupting politely to ask questions
3	Both learners usually − Work together on most parts of the tasks − Respond to each other and engage each other's ideas Offer feedback	− Good completion of the task; almost all required elements are present − Responses appropriate and with some elaboration and detail; overall task outcome is satisfactory	− Good ability to state an opinion − Show good skills in using narrative techniques − Show good skills in interrupting politely to ask questions

(continued)

2	– Some engagement in the interaction but only one student generally leads participation during tasks – Sometimes the learners ignore each other's responses – Both learners or one learner sometimes do not offer any feedback	– Acceptable completion of the task; some required elements are missing – Responses mostly appropriate and adequately developed; overall task outcome is acceptable	– Adequate ability to state an opinion – Show adequate skills in using narrative techniques – Show adequate skills in interrupting politely to ask questions
1	– One learner always takes lead in discussion during tasks or neither of them often try to engage in tasks – Both learners often ignore each other's responses and have high level of disagreements and inability to reach consensus; only claim own opinion – Both learners provide very little feedback to each other	– Partial completion of the task; many required elements are missing – Responses appropriate yet undeveloped; only basic ideas expressed without any elaboration or detail; overall task outcome is poor	– Try to state an opinion – Try to use narrative techniques – Try to interrupt politely to ask questions
0	– Bother learners show no evidence of working with partners – Both learners never pay attention or respond to each other – Both learners demonstrate no evidence of ability to provide feedback to each other	– Unable to complete the task; few or no required elements are present – Responses are inappropriate; overall task outcome is not comprehensible	– Cannot state an opinion – Show no skills in using narrative techniques – Show no skills in interrupting politely to ask questions

Version B

	4	3	2	1	0
Delivery	Clear and automatic speech with a few short pauses and hesitations. Intonation and stress help communicate meaning. Typically correct pronunciation of words. The listener has little difficulty decoding speech.	A few awkward pauses, slow speech, more than a few mispronounced words. Some use of intonation and stress may distort meaning. Listener occasionally needs to attend to speech carefully.	Multiple long pauses, very slow speech, consistent mispronunciation of words. Some intonation and stress usage distort meaning. Listener needs to attend to speech carefully.	Attempts to address the prompt but has long periods of silence and unintelligibility.	Speaker makes no attempt to respond.
Content	Generally accurate information relevant to topic. Sufficient number of ideas presented but might lack elaboration or specificity to some extent. Connections of ideas are generally clear.	General information is relevant to topic. Ideas are limited and usually lack elaboration or specificity. Connections of ideas maybe unclear.	Information needs to be more relevant to topic. Very limited number of ideas and repetitious.	Needs to make connections with listening information. Most information is unrelated to topic.	Speaker makes no attempt to respond.

(continued)

Language use	Uses most required vocabulary and some additional vocabulary terms related to the topic. Consistent use of required grammatical features. Grammar and vocabulary use are accurate in general.	Uses several required vocabulary and some additional vocabulary terms related to the topic. Language often recycled. Use of required grammatical features. Frequent errors in grammar and vocabulary use.	Uses only a few required vocabulary terms. Relies on several vocabulary words from prompt; Has Noticeable errors in grammar and vocabulary use	Very limited range of vocabulary. Has problems with using the required grammatical features. Repetition of prompt. Frequent errors in grammar and vocabulary use.	Speaker makes no attempt to respond.

Scholarship (Task #19)

Level: 1
Task versions: 1
Administration time: A: F9wk10; B: SP10wk9
Planning time: A: 2 minutes; B: 1 minute
Planning type: Individual
Task completion time: 3 minutes
Rubric types: 1

Task

Directions: Your American friends, Tom and Sarah, got a scholarship to visit a different country for one week. Tom and Sarah have different expectations for this trip. You talked with Tom, and your partner talked with Sarah about what they would like to see/do.
Step 1 Version A: 2 minutes planning time; Version B: one minute planning time

(1) Look at what Tom/Sarah would like to see/do and think of <u>two places</u> that you think Tom/Sarah will be satisfied with. Tell your partner what Tom would like to see/do during his visit.

Tom: Student A
- Very interested in popular tourist attractions
- Wants to buy many souvenirs
- Wants to meet local people

Sarah: Student B
- Wants to learn about new cultures
- Wants to visit controversial tourist attractions
- Wants to visit a well-preserved areas

(2) Listen to your partner's story about what Tom/Sarah wants to see/do during the trip. After listening to your partner, find one place that you would like to take both Tom and Sarah considering what they would like to do/see. You have to consider both Tom and Sarah's ideas.

Rubric

	Collaboration	Task completion	Style
4	Both learners often - Work together on almost all parts of the task - Carefully respond to each other and engage each other's ideas - Offer constructive feedback	- Excellent completion of the task; all required elements of the task are present - Content is rich; ideas developed with elaboration and detail; overall task outcome is outstanding	- Excellent skills as a discussion leader - Have excellent skills in using transition words - Have excellent skills in asking for partner's opinion
3	Both learners usually - Work together on most parts of the tasks - Respond to each other and engage each other's ideas - Offer feedback	- Good completion of the task; almost all required elements are present - Responses appropriate and with some elaboration and detail; overall task outcome is satisfactory	- Good skills as a discussion leader - Have good skills in using transition words - Have good skills in asking for partner's opinion

(continued)

2	– Some engagement in the interaction but only one student generally leads participation during tasks – Sometimes the learners ignore each other's responses – Both learners or one learner sometimes do/does not offer any feedback	– Acceptable completion of the task; some required elements are missing – Responses mostly appropriate and adequately developed; overall task outcome is acceptable	– Adequate skills as a discussion leader – Have adequate skills in using transition words – Have adequate skills in asking for partner's opinion
1	– One learner always takes the lead in discussion during tasks or neither of them often try to engage in tasks – Both learners often ignore each other's responses and have high level of disagreements and inability to reach consensus; only claim own opinion. – Both learners provide very little feedback to each other	– Partial completion of the task; many required elements are missing – Responses appropriate yet undeveloped; only basic ideas expressed without any elaboration or detail; overall task outcome is poor	– Have some skills as a discussion leader – Have difficulties in using transition words – Have difficulties in asking for partner's opinion
0	– Bother learners show no evidence of working with partners – Both learners never pay attention or respond to each other – Both learners demonstrate no evidence of ability to provide feedback to each other	– Unable to complete the task; few or no required elements are present – Responses are inappropriate; overall task outcome is not comprehensible	– Cannot lead discussion – Have no skills in using transition words – Have no skills in asking for partner's opinion

Sleep Clinic (Task #20)

Level: 2
Task versions: 1
Administration time: A: F09wk5; B: SP10wk5; C: SU10wk5
Planning time: 2 minutes

Planning type: A: Individual
Task completion time: A: 3 minutes; B: 2 minutes; C: 3–4 minutes
Rubric types: 1

Task

Directions:
You and your partner will pretend to be doctors. You both work at a Sleep Therapy Clinic; you work with people who have sleep disorders.

You have room at your clinic for one more patient. You and Student B must discuss two possible patients and decide whom to let in to the clinic.

You want to admit John Smith/Linda Evans, but Student A/B wants to admit Linda Evans/John Smith.

You and Student B must exchange information about each patient, and choose ONE patient to admit.

(1) You want to admit John Smith/Linda Evans. Tell a story about John Smith/Linda Evans to your partner.

Do not just read the information. Make a story about John/Linda.

John Smith: Student A	Linda Evans: Student B
– Is a high school student	– Works at a bank
– Stays up until 2:00am to study	– Her husband's snoring keeps her up all night
– Suffers from insomnia	– Has to go to work at 7:00am
– Wants to go to law school	– Cannot focus on her job during day time
– Received a scholarship	– Bought many sleeping pills

(2) While listening to your partner, fill out the following table about Linda.
(3) Talk with Student B and make a decision about whom to let in to the clinic. Make sure to provide reasons to support your ideas.

Rubric

	Collaboration	Task completion	Style
4	Both learners almost always – Work together on almost all parts of the task – Carefully respond to each other and engage each other's ideas. – Offer constructive feedback	– Excellent completion of the task; all required elements of the task are present – Content is rich; ideas developed with elaboration and detail; overall task outcome is outstanding	– Outstanding ability to state an opinion – Show excellent skills in using narrative techniques – Show excellent skills in interrupting politely to ask questions
3	– Both learners usually – Work together on most parts of the tasks – Respond to each other and engage each other's ideas – Offer feedback	– Good completion of the task; almost all required elements are present – Responses appropriate and with some elaboration and detail; overall task outcome is satisfactory	– Good ability to state an opinion – Show good skills in using narrative techniques – Show good skills in interrupting politely to ask questions
2	– Some engagement in the interaction but only one student generally leads participation during tasks – Sometimes the learners ignore each other's responses. – Both learners or one learner sometimes do not offer any feedback	– Acceptable completion of the task; some required elements are missing – Responses mostly appropriate and adequately developed; overall task outcome is acceptable	– Adequate ability to state an opinion – Show adequate skills in using narrative techniques – Show adequate skills in interrupting politely to ask questions
1	– One learner always takes lead in discussion during tasks or neither of them often try to engage in tasks – Both learners often ignore each other's responses and have high level of disagreements and inability to reach consensus; only claim own opinion. – Both learners provide very little feedback to each other	– Partial completion of the task; many required elements are missing – Responses appropriate yet undeveloped; only basic ideas expressed without any elaboration or detail; overall task outcome is poor	– Try to state an opinion – Try to use narrative techniques – Try to interrupt politely to ask questions

(continued)

0	– Bother learners show no evidence of working with partners – Both learners never pay attention or respond to each other – Both learners demonstrate no evidence of ability to provide feedback to each other	– Unable to complete the task; few or no required elements are present – Responses are inappropriate; overall task outcome is not comprehensible	– Cannot state an opinion – Show no skills in using narrative techniques – Show no skills in interrupting politely to ask questions

Spanking (Task #21)

Level: 1
Task versions: 1
Administration time: F09wk15, F10wk15, SP11wk15
Planning time: 2 minutes
Planning type: Individual
Task completion time: 3 minutes
Rubric types: 1

Task

Student A

Background information: You and your partner are talking about spanking and other kinds of discipline. You have 2 minutes to plan and 3 minutes to record with your partner.

Step 1 Student A: (2 minutes): You believe that parents should never spank their children. You think it should be illegal to spank children. Tell your partner why people should never spank their children. Think of at least 3 points to support your main idea.

Step 1 Student B: (2 minutes): You believe that parents should spank their children sometimes. You do NOT think it should be against the law to spank your children. Tell your partner why spanking is not child abuse and it is a good way to discipline children. Think of at least 3 points to support your main idea.

Both students A and B:

Step 2 (3 minutes): Explain your points to your partner. Listen to your partner's points for why parents should be allowed to spank their children.

Step 3 Decide together the best way for parents to discipline their children. Support your conclusion with details.

Rubric

	Collaboration	Task completion	Style
4	Both learners almost always – Work together on almost all parts of the task – Carefully respond to each other and engage each other's ideas – Offer constructive feedback	– Excellent completion of the task; all required elements of the task are present (see "requirements for completing tasks" below) – Content is rich; ideas developed with elaboration and detail; overall task outcome is outstanding	– Outstanding ability to state an opinion – Show excellent skills in supporting opinions in different ways – Show excellent skills in using voice qualities to express emotion
3.5	Both learners usually – Work together on most parts of the tasks – Respond to each other and engage each other's ideas – Offer feedback	– Good completion of the task; almost all required elements are present – Responses appropriate and with some elaboration and detail; overall task outcome is good	– Good ability to state an opinion – Show good skills in supporting opinions in different ways – Show good skills in using voice qualities to express emotion
3	– Some engagement in the interaction but only one student generally leads participation during tasks – Sometimes the learners ignore each other's responses – Both learners or one learner sometimes do not offer any feedback	– Acceptable completion of the task; some required elements are missing – Responses mostly appropriate and adequately developed; overall task outcome is acceptable	– Adequate ability to state an opinion – Show adequate skills in supporting opinions in different ways – Show adequate skills in using voice qualities to express emotion

(continued)

2.5	– One learner always takes lead in discussion during tasks or neither of them often try to engage each other in tasks – Both learners often ignore each other's responses and have high level of disagreements and inability to reach consensus; only claim own opinion – Both learners provide very little feedback to each other	– Partial completion of the task; many required elements are missing – Responses appropriate yet undeveloped; only basic ideas expressed without any elaboration or detail; overall task outcome is poor	– Try to state an opinion – Try to use skills in supporting opinions in different ways – Try to use skills in using voice qualities to express emotion
0	– Both learners show no evidence of working with partners – Both learners never pay attention or respond to each other – Both learners demonstrate no evidence of ability to provide feedback to each other	– Unable to complete the task; few or no required elements are present – Responses are inappropriate; overall task outcome is not comprehensible	– Cannot state an opinion – Show no skills in supporting opinions in different ways – Show no skills in using voice qualities to express emotion

Requirements for completing tasks: (1) present at least 3 main points to support his/her own idea. (2) Make a decision by exchanging information/expressing opinions to each other (3) quality of discussion/decision making process

Selecting and Opening a Store (Task #22)

Level: 2
Task versions: 1
Administration time: A: F12wk14; B: SP12wk14; C: SU12wk10
Planning time: 2 minutes individual; 2 minutes with partner
Planning type: Individual and Collaborative
Task completion time: 2–3 minutes
Rubric types: 2 (different items in "Style Checklist.")

Task

You and your partner will have a conversation to decide what type of store you should open in the mall.
1. You will have 2 minutes to think about your idea on your own. You can use the SWOT analysis to help organize your thoughts.
2. You will then meet with your partner and have 2 minutes to prepare your conversation.
3. Then, you and your partner will have 2–3 minutes to record your conversation. You should discuss your idea and your partner's idea and then decide which type of store is best.

My store idea: _____

SWOT Analysis

Strengths	Weaknesses
Opportunities	Threats

Rubrics

Version A

	Collaboration	Task completion	Style checklist
4	Both learners almost always – work together on almost all parts of the task – carefully respond to each other and engage each other's ideas	– Excellent completion of the task; all required elements of the task are present – Content is rich; ideas developed with elaboration and detail; overall task outcome is outstanding	☐ Declare/reject ideas (e.g., in my opinion, I'm not sure that's…) ☐ Asking for information (e.g., like what, what does x mean?) ☐ Giving information (e.g., for example, I mean) ☐ Persuading (e.g., don't you agree/think) ☐ Countering (e.g., but, even though)

(continued)

3.5	Both learners usually – work together on most parts of the tasks – respond to each other and engage each other's ideas	– Good completion of the task; almost all required elements are present – Responses appropriate and with some elaboration and detail; overall task outcome is satisfactory	☐ Conceding (e.g., I see what you mean, that makes sense) ☐ Transition words (e.g., first, second, next, in addition, also)	
3	– Some engagement in the interaction but only one student generally leads participation during tasks – Sometimes the learners ignore each other's responses	– Acceptable completion of the task; some required elements are missing – Responses mostly appropriate and adequately developed; overall task outcome is acceptable	**No. of Features**	**Score**
			4	4
			Strong 3 or Weak 4	3.5
			3	3
			Strong 2 or Weak 3	2.5
2.5	– One learner always takes lead in discussion during tasks or neither of them often try to engage in tasks – Both learners often ignore each other's responses and have high level of disagreements and inability to reach consensus; only claim own opinion	– Partial completion of the task; many required elements are missing – Responses appropriate yet undeveloped; only basic ideas expressed without any elaboration or detail; overall task outcome is poor	2	2
			Strong 1 or Weak 2	1.5
			1	1
			0	0

Versions B and C

	Collaboration	Task completion	Style checklist
4	Both learners almost always – work together on almost all parts of the task. – carefully respond to each other and engage each other's ideas – offer constructive feedback	– Excellent completion of the task; all required elements of the task are present – Content is rich; ideas developed with elaboration and detail; overall task outcome is outstanding	☐ Declare/reject ideas (e.g., in my opinion, I'm not sure that's…) ☐ Hedges (e.g., perhaps, maybe, I guess, it seems) ☐ Express lack of information (e.g., I'm not sure, I can't remember, I have no idea)

(continued)

3.5	Both learners usually – work together on most parts of the tasks – respond to each other and engage each other's ideas – offer feedback	– Good completion of the task; almost all required elements are present – Responses appropriate and with some elaboration and detail; overall task outcome is satisfactory	☐ Asking for information (e.g., like what, what does x mean?) Giving information (e.g., for example, it means) ☐ Persuading (e.g., wouldn't you agree, don't you think) Countering (e.g., but, even though that may be true) Conceding (e.g., I see what you mean, that makes sense) ☐ Boundary signal words (e.g., first, second, before, after, now)
3	– Some engagement in the interaction but only one student generally leads participation during tasks – Sometimes the learners ignore each other's responses – Both learners or one learner sometimes do not offer any feedback	– Acceptable completion of the task; some required elements are missing – Responses mostly appropriate and adequately developed; overall task outcome is acceptable	
2.5	– One learner always takes lead in discussion during tasks or neither of them often try to engage in tasks – Both learners often ignore each other's responses and have high level of disagreements and inability to reach consensus; only claim own opinion – Both learners provide very little feedback to each other	– Partial completion of the task; many required elements are missing – Responses appropriate yet undeveloped; only basic ideas expressed without any elaboration or detail; overall task outcome is poor	

No. of Features	Score
4	4
Strong 3 or Weak 4	3.5
3	3
Strong 2 or Weak 3	2.5
2	2
Strong 1 or Weak 2	1.5
1	1
0	0

(continued)

2	– Bother learners show no evidence of working with partners – Both learners never pay attention or respond to each other – Both learners demonstrate no evidence of ability to provide feedback to each other	– Unable to complete the task; few or no required elements are present – Responses are inappropriate; overall task outcome is not comprehensible

Voluntary Simplicity (Task #23)

Level: 1
Task versions: 3
Administration time: A: F10wk10, SP10wk15, SP11wk10; B: F11wk15, SU11wk8; C: SU10wk10
Planning time: 2 minutes
Planning type: Individual
Task completion time: A, C: 3 minutes; B: 2 minutes
Rubric types: 1 (2 points the lowest score)

Task

Student A

Background information: You and your partner are talking about voluntary simplicity. You have 2 minutes to plan and 2/3 minutes total to discuss with your partner.

Step 1 (2 minutes): You believe that living a simple life has many advantages. You think people become healthier and happier if they choose this life style. Tell your partner why people should live a simple life. Think of at least 3 main points to support your idea.

Step 2 (2/3 minutes): Explain your points to your partner. Listen to your partner's main points for why people should live a modern life. You and your partner only have 3 minutes to discuss this information.

Step 3: Decide together which life style is better.

Student B

Background information: You and your partner are talking about voluntary simplicity. You have 2 minutes to plan and 2/3 minutes total to discuss with your partner.

Step 1 (2 minutes): You believe that living a modern life is better than living a simple life. You do NOT think that simple life makes people happier and healthier. Tell your partner why people should live a modern life. Think of at least 3 main points to support your idea.

Step 2 (2/3 minutes): Explain your points to your partner. Listen to your partner's main points for why people should live a simple life. You and your partner only have 3 minutes to discuss this information.

Step 3: Decide together which life style is better.

Rubric

	Collaboration	Task completion	Style
4	Both learners: – Work together on almost all parts of the task – Carefully respond to each other and engage each other's ideas – Offer constructive feedback	– Excellent completion of the task; all required elements of the task are present – Content is rich; ideas developed with elaboration and detail; overall task outcome is outstanding	– Excellent use of attention grabbers – Have excellent skills in providing reasons and elaborating ideas – Have excellent skills in utilizing positive and/or negative appeals
3.5	Both learners: – Work together on most parts of the tasks – Respond to each other and engage each other's ideas – Offer some feedback	– Good completion of the task; almost all required elements are present – Responses appropriate and with some elaboration and detail; overall task outcome is satisfactory	– Good use of attention grabbers – Have good skills in providing reasons and elaborating ideas – Have good skills in utilizing positive and/or negative appeals
3	– Both learners: – Engage in interaction, but only one student generally leads participation during task. – Sometimes ignore each other's responses. – Sometimes do not offer any feedback	– Acceptable completion of the task; some required elements are missing – Responses mostly appropriate and adequately developed; overall task outcome is acceptable	– Adequate use of attention grabbers – Have adequate skills in providing reasons and elaborating ideas – Have adequate skills in utilizing positive and/or negative appeals

(continued)

2.5	Both learners: – Engage each other very little in the task – Often ignore each other's responses and have high level of disagreements and inability to reach consensus – Provide very little feedback to each other	– Partial completion of the task; many required elements are missing – Responses appropriate yet undeveloped; only basic ideas expressed without any elaboration or detail; overall task outcome is poor	– Have some difficulties in using attention grabbers – Have difficulties in providing reasons and elaborating ideas – Have difficulties in utilizing positive and/or negative appeals
2	Both learners: – Show no evidence of working with their partner – Never pay attention or respond to each other – Demonstrate no evidence of ability to provide feedback to each other	– Unable to complete the task; few or no required elements are present. – Responses are inappropriate; overall task outcome is not comprehensible	– Cannot use attention grabbers – Have no skills in providing reasons and elaborating ideas – Have no skills in utilizing positive and/or negative appeals

Workplace Monitoring (Task #24)

Level: 3
Task versions: 1
Administration time: A: SP10wk15; B: SU10wk10
Planning time: 3 minutes
Planning type: Individual
Task completion time: 3 minutes
Rubric types: 2

Task

For this speaking part of the test, you will work with your partner.
Scenario: You and your partner are owners of a large company. You manage 300 employees. Recently, you have noticed problems with employee productivity and theft. Your company is losing money because employees are not selling enough products. Additionally, employees complain that their personal belongings have been stolen.

You decide to hold a meeting with your partner to solve this problem.
<After your teacher says to, please continue to the next page>

Student A
Your opinion: You *oppose monitoring* in the workplace. You *do not want* to use video cameras, phone taps, and email monitoring in your company.
You have three minutes to individually prepare your own ideas before discussing it with your partner. You have three minutes to complete this task with your partner.

Student B
Your opinion: You *support monitoring* in the workplace. You want to use video cameras, phone taps, and email monitoring in your company.
You have three minutes to individually prepare your own ideas before discussing it with your partner. You have three minutes to complete this task with your partner.

Explain your opinion. Listen to your partner and ask questions. Remember to take turns.

Rubric

Version A

	4	3.5	3	2.5	0
Collaboration	Both consistently and actively work toward group goals. Value the knowledge, opinion and skills of group members and encourage contribution. The amount of contribution is fairly equal.	Both work toward group goals without prompting. Value the knowledge, opinion and skills of group members. The amount of contribution is fairly equal but interaction is clearly controlled by one member.	One works toward group goal but the other contributes only occasionally. Opinion and knowledge of group members do not receive equal attention. There is a clear difference in the amount of contribution.	One works toward group goal but the other contributes only when prompted. Only the dominant member's opinion is valued; or the other member is disinterested. One member largely dominates the conversation.	Both learners show no evidence of working with partners. Both learners never pay attention or respond to each other. Both learners demonstrate no evidence of ability to provide feedback to each other.

(continued)

Task completion	Both complete task with excellent ideas relevant to topic. (see "task completion requirements" below) Good use of examples to illustrate idea. Ideas are exceptionally well developed and coherent; relationship between ideas is clear.	Both complete the task with valid ideas relevant to topic. Sufficient number of ideas but may lack elaboration or specificity. Relationships between ideas may not be immediately clear.	Both complete part of the task with ideas relevant to topic, but with an insufficient number. Some ideas lack elaboration or specificity. Connections of ideas may not always be clear.	Both complete part of the task with only a few ideas relevant to topic. Ideas are limited and lack elaboration or specificity. Unclear connection between ideas.	Unable to complete the task; few or no required elements are present. Responses are inappropriate; overall task outcome is not comprehensible
Style	Variety of expressions for emphasizing points, giving opinions, agreeing, disagreeing, and building on other member's idea. Shows appropriate use of the expressions and vocabulary. Exhibits a fairly high degree of automaticity. Some errors are noticeable but do not obscure meaning.	A few expressions for emphasizing points, giving opinions, agreeing, and disagreeing, and building on other member's idea. Show fairly automatic and effective use of the expression and vocabulary.	Demonstrate limited range and control of expressions for emphasizing points, giving opinions, agreeing, and disagreeing, and building on other member's idea. May rely on one or two general expressions. Show difficulty using the more complex expression and can be inappropriate at times.	Demonstrate a very limited range of expressions for emphasizing points, giving opinions, agreeing, and disagreeing, and building on other member's ideas. Rely heavily on one or two general expressions. Show limited use of the more complex and specific expressions.	No use of more complex and specific expressions for emphasizing points, giving opinions, agreeing, disagreeing, and building on other member's ideas.

Task completion requirements: Have to discuss opinion of monitoring in the workplace and come to an agreement.

Version B

	Collaboration	Task completion	Style
5	Both learners often – Work together on almost all parts of the task – Carefully respond to each other and engage each other's ideas. – Offer constructive feedback	– Excellent completion of the task; all required elements of the task are present – Content is rich; ideas developed with elaboration and detail; overall task outcome is outstanding	– Excellent skills as a discussion leader – Have excellent skills in using transition words – Have excellent skills in asking for partner's opinion
4	Both learners usually – Work together on most parts of the tasks – Respond to each other and engage each other's ideas – Offer feedback	– Good completion of the task; almost all required elements are present – Responses appropriate and with some elaboration and detail; overall task outcome is satisfactory	– Good skills as a discussion leader – Have good skills in using transition words – Have good skills in asking for partner's opinion
3	– Some engagement in the interaction but only one student generally leads participation during tasks – Sometimes the learners ignore each other's responses. – Both learners or one learner sometimes do/does not offer any feedback	– Acceptable completion of the task; some required elements are missing – Responses mostly appropriate and adequately developed; overall task outcome is acceptable	– Adequate skills as a discussion leader – Have adequate skills in using transition words – Have adequate skills in asking for partner's opinion
2	– One learner always takes the lead in discussion during tasks or neither of them often try to engage in tasks – Both learners often ignore each other's responses and have high level of disagreements and inability to reach consensus; only claim own opinion – Both learners provide very little feedback to each other	– Partial completion of the task; many required elements are missing – Responses appropriate yet undeveloped; only basic ideas expressed without any elaboration or detail; overall task outcome is poor	– Have some skills as a discussion leader – Have difficulties in using transition words – Have difficulties in asking for partner's opinion

(continued)

1	- Bother learners show no evidence of working with partners - Both learners pay little attention or barely respond to each other - Both learners demonstrate no evidence of ability to provide feedback to each other	- Unable to complete the task; few required elements are present - Responses are inappropriate; overall task outcome is not comprehensible	- Difficulty leading discussion - Have few or no skills in using transition words - Have few or no skills in asking for partner's opinion

Crime and Economy (Task #25)

Level: 3
Task versions: 1
Administration time: SP10wk9
Planning time: 1 minute
Planning type: Individual
Task completion time: 3 minutes
Rubric types: 1

Task

Scenario: You and your partner are taking Sociology at NAU. Your assignment is to find two different statistical reports on the relationship between crime rates and economy. You and your partner have chosen two different reports.

You have one minute to individually prepare your own ideas before discussing it with your partner. You have three minutes to complete this task with your partner.

Directions:
Step 1: In pairs, explain what your report presents.
Step 2: Based on the amount of information that each report includes, choose one report that you would like to present to the class. Make sure to discuss why you would like to choose one report over the other.
Step 3: Discuss two possible reasons for crime rates.

Student A

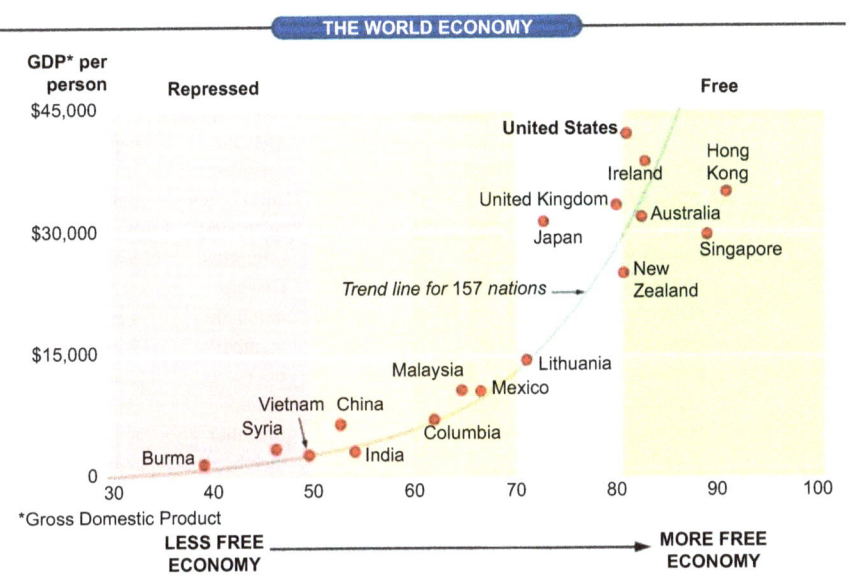

Student B

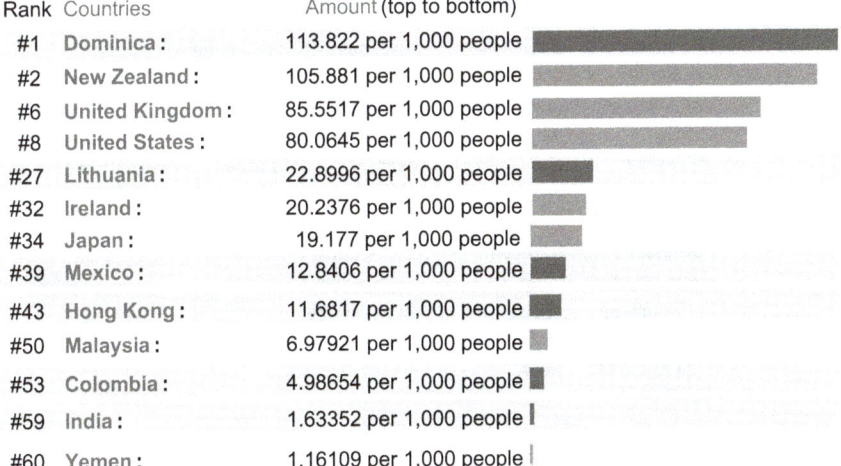

Rubric

	4	3	2	1	0
Collaboration	Both consistently and actively work toward group goals. Value the knowledge, opinion and skills of group members and encourage contribution. The amount of contribution is fairly equal.	Both work toward group goals without prompting. Value the knowledge, opinion and skills of group members. The amount of contribution is fairly equal but turn is clearly controlled by one member.	One works toward group goal but the other contributes occasionally. Opinion and knowledge of group members do not receive equal attention. There is a clear difference in the amount of contribution.	One works toward group goal but the other contributes only when prompted. Only the dominant member's opinion is valued; or the other member is disinterested. One member largely dominates the conversation.	Both learners show no evidence of working with partners. Both learners never pay attention or respond to each other. Both learners demonstrate no evidence of ability to provide feedback to each other.
Task completion	Both complete task with excellent ideas relevant to topic. Good use of examples to illustrate idea. Ideas are exceptionally well developed and coherent; relationship between ideas is clear.	Both complete the task with valid ideas relevant to topic. Sufficient number of ideas but may lack elaboration or specificity. Relationships between ideas may not be immediately clear.	One or both complete part of the task with ideas relevant to topic, but with an insufficient number. Some ideas lack elaboration or specificity. Connections of ideas may not always be clear.	Both complete part of the task with only a few ideas relevant to topic. Ideas are limited and lack elaboration or specificity. Unclear connection between ideas.	Unable to complete the task; few or no required elements are present Responses are inappropriate; overall task outcome is not comprehensible

(continued)

Style	Both demonstrate use of a variety of expressions for giving opinions, agreeing, disagreeing, and building on other member's idea. Shows appropriate use of the expressions and vocabulary. Exhibits a fairly high degree of automaticity. Some errors are noticeable but do not obscure meaning.	Both demonstrate use of a few expressions for giving opinions, agreeing, and disagreeing, and building on other member's idea. Show fairly automatic and effective use of the expression and vocabulary.	One or both demonstrates limited range and control of expressions for giving opinions, agreeing, and disagreeing, and building on other member's idea. May rely on one or two general expressions. Show difficulty using the more complex expression and can be inappropriate at times.	Both demonstrate a very limited range of expressions for giving opinions, agreeing, and disagreeing, and building on other member's ideas. Rely heavily on one or two general expressions. Show limited use of the more complex and specific expressions.	No use of more complex and specific expressions for giving opinions, agreeing, disagreeing, and building on other member's ideas.

About the Contributors

Mohammed Alquraishi, Ph.D. is an assistant professor at the Arabic Linguistics Institute at King Saud University, KSA. He is interested in analyzing patterns of language use within language teaching contexts through the utilization of corpus linguistic methods, both in English and Arabic. He is also interested in developing teaching materials and tools for teaching Arabic as a second language that utilize corpus linguistic methods.

Anthony Becker is an Associate Professor in the English Department at Colorado State University where he teaches courses within the TEFL/TESL graduate program and the undergraduate Linguistics program. He holds Ph.D. and M.A. degrees in Applied Linguistics from Northern Arizona University and Georgia State University, and an undergraduate degree in Psychology from Millersville University of Pennsylvania. His current research/teaching interests focus on second language assessment, corpus linguistics, English for specific purposes, and research methods in applied linguistics.

SungEun Choi is a Ph.D. student of Applied Linguistics at Northern Arizona University. Her research interests include spoken interaction of second language (L2) learners of English with a specific focus on prosody use and pronunciation. She explores the linguistic variation in second language speech in relation to situational factors and speaker characteristics, including communicative purpose and proficiency levels. The aim of her research is to understand L2 spoken interaction and to promote communication in English as a second language.

William Crawford is a Professor of Applied Linguistics and the Academic Director of the Program in Intensive English at Northern Arizona University. His research interests include interaction/collaboration, L2 writing and learner corpus research.

Romy Ghanem is an Assistant Professor of Applied Linguistics in the English department at the University of Memphis. Her research explores topics in second language speech perception and production as well as various aspects of pronunciation teaching and learning. Her studies have examined issues related to nonnative speaker accentedness, the acquisition of second language phonology, ESL pronunciation instruction, linguistic stereotyping, and phonological convergence.

Okim Kang is Professor of Applied Linguistics at Northern Arizona University. Her research interests are speech production and perception, L2 pronunciation and intelligibility, L2 oral assessment and testing, automated scoring and speech recognition, World Englishes, and language attitude.

Mark McAndrews is an assistant professor in the Department of English at Western Kentucky University. His research focuses on second language speaking and listening for specific purposes. His work has been published in *Language Teaching*, *the Journal of Second Language Pronunciation*, *System*, and *the International Journal of Learner Corpus Research*.

Tatiana Nekrasova-Beker is an Associate Professor in Applied Linguistics and TEFL/TESL (Teaching English as a Foreign/Second Language) in the English Department at Colorado State University, where she teaches graduate courses in the TEFL/TESL program, including *Teaching English as a Foreign/Second Language*, *Theories of Foreign/Second Language Learning*, and *Curriculum Development in English for Specific Purposes*. She holds a doctorate in Applied Linguistics from Northern Arizona University. Her research focuses on usage-based approaches to second language acquisition, learner language development, corpus-based analyses of ESP (English for Specific Purposes) texts, and assessment of second language skills.

Kim McDonough is a Professor of Applied Linguistics in the Education Department at Concordia University. Her current research interests include the role of visual cues in task-based interaction, collaboration in L2 writing, and L2 written language development.

Shelley Staples is Associate Professor of English/Second Language Acquisition and Teaching at University of Arizona. Her research focuses on corpus-based analyses of writing and speech, with a particular emphasis incorporating fluency and prosody into analyses of spoken corpora. Her work can be found in journals such as *Applied Linguistics*, *English for Specific Purposes Journal*, *Journal of English for Academic Purposes*, *Modern Language Journal*, and *TESOL Quarterly*. She is also a PI of the Corpus and Repository of Writing project: http://writecrow.org.

Pakize Uludag is a Ph.D. candidate in Applied Linguistics in the Education Department at Concordia University in Montreal, Canada. She has an MA degree in TESL from Northern Arizona University in the USA (2009–2011) and worked as an English language instructor at Qatar University from 2012–2018. Her research interests include L2 writing, language assessment and corpus linguistics.

Index

Accentedness 173, 176, 178
Accuracy 17, 61, 74, 75, 77, 124, 146–147, 179, 193
Acquisition 7, 41, 45, 173
Adjectives 30, 31, 95, 97, 100, 103–104, 106–107, 153
– Attitudinal 29–30
– Attributive 19, 29–30, 32, 95, 100, 102, 104–105, 107, 123, 131, 133–134, 136, 140
– Evaluative 29–32, 40
– Predicative 100, 103–104, 106–107
Adverbials 100, 102, 104, 105, 107, 125, 131, 133
Adverbs 23, 40, 153
– Linking 71
– Place 100, 102, 103–104, 106–107
– Stance 125
Alignment 3, 145–146, 149–150, 153–155, 156, 159–160, 162– 164
ANOVA 99, 103, 155, 157
Anxiety 70
Argumentation 141, 193
Argumentative 129, 130, 132–142, 181, 184
Articulation 146–147, 152–153, 155–160, 163, 176
Aspect see Perfect
Aspirates 132
Assessment 3, 8, 11, 14–15, 18, 36, 69–72, 74, 76, 79, 82–83, 91, 93, 96, 112–113, 123–128, 130, 140, 142, 173–175
Asymmetric 69, 71, 93, 94
Attributive see Adjectives
Authentic 42, 61, 69, 82
Authenticity 69–70
Awareness 70, 81

Backchannels 123, 126, 129, 131–132, 136–137
Bootstrapping 3–4, 132–139

Clauses
– Adverbial 125, 131
– Conditional 132, 134
– Dependent 111
– Finite 125, 131
– *If* 125
– Relative 29, 95, 100, 103–107, 111–112, 125, 130
– Subordinate 111, 133
– *That* complement 21–23, 32, 97, 100, 103–107, 125, 130–131, 133, 141
– *To* complement 33–34, 125
– *Wh* complement 100, 102–107, 112–113
– *Wh* relative 100, 102, 104, 107
Cluster Analysis 3–4, 91–92, 96, 99–101, 113
Cognitive 160–161, 163
– Demands 161
– Effort 149
– Fluency, see Fluency
– Processes 146, 162
Communicative 42, 58, 182
– Competence see Competence
– Function 33, 36
– Goal 81
– Purpose 2–3, 9–11, 125, 127–130, 132, 140–141, 148, 150–152, 155, 157–158, 160–163
Competence
– Communicative 177
– Interactional 70, 93, 126, 140
– Linguistic 178
Complement see Clauses
Complexity 2, 17–18, 23, 41, 58, 74–75, 77, 86–89, 124, 147, 176, 178–179
– Task 2, 15, 58, 145, 147–148, 151, 163, 168, 178
Comprehensibility 93, 173–174
Comprehension 177–178
– Checks 149
Conjunctions 94, 100, 103–104, 106–107
– Coordinate 109–110, 153
– Subordinate 75–79, 95, 100, 102–105, 107–110
Conversation 23, 26, 29, 31, 44, 49–50, 54–56, 58, 69–70, 92–94, 111, 125–126, 177–178
– Analysis 93, 126, 128, 140, 176

Conversational 57, 60, 82, 113, 148
- Expressions 50, 54,
- P-frames 42, 54, 57-58
Coordination 111
Coordinators 110-111
Correlation 45, 78-79, 82, 176, 184-192
- Coefficient 75-76, 78, 184-185, 187-188
- Intraclass 131

Deletion
- *That* 21, 23, 32, 35, 39, 95, 100, 102, 104-105, 107, 111
Determiners 133-134, 141
Development
- Content 74-75, 77, 86-89
- Language 3, 17-18, 41-45, 60-61, 124, 127, 147-148, 160, 173
- Task 123
Dialogic 17, 124, 126, 145, 147-148, 162-163, 176-179, 181, 184, 190-191, 194
Discourse 20-21, 24, 26, 27-28, 43, 50, 57, 60, 69, 71, 74, 76, 77-79, 87-89, 91, 93-94, 111, 123-125, 130, 136, 140, 179, 190
- Function 18, 26, 44, 50, 60, 142
- Marker 23, 35, 71, 74, 76-79, 86-89, 123, 126, 131, 136-137, 176
- Organizer 50, 54, 56-57, 60
- Particle 24-26
Disfluency 176
Downtoners 100, 102, 104-105, 107

Emphatics 39, 95
Engagement 81, 89, 118, 170
Epistemic 23, 100, 103-104, 106-107
Equality 69, 71, 74, 76, 94
Evaluative 30, 58, 173, 180
- Functions 23, 29, 31-33, 35
- See Adjectives

Female see Gender
Fillers 49-50, 59
Finite see clauses
Fluency 3, 17, 123-124, 126-127, 131, 137-138, 141, 145-151, 155-157, 159-164, 174-177, 179-180, 182, 184-185, 189-191, 193-194

- Cognitive 146,163
- Perceived 146
- Repair 146
- Utterance 145-146, 152-153, 155, 157-164
Fluent 145, 147-148, 160, 162-163
Formulaic 3, 23, 26, 28, 33-35, 41, 43-45, 58
Functional 2, 9, 17-19, 45-46, 49, 51, 54, 56-58, 60-61, 123-124, 128, 130

Gender 3, 11, 13, 15, 43, 73, 82, 93, 98, 128, 145-146, 148-150, 152, 155-156, 158-164
- Female 13, 128, 149, 152, 158, 162-163, 181
- Male 13, 15, 73, 128, 148-149, 158, 152, 162-163, 181
Genre 58, 161
Grammaticalization 23
Grams see N grams

Hesitations 49, 86-88, 126, 131, 137, 141, 153, 164

Inductive 43, 48
Infinitives 33-34, 39
Interactional 2-3, 19, 24, 35-36, 70-71, 91-93, 123-124, 126-127, 129, 131, 136-137, 140-141, 149, 163
Interactive 18, 20, 24-26, 32, 35-36, 49, 58, 69-70, 92-94, 108, 130, 140, 145, 147-149, 157
Interactivity 71-72, 76, 78
Interlanguage 18
Interpersonal 50, 71, 95, 108, 160-161
Interruptions 110, 118, 129-130, 141, 170, 175, 177, 181, 190, 193
Intonation 127, 173, 177
Involvement 35, 95, 128, 130, 132-133, 140-141

Lexical 17, 22, 26, 29, 33, 35, 37, 41, 43, 52, 76, 95, 145, 149, 162, 178, 192
- Lexical alignment 149-150, 153-156, 159-160, 162
- Lexical bundles 43, 50
Lexico grammatical 2-3, 17, 19, 35-36, 41, 69, 71-72, 75-81, 83, 91, 95, 123-125, 127, 130-133, 178-179, 193

Male see Gender
Multi-Dimensional Analysis 3, 18–20, 29, 31, 35–36
Modals
– Necessity 40, 100, 102, 103–107, 112, 131, 133, 135
– Possibility 100, 103–104, 106–107, 112–113, 131, 133
– Prediction 131, 133
Mode 2, 124, 126, 147–148, 163
Monologic 7, 17, 39, 70, 140, 145–147, 163, 176, 178, 193
Multiword 41–44, 50, 61, 164
Mutuality 71, 74, 76, 81, 94

N Gram 43–44, 46
Narration 20, 29–30, 32, 112
Narrative 28, 31–33, 35, 110, 118–119, 148, 169–171, 192
Negotiation 2, 75, 86–89, 93, 148–149, 163
Nominalization 19, 26–29, 35, 40, 71, 95
Noticing 93
Noun 19, 26–33, 35, 37, 40, 71, 95, 97, 100, 102–107, 112–113, 123, 125, 131–134, 136, 140, 153
– Premodifying 133–134

Opinion 9, 59, 75, 95, 110, 112, 118–119, 125, 130, 141, 169–171, 195
– see also Tasks

Participation 76, 117, 170
Passives 71, 75, 94
– Voice 29, 95, 100, 102–107, 125, 130
Pauses 124, 126, 131, 138–139, 141, 146–147, 152–153, 174, 176–177, 182, 183–191, 193, 195
– Filled 36, 80, 127, 147, 175–176, 182–183, 185–193
– Silent 127, 131, 137–138, 175–178, 182–183, 190, 192–193
– Unfilled 80
Perfect 29–31, 40
Persuasion 3, 9, 32, 148, 160
– see also Tasks
Phonation 127, 175
Phonological 2–3, 36, 182, 193

Phrasal 95, 100, 102–105, 107, 177
Phrase 23, 41, 44, 60, 123, 140, 146, 177
– *By* phrase 100, 102, 104, 106–107
– Noun phrase 2, 58–59
– Prepositional phrase 111, 123, 125
– Verb phrase 29
Phraseology 41–46, 45, 60–61
Pitch 124, 127, 131–132, 138, 141, 177–178, 182–183, 185–193, 195
Planning 11, 17, 73–74, 128–130, 138, 141–142, 148, 151, 161, 168, 181
Politeness 50, 60, 195
Possessive (see Pronouns)
Pragmatics 49
Predicative see Adjectives
Preposition 39, 100, 103–107, 111, 155
Priming 145
Processing 141, 162
Productivity 45, 60–61
Proficiency 2–3, 8, 10–11, 13, 17, 35, 41–48, 50–52, 55–61, 69, 81–82, 92–93, 99, 112, 114, 125–127, 145–146, 150, 161, 173, 175–178, 180–181, 190–191, 193
Prominent 33, 127, 173, 177, 183
Pronunciation 4, 123–124, 126–127, 131, 138, 172–194
Pronouns 23, 30, 32, 71, 75, 76–79, 95, 99–100, 102, 104–105, 107
– Demonstrative 99
– First person 22–23, 28, 36, 75–76, 78–79, 95, 99, 102–105, 107, 109–110, 112, 132–133, 141
– Indefinite 99
– *It* 29–32, 39, 99
– Personal 75, 110–112, 153, 155
– Possessive 99, 153
– Second person 20, 28–32, 35, 71, 75–76, 78–79, 95, 99, 102, 105, 107, 109–110, 132–133
– Third person 29, 30–31, 35, 39, 95, 99, 100, 102–104, 105, 107, 109–110, 112–113
– WH-pronoun 155
Prosody 173, 175, 177, 179–180, 182, 184, 193–194
Purpose (see Communicative)

Qualitative 1, 71, 75, 82, 91, 111
Quantitative 1, 4, 59

Ratings 3, 71–72, 74–80, 82–83, 96, 174, 176–177
Referential (see pronouns)
Register 2–3, 17–19, 23, 26, 28, 50, 123–130, 141, 148, 161
Relative (see Pronoun)
Repair 147, 163
Repetition 30, 40, 80, 146
Representation 15, 37, 41, 61, 69, 108

Segmental features 173–175, 183, 194
Situational characteristics 2, 19, 42, 123–124, 127–130, 132, 141, 148, 161
Sociocultural 2
Sociolinguistic 149
Strategy 111, 148
Subordinate (see Conjunction and Clause)
Subordination 79
Suprasegmental features 4, 173–179, 183, 189, 191, 193–194
Syllable 126–128, 151–153, 157, 159, 175, 177, 183

Tasks
– Argumentative 181
– Difficulty 163
– Decision 3, 10–11, 151–152, 157–158, 168
– Information 4, 179–180, 184, 191–192, 194
– Opinion 4, 82, 173, 179–181, 184, 187–194
– Persuasion 3, 10–11, 12, 151–152, 157–158, 161, 168
– Repetition 2
– Selecting from alternatives 10–11, 157–158, 168
Tense
– Past 29–31, 40
– Present 22–23, 26–28, 100, 102, 104–105, 107–110, 153, 155
Tone 177, 183, 192
Turns 21, 24–26, 35, 39, 41, 70, 81, 108, 110–111, 126, 128–129, 131–132, 136–137, 148, 153–155, 162, 164, 182

Unanalyzed 23, 164

Variable 2, 7, 11, 15, 17–20, 35–37, 39–41, 43–44, 46, 48–50, 52–61, 82, 96, 103, 124, 126, 130–133, 137–138, 140–142, 149, 155–157, 161–163, 174–176, 179–180, 182, 184–185, 187, 192, 194
Variation 2–4, 11, 17–21, 35–37, 41–42, 44, 49, 56, 72, 105, 111–112, 123, 128, 140, 155, 161, 163, 177, 179, 183, 194
Verb 19, 21–23, 26–31, 33–37, 39–40, 44–45, 60, 95, 97, 100, 102–110, 112–113, 125, 130–131, 133, 153, 155
Voice see Passive

Writing 2, 7–8, 17–19, 26, 42, 44–46, 57–58, 80, 96, 111, 123–125, 127, 130, 151, 153, 173, 178

www.ingramcontent.com/pod-product-compliance
Lightning Source LLC
Chambersburg PA
CBHW071423150426
43191CB00008B/1029